CW01337603

HALFBACK, HALF FORWARD

GEORGE GREGAN

HALFBACK, HALF FORWARD

MACMILLAN

Pan Macmillan Australia

First published 2008 in Macmillan by Pan Macmillan Australia Pty Ltd
1 Market Street, Sydney

National Library of Australia
cataloguing-in-publication data:

Gregan, George.

Halfback, half forward : an autobiography / George Gregan.

ISBN 9781405038614 (hbk.)

Gregan, George.
Rugby Union football–Australia.
Rugby Union football–Australia–Anecdotes.
Rugby Union football players–Australia–Biography.

796.333092

Set in 11.5/16.5 pt Sabon by Midland Typesetters, Australia
Printed in Australia by McPherson's Printing Group
Quotes from *One Step Ahead: On the Field and in the Boardroom* by
Rod Macqueen, published in 2001, reprinted by permission of
Random House Australia

To my wife and family

CONTENTS

ACKNOWLEDGMENTS

It seems like only yesterday that I turned up for my first training session for St Edmund's College under-10s in April 1983. Since that moment I have been extremely lucky and fortunate to have this wonderful game called rugby play a major part in my life. I can honestly say that, outside of my loving family, it has been one of the strongest influences that have shaped the person I am today. It has taught me important life skills that have and will continue to aid me in my day to day life. Teamwork, responsibility, humility, fun, laughter, triumph, failure, family and trust are just some of the things that I have been lucky enough to share with an incredible group of players and coaches over the years. For this I feel truly blessed, because it is not until you spend time away from your regular routine that you fully appreciate just how lucky you were to be playing professionally a sport that you have loved since childhood.

My family is the most important thing in my life and I owe them all so much for their incredible support over the past 35 years. This extends to the Gregans – Dad, Mum, Tendai, Shaye and Susannah Gregan and all the other Gregan's (you know who you are!) – as well as my incredible wife, Erica, children Max, Charlie and Jazz, and Erica's amazing family: Melanie and Anthony (and their little tribe of Oliver, Isabelle and India), Joe, Ivy, Karen, Rebecca, Carole, Leonora and Freddie. Without their support I could not have kept playing for as long as I did; whenever I was away from home (and I was away a hell of a lot!), I always knew that my family would look after each other. This gave me a great deal of solace whenever I had to leave, as I knew they would cope more than adequately (particularly once Erica's social calendar was aligned with that of our extended rugby family, including the Burkes, Kearns, Littles, Blades, Harrys, Wilsons, Mehrtens, Neills, Barnes and so on!).

I always felt uneasy about writing a book because I have always thought that a sportsperson only starts their life when their career ends. So how could someone talk about anything other than their time playing sport, which did not seem that interesting to me? However, when I was approached by Pan Macmillan to do this autobiography we had a good discussion about this concern and we agreed to change things up a little. This is reflected in the 'me on them, them on me' chapters, which are a funny and also serious look at the incredible friends I have come to know throughout my career. They are all a little different and it was the part of the book that I loved doing most – in fact if it was not for time and word constraints I could have written a whole book on all my great mates in and out of rugby.

Also enormous thanks to those who have supported the George Gregan Foundation – you have all helped many dreams come true and will continue to do so in the future. In particular, thank you to Meagan Bryant and The George Gregan Foundation Board, lead by David Clarke, Bob Mansfield, Jane Kennedy, Jessica Rowe, Martin Lakos, Kylie Virtue, Paul Ramsey and my wife, Erica. We also have many amazing ambassadors who help make our fundraisers exciting, Thanks to Phil Kearns, Pat Rafter, Melissa Doyle, Rob Sitch, Sam Neill, Bryan Brown, Rachel Ward, Peter Overton, Matthew Burke, Richard Harry, Tim Horan, Jason Little, David Wilson, Andrew Blades, John Eales, George Smith, Phil Waugh, Stephen Larkham, Stirling Mortlock, Peter O'Malley, Michael Campbell, Jimmy Barnes, Mark Lizotte, Jenny Morris, Jon Stevens, Melissa Brydon and Katie Powers, plus many more of my Wallabies and Brumbies team-mates and others who have given up their time and sponsorship. Thank you also to our committee, Phil Harte, Allens Arthur Robinson and PDY.

There are so many more people I would love to thank in and away from rugby, but I want you to start reading this book! To all those people I have worked with over the years – players, coaches, managers, medical staff, gear handlers, administrators and so on – I thank you. But I think it's time for you to turn the page and start reading about my 'rugby life' – enjoy!

Prologue

FOR THE LOVE OF THE GAME

2005

'It would have been easy to let this one go by, but it would have been wrong to do so.'

John Smit, South African captain, February 2005

I was playing cricket at the time, in a charity game – it was the Brumbies against the Canberra Raiders rugby league team – when a media statement was issued revealing I was going to England for the International Rugby Board's North versus South Rugby Aid match. The principal objective of the game was to raise money for the United Nations World Food Program, and their efforts to assist communities devastated by the tsunami that hit Asia on Boxing Day 2004, but even though the cause was so important, the match had been caught up in a small game of rugby politics. The IRB had been accused of hijacking other rugby bodies' attempts to raise money for the disaster relief, and as a result pressure was being put on players from the Southern Hemisphere not to get involved. I didn't care about any of that. At this point, as the bats and pads were put away and we toasted yet another convincing victory over the league boys, I didn't realise that as well as being ready to do my bit for a very worthy cause, I was about to have just about the best week of my rugby life, an experience which would remind me what it was I loved about the game.

I'd first officially heard about the game through Brumbies chief executive Rob Clarke, though ever since international cricket had staged a successful one-day game that raised more than $14 million, there had been whispers that rugby would try something similar. While the Australian Rugby Union (ARU) supported the concept, the provinces – Australian Capital Territory, New South Wales and Queensland – were less keen, because they feared the game's timing, 5 March, and the fact it was being staged in London would hurt the Super 12 competition. Rob told me he believed there would a 'one player from each Super 12 team' compromise, but warned me that nothing had been confirmed yet.

For me, it was a no-brainer. I'd seen footage of the devastation the tsunami had caused and put my hand up straight away. 'Clarkey, I'm playing in this,' I said. 'I don't care if I miss a game in the Super 12. I'll play round one, go for round two and be back for round three. The squad is good enough to win without me. I've got the utmost faith in them.'

I had been involved in some pretty weird rugby politics during the previous decade, but the way the administrators tried to hijack this game amazed even me. Their lack of perspective, and sense of charity, was disappointing. As I was making my decision, some other notable identities were doing the same. The New Zealand captain, the great Tana Umaga, rang me from Wellington to say,

'Excellent decision, good on you.' He was coming, too. So was Andrew Mehrtens, the Canterbury Crusaders and All Blacks No. 10. Momentum built from there, and the Southern Hemisphere team would be a strong one, featuring Tana, Mehrts, Queensland and Australia's Chris Latham, and South Africa's John Smit, Victor Matfield and Schalk Burger.

Round one of the 2005 Super 12 for the Brumbies was a Saturday-night home game in Canberra against the Crusaders. Mehrts and I drove up to Sydney after the game, and we flew out to the UK on the Sunday night. We laughed about the memory of the previous year's Super 12 final, when the Brumbies scored 33 points in the first 20 minutes to pretty much win the game. Mehrts had been on the bench, but after 25 minutes their coach, Robbie Deans, had sent him on. I wasn't the skipper, but I'd sensed the mood was about to change. 'Listen, these guys are going to start playing really well now, boys,' I'd said during the next break in play. 'Mehrtens will get them organised. We've got to be patient, we've got to defend well.'

Sure enough, the Crusaders had dragged themselves back into the game, and then there had been a bit of push and shove. Mehrts had run over to me and I'd seen him out of the corner of my eye and had grabbed him. Then we'd pretended we were having a bit of a scuffle. If anyone hadn't known that the two of us were mates, they'd have thought we'd been about to have a stink, and the touch judge, ignoring the real fracas, had run in and put his flag out. We'd pissed ourselves laughing. 'Mate,' we'd said as one, 'We're just mucking around.'

This sense of camaraderie would be characteristic of the whole experience. From the moment the South team got together at our hotel in London, the mood was buoyant. The first night, we had a couple of beers and got to know each other, something that rarely happened given the breakneck pace of modern professional rugby.

Until now, we had barely crossed paths, except as opponents on the field, but that quickly changed. Someone – it might have been Mehrts – said we needed to start planning for a twelve-month reunion.

Of course, it required an enormous amount of planning for a game like this to work. From the South's perspective, much of this was the responsibility of our manager, one of rugby's finest gentlemen, the great South African Morne du Plessis. When Morne wasn't getting any love from the Northern Hemisphere clubs – he even had a battle getting the okay for my old Wallabies team-mate Matty Burke to come down from Newcastle in the north of England and act as our 'waterboy' – there was never any angst, just a calm determination to find a solution. If only all rugby administrators were so shrewd and straight.

Our coach was Rod Macqueen, a man who had had a great influence on my career. Coach of the Wallabies team that won the 1999 World Cup and beat the Lions in 2001, he had been away from the coaching scene for a couple of years, but in the lead-up to this game he had been in classic form, devising plays and looking for innovations that would set his team apart. Rod always loved it when his players were involved in building the game plan, and he asked Tana, Mehrts and me to each come up with a series of backline plays from scrums and lineouts. He laughed when he saw how similar our strategies were.

I was captain of the South team and, as leadership assignments go, it was an easy one – we had five national captains within our group (Tana, John Smit, Moses Rauluni of Fiji, Samoa's Semo Sititi and me) and the coach was keen to enjoy the week. There were no heavy training sessions, just plenty of time to get to know each other and revel in Rod's predilection for drawing plays on butcher's paper.

I had never worked with Rod as a captain before, though I had been vice-captain behind Brett Robinson when Rod coached the Brumbies in 1996–97, and behind John Eales and David Wilson when he was in charge of the Wallabies from 1997 to 2001. When Rod was Australian coach there were numerous occasions when, within the leadership group, we debated tactics, strategies, a whole range of things. It might have been that I was voicing the concerns of the entire playing group, or maybe it was just my own opinion, but there were times when he took our disagreement personally, and times when I did the same. Looking back, though, while they might have been animated debates, they were productive, and we always seemed to find some middle ground eventually. That process built a respect between us that wouldn't have existed if we'd just agreed with each other all the time. But it wasn't until after Rod left the Wallabies set-up, when we could look back on our five years together, that we really came to appreciate the time we had worked with each other. In his autobiography, *One Step Ahead*, from 2001, he wrote:

> *I found George Gregan almost a contradiction. In the public eye, he was the talkative livewire on the field, often flashing a huge smile either to taunt the opposition or respond to a reaction from the crowd. Yet off the field he was very serious and set very high standards for himself. More than anyone else, he worked hard to make sure he was always at the peak of physical fitness for every match. He did everything possible at all times to improve every aspect of his game and when playing he led by example. I thought George would have to be one of the best foot-ballers in the world, but in his early playing days George had several detractors and was continually being compared and judged by the standards of the past. The fact is he was a product of the future . . .*

Of all the things written about me over the years, that brief analysis is one I appreciate most.

Ironically, we didn't disagree on anything during the week of the tsunami game, except for the wine selection for the team dinner. In the end, I left Rod to order the white, while I took care of the red: a Coldstream Hills Reserve Pinot Noir, which all but the South African boys enjoyed. (They stuck to their beer.) It says something of the impact this week had on me that I can still remember clearly the wine we enjoyed at the team dinner.

On match day, it wasn't a Test, it wasn't Super 12 or Super 14, but it was still a genuine contest, with the North led by England's Lawrence Dallaglio and coached by the man who had steered England to a World Cup victory in 2003, Sir Clive Woodward. We all wanted to win, but more than anything it was a celebration of rugby. Usually, in the professional era, when you stop to celebrate the game, it is only briefly – the day after a big final, or maybe to recognise an important milestone or the end of a notable career. This time, we lived it for the whole week. And afterwards, everyone said, 'How good was that?'

The biggest pressure came from wanting to play well in front of such celebrated team-mates. I didn't want to throw a terrible pass to Mehrts, or to have someone remind me of how they had to clean up after I missed a crucial tackle. At one point, a couple of the Kiwis were into Mehrts about his defence, but on game day Mehrts tackled like a beast. Tana said he'd never seen him defend that well. It's always satisfying when you meet your own standards, or improve upon them.

Rod gave us a basic strategic framework so that we weren't running around not knowing what each other was doing, but within that we were free to express ourselves and that's what we did. At times, I felt I was back playing sevens, where the pressure is on to create space, use space and defend big space. We played really well, scoring some crackerjack tries and eventually prevailing 54–19. Even though the stadium wasn't full, those who were there made plenty of noise, creating a wintry carnival atmosphere. I've played quite a few times in front of a full house at Twickenham Stadium, including a World Cup semifinal that went to extra time, but when I was in 'Test-match mode' I really didn't know who was in the crowd, or how big or small it was. It was just noise; everything outside the contest just became a bit of a blur. The fact that I checked out the crowd this time reflected the fact that it wasn't quite a full-blooded encounter. But it was still good. And, most importantly, it was all for a very good cause, raising money for – and awareness of – the disaster and its aftermath. I feel like we made a difference.

There was genuine disappointment when it was time to come home. I'd been playing the game for more than twenty years, been a Test halfback for more than ten, and experienced plenty in that time – a little of which was difficult, most of it good, some glorious – that tested me in a wide variety of ways. I needed this experience to remind me of what it is that I actually love about rugby: the mateship, the shared experience, the contest, testing yourself and winning all matter. When you put on top of that the reason why this particular game was played – to help others – that's what made it a unique rugby experience. That's why I wanted to open this book with the story of the 'tsunami match'.

The next time I met Tana Umaga was in a Test, and as usual I was dreading having to try to tackle him. It had to happen eventually, and when it did all I could do was grimace, try my best and afterwards say just loudly enough for him to hear, 'Hey, mate, I thought we had a gentlemen's agreement. You don't run at me, I won't run at you.'

He looked at me and smiled. We both know top-level rugby isn't quite like that.

1

GROWING UP

1973–1990

'The best dreams are the ones that come true.'
RICKY PONTING, AUSTRALIAN CRICKET CAPTAIN

I am the son of a white Australian father and a black Zimbab-
wean mother, but if you're expecting to find tales of racism in
sport or of the prejudice I encountered growing up in Australia in
the 1970s and 1980s, I'm afraid you are going to be disappointed
– I never experienced it.

My parents, John and Jenny, met in London, came to
Australia, where they had two children, then journeyed to Zambia
in Africa, where in 1973 they had a third child: me. I can't
remember anything of Zambia, which we left before my first
birthday. Corné Krige, a South African captain when I led the
Wallabies, was born in the same Lusaka hospital two years later,

9

but until that coincidence was pointed out to me I'd hardly ever thought about my birthplace. I know I have *African* blood in me – I see it in my skin colour, and every time I see my mother – but my memories of growing up, barring two trips to Zimbabwe, one when I was five, the other at eleven, are all Australian. My earliest childhood memory is of Miranda, in the Sutherland Shire, on the southern fringe of Sydney, where we stayed for six months before the family headed three hours south to our new home at Kambah, in the Tuggeranong Valley, a new suburb twenty minutes south of the centre of Canberra.

Obviously, my skin was a different colour to that of most of the other kids, but I was never faced with a situation where it seemed like a negative – which says a lot about my parents and also the new 'multi-national' community we were living in. It was more of a deal being short than being black. For this reason, I never thought of myself as a 'trailblazer' of any kind. When I go overseas, especially to South Africa, and hear people say how important it is that I 'rose' to the Australian captaincy with my 'background', then I think, *Maybe I have had an impact*. But, really, it's not something I think about; I'll leave that kind of social analysis to others.

If anything, my skin colour has always caused more confusion than angst. In 1996, I was at a function in Brisbane after an All Blacks Test, talking to an older 'white' Australian, when Andrew Mehrtens came up and gave me a subtle nudge. 'Mate, do you need a beer?' he asked me.

'Mate, I've got a beer, you just got me a beer,' I replied.

Then, when the guy I was talking to looked away for a moment, Mehrts whispered, 'Do you need me to save you?' It's a time-honoured tradition that when a player is being hassled by a member of the public, someone else will attempt a rescue.

'Mehrts,' I said, 'this is my old man. John Gregan, meet Andrew Mehrtens.'

'Andrew Mehrtens! I've been watching you since the under-19s. I first saw you play when George played for Australia in Dunedin with the under-21s . . .' Dad was away. Few men love talking about rugby and his son's career as fervently as he does. He has been a loyal and committed supporter of my career since day one.

I quietly slipped away, leaving the two of them to chat away for 20 minutes, before catching up with Mehrts later in the night. 'It was your fault,' I told him. 'That's my dad.'

There was plenty of open ground around where I lived – parks with bike tracks, footy posts, cricket pitches, basketball hoops and plenty of bushland. Exploring was a habit. Canberra Nature Park's Mount Taylor – more a large hill than a mountain – was literally outside the front door and I used it as an extension of our backyard. I was a naturally fit kid and I had plenty of mates to share my love of sport, whether through backyard cricket, kicking the footy or just running around as kids are prone to do.

I know I had a competitive spirit from a very young age. I suspect that, being the youngest of three, it grew out of a desire to beat my older sister and brother. I remember when I was seven or eight years old and in Little Athletics, running my first 100-metre race. Two longer-legged rivals ran past me and I ended up finishing third. Sadly, I'd become a bit used to winning and when the official came up to me and handed over the green certificate (the 'bronze', if you like) I ripped it up in front of him. 'Sorry, Mr Burns,' I said tearfully. 'I only take blue ones.'

If my skin colour was never an issue when I was a kid, my size could have been – I was a little guy. But although being short might have made a few selectors shy away from me as I was growing up, and maybe a few people feared for my safety, I never felt disadvantaged. It meant I was noticed immediately – how could you not be when the cricket pads are too tall for you or

11

you look tiny in a rugby league 'Midgets' competition? Being small, I had to find ways to survive, and the survival instinct is a strong one. When I was in primary school, I followed my brother Tendai into judo, which taught me how to use my body and to not be intimidated when I came up against a bigger opponent. It's all about learning how to put a rival, whatever their size, on the mat and finding the right way to do it. The big man with poor technique is no match for the little guy with good technique, a lesson that I have found applies to all sports, as long as you have the courage and faith to believe it.

I went to high school at St Edmund's College in Griffith, a Canberra suburb a couple of kilometres east of Manuka Oval (which, before the advent of the Australian Institute of Sport, was the main sportsground in the city). I found myself part of a really great group of mates. We weren't too academically inclined, just enough, and we shared a love of sport. I remember especially the banter between us and the PE teachers. They were good at sledging you in a way that got you heading in the right direction.

One of the worst injuries I suffered in my sporting life occurred while I was at school, when I dislocated my thumb as I was practising my ankle-tapping. Some innocent party would be running along on the oval when, all of a sudden, there'd be an ankle-tap and he'd fall face first. We all thought it was quite funny, though with hindsight and a bit of maturity it seems stupid. Fate got me in the end, as the groundsman had replaced some turf but hadn't put it back in flush, and as I went for the ankle-tap I tripped on the loose sod, missed my mark and my thumb hit the ground at just the wrong angle. It was such a bad dislocation the hand was in plaster for a month and I missed a large chunk of the cricket season.

Cricket and rugby league were the team sports I loved most as a boy. I was playing league until I went to St Edmund's, and that I focused on the professional code was hardly surprising, as this was the reality of Canberra as a sporting town in the early 1980s. Football-wise, my earliest heroes were league players such as Canterbury's Steve Folkes and Steve Mortimer; the fact that the two Steves came to a league presentation day when I was playing in the Midgets had to make an impact on me. We watched the Sydney premiership on television, and then the Raiders came into existence and we could see the stars in the flesh. David Campese was a Wallabies star and a Canberra product, but by the time I started paying attention he was playing his club rugby in Sydney and wearing the NSW blue, so it wasn't until local players such as Ricky Stuart, Brad Girvan, Paul Cornish and Geoff Didier started making representative teams while playing in Canberra that local rugby won some consistent media exposure – or at least enough exposure for an impression-able teenager like me to notice.

But if you'd asked me to nominate my number one sporting hero in the 1980s, the first man I'd have mentioned would be Viv Richards, the legendary West Indian batsman. I used to love how Viv went about his work. It was his presence that got me, the way he could have been in bad nick, but you'd never know from his body language. He always looked as though he was going to dominate the poor bowler at the other end, and the fact that he could play a front-foot pull shot off guys such as Dennis Lillee and Jeff Thomson was special. Even the way he used to play across the line. The experts used to sneer that he needed to play straight, but he would back himself. He trusted his technique and it came through for him.

Observing the positive approach to sport adopted by heroes such as Viv Richards shaped me a little bit as a footballer. I came to realise that when you are going about your business, you need to be confident and positive. The good players are always learning, and on their occasional bad days they never lose faith that they are one innings or one game away from performing well. It taught me that if I wanted to win I had to work hard at it. One kick wouldn't improve my goal kicking, but one hundred might.

I played a fair amount of representative footy while I was at school, the highlight of which was probably a trip to Darwin in 1989 for the Australian under-17 championships, when we were billeted out with local rugby families. I stayed with a really nice Kiwi family, who showed me a few sides of life that I'd barely experienced before. The father worked on a boat and used to bring back this fantastic fresh fish all the time, and I remember one hangi where everyone seemed really loose. I was just about to help myself to the sauce when someone said to me, 'Hey bro, don't touch that.' Then he explained there was ganja in it, which was why everyone was chilling out. 'Okay,' I said, trying to sound as adult and unsurprised as I could, 'I'll stay away from that.' A little earlier, they'd opened up the big hot coals they had placed in a hole they'd dug in the backyard, then folded back a big banana leaf to reveal a massive, perfectly cooked barramundi. Another night, we had the best tiger prawns I'll ever have in my life.

The football was good, too. I was the number two halfback, behind Stephen 'Scruffy' Scahill, a great guy who ended up playing some first-grade rugby league for Balmain. He was bigger than me – not much taller, but stronger physically – at that time he played a more robust game, which I think was why the selectors liked him. A future Wallabies team-mate, Andrew Walker, was kicking goals over from 50 metres for NSW Country, just one of a number of really good young talented players on show. I got limited game time from that tournament, but somehow made an Australia under-17 B team.

In the late 1980s, St Edmund's College was strong in the state-wide Waratah Shield schools competition. In 1990, my one year in the first XV, we were beaten by Scots College in the final. The opponent I remember most from my year in the first team was Stuey Pinkerton, who was a genuine standout, amazing at that level. In the final, playing No. 8, he put on a one-man show, pulling off cover tackles, line breaks, everything.

I finished high school in 1990 and enrolled in a Bachelor of Education, with a major in physical education at Canberra University. I always wanted to scratch that sporting itch. A career playing either cricket or rugby was by no means a certainty, but I knew that one way or another my future lay in sport.

2

TRAINING EFFECT

1991–1994

'George's ability was inherent, but his desire to play the game hadn't been tapped. He was just playing the game, like a lot of fellows do. But we showed him a new way to approach the sport, to develop both the physical and the mental side, and he blossomed, particularly in the physical side . . .'

DAVID CLARK, AIS HEAD RUGBY COACH, 1986–1996

The biggest break of my sporting life came in 1992, when I won a rugby scholarship to the Australian Institute of Sport (AIS). Until then, I was divided as to whether my sporting ambitions lay with rugby or cricket. Maybe the summer game held the edge until the 1991–92 season, during which I'd represented the ACT in the Australian under-19 cricket championship in Perth. I'd worn the ACT cap at the under-17s carnival two years earlier, had played a lot of junior representative cricket in Canberra, and had seen a slightly older local batsman named Michael Bevan win the man-of-the-match award for the Prime Minister's XI against the touring Pakistanis and then start scoring a truckload of runs in first-class cricket. I had visions of one day wearing the baggy green cap, but at the under-19s championship I saw gifted young players such as Ricky Ponting, Martin Love, Jimmy Maher, Michael Di Venuto and Shane Lee in action, and concluded ruefully that while they were future international cricketers, I wasn't. Quick bowlers sending down big leg-cutters on those bouncy Perth wickets were my undoing. I managed one half-century, against the Northern Territory, and the biggest mark I made was underneath Ponting's chin, when I clipped a ball to the leg side in our game against Tasmania, only to see the ball crash into the throat of the Tassie short-leg fieldsman.

Ricky was fielding there because he was the youngest member of the Tasmanian team – short leg is where you traditionally put the upstart of the team – but after he was hit his skipper moved him back to field at backward square. Soon after, I pushed a ball into the leg side, called for the single, and was mortified when Ricky dashed in, picked the ball up on the run and threw down the stumps at the bowler's end. It's funny – talk to Punter today and he remembers clearly the moment when I hit him in the throat, but can't recall anything of the gobful he gave me after he ran me out!

I loved my cricket, absolutely loved it.

I came back to Canberra and at the start of the 1992 rugby season I broke into Easts' first-grade side, playing five-eighth. I'd started playing my club football with Easts the previous year, largely because it was just down the road from St Edmund's and was where all my ex-schoolmates were playing. It was a social club, and we had a very good time. In 1991 we'd made the grand final, where we'd faced Tuggeranong – the form team of the competition – whom we'd defeated. The following year, however, I had a very different experience of a big match when, in the opening minutes of the semifinal, we ran a set play at the back of a lineout and our winger, Gordon Scott, ran into me. I can remember getting the ball, running across the field and then BANG! Next thing, I'm waking up in hospital. Apparently there had been some blood and it had looked ugly for a little while – one of those incidents where the game stops for minutes while the injured player is stretchered from the field. My skull was fractured, the most brutal injury I ever suffered during my career. The coaches at St Edmund's had always reminded us that rugby was a *collision* sport, not a *contact* sport (basketball, they explained, was a contact sport), and this was one of the few collisions where I came off second best. Fortunately, there was no long-term hangover.

Not long after, in August 1992, I was selected to go to New Zealand with the Australian under-19 team as the team's number one halfback. The New Zealand team included Andrew Mehrtens and Justin Marshall, and our No. 10 was Queensland's Pat Howard. The improvement in my game after just a few months at the AIS was substantial – we had really good trainers, with a wonderful understanding of the game, and I just worked their program as best I could. I got bigger, stronger, faster, and was in much better athletic shape than I had been twelve months before. The confidence I gained helped transform my game, and I increased the intensity of my individual training. I didn't see this as a time to rest on my laurels; rather, I did some extra work. That was my mindset.

I learned two inexorable facts about New Zealanders on my first trip across the Tasman. One, they are consumed by rugby. They certainly loved beating us and they just as certainly played a different level of rugby to what I'd been used to in junior rugby back home. It was very intense, especially straight after the opening kick-off. I quickly discovered that if you don't start well against Kiwi teams, they have twenty points on you quick-smart.

The second thing is that although they (kind of) hate us, we enjoy a special kinship, too. We really enjoyed each other's company, once the Test had been won and lost. I recall the drinking games in particular, and how they stitched us up off the field as well as on it!

The tour involved three games: a 9–all draw against Canterbury under-21s at Christchurch, then 40–0 versus Southland in Invercargill, then the under-19 Test, which we lost 23–3 on a really boggy ground in Dunedin. Though we didn't play as well as we could have, the reason they beat us in the Test was simply because they were a lot better than us. They camped in our half, as Mehrts dominated field position with his right boot and kicked goals. He made a career out of that. They smashed us up front, too, and we ended up having our reserve hooker going on as prop. We were just on the back foot the whole time. I flew home thinking how nice it would be to beat them some day.

By late 1992 I was training with the ACT under-21s and had been picked for the Kookaburras, the ACT senior rugby squad. I might not have been getting paid to play rugby, but at the AIS I was certainly training in the manner of a professional athlete. I saw how top-level sportspeople go about their business and, most importantly, how that commitment to excellence translates into performance. The players who went into that AIS program came from all over the country, but there were a number of footballers from Canberra, including some guys who went on to play for the Wallabies, such as Rod Kafer, Matt O'Connor and Marco Caputo. They were in the first intake; I was in the next batch.

These more experienced locals were fantastic in the way they supported us young players, setting a standard that never wavered during my football career. For me, it was a real eye-opener to see how elite athletes prepared for competition. A lot of the practices I learned at the AIS remained important to me throughout my life in sport. I recall a lecture on 'training effect', on how to get the most out of training. It is one thing to work hard on the training ground or in the gymnasium, but I also needed to work hard on my recovery from that effort, so that my next training session would be as effective as the last. The best athletes 'recover harder'.

Recovering harder is about concepts such as flexibility, about preserving your range of movement. It is important to recover neurologically and mentally as well as physically. At the AIS, I was introduced to practices such as massage, the use of hot and cold hydrotherapy to minimise the impact of games and heavy training, flotation tanks for physical and mental relaxation, and strengthening key parts of the body such as your shoulders, your hips and your back, which were generally ignored back in the early 1990s. Things that have been part of my routine since 1992 did not become common practice in top-level rugby until years later.

AIS experts such as Ian King, a world-renowned strength coach, offered me fantastic guidance. Ian tailored different programs to suit different athletes; he wasn't going to prescribe the same program for me, a rugby footballer, as he would for a hockey player. Crucially, he didn't want one of his athletes to waste a single repetition in the gym. He also stressed the importance of warming up right before you did a strenuous exercise. I'd seen mates in the gym at the rugby club stride in and immediately attempt large lifts, while I was being ribbed by those same people when I commenced my routine with a range of light exercises before I did my main lifts. But over a period of weeks, the increase in my strength quietened the critics.

Before I went to the AIS, I'd been dedicated to my training, but not in such a precise, systematic and logical way. When I saw the results my new methods brought, it was really invigorating, as was seeing elite athletes such as the great British track and field athletes Colin Jackson and Linford Christie training along similar lines. I'd think, 'Gosh, that's a world-record holder, winner of Olympic gold.' There is always a certain joy in discovering something works. Over the summer of 1992–93, a group of AIS scholarship holders played in a touch footy competition, and by observing each others' evasion skills and speed off the mark we could see that we were improving in that way, too. Simply put, I was inspired.

I could see my life heading in a number of ways, but the common denominator always was sport. Phys ed teaching was my back-up, top-level rugby union was my preference, but playing for a living was the ideal, which was why rugby league remained an option. The Canberra Raiders of the early 1990s were a special team, featuring the likes of Mal Meninga, Laurie Daley and Ricky Stuart, all at the top of their games. In 1993, I had a quiet coffee with Raiders coach Tim Sheens and Ricky. They tabled a three-year proposal which would initially see me as the 'back up' to Ricky with a view to eventually becoming his successor in the top side. I was humbled by the approach, but in the end it came down to a choice between playing at least the next couple of years in rugby league reserve grade, or having a real crack at union and then looking again at league. The Raiders respected my ultimate decision, and I came away impressed by them. It wasn't as if the money they were offering was life-changing, but I was a student whose main source of income was working as a tour guide at the AIS or putting in some hours at an after-school daycare facility, so it didn't look too bad a deal at all. Near the end of our conversation, Ricky said, 'In rugby league, in the long run, you get rewarded based on how you perform.' That was something I remembered when rugby union did go professional in 1995.

I made my debut on the sevens circuit (playing seven-a-side rugby in a variety of city and country locations) with the AIS team in early 1993. In the years since, I have read stories of prominent rugby identities such as Wallabies coach Bob Dwyer and television commentator Gordon Bray noticing me play during these games – specifically at the tournament at Terrigal, on the Central Coast north of Sydney. My clearest memory of my first tournament, however, is of missing the plane for our flight from Canberra to Brisbane because I mucked up the departure time, then catching a later flight and getting changed into my playing kit as we ran out onto the field. We ended up making the final that day.

My senior ACT debut with the Kookaburras came in 1993, when we defeated the Northern Transvaal Bulls from South Africa. My main memory is of a try we scored using a move that we still use today, nicknamed 'blue bulls', a sharp, precise play that starts with the No. 12 getting the ball and ends with the fullback going through the gap created by the 12 and 13 changing their running lines. (I won't be providing too much information about set plays through this book. Many of them are still used by the teams I played for, and I'd be betraying a trust if I gave up all the details.) This victory was the start of an important season for ACT rugby at a provincial level. The inclusion of a few young guys from the AIS program blending with a core group of experienced men helped instil a confidence within the playing group, but it was impossible to get the game's bigwigs in Sydney to give us any attention. Northern Transvaal had beaten NSW by plenty the week before they came to Canberra, so they could obviously play, yet our victory was downplayed in official circles. We lost a competitive game to the New Zealand side, Otago, after leading by fourteen points at one stage, and then we beat Tonga, after which a forty-two-man Wallabies squad was announced that included precisely *zero* ACT players. Maybe the selectors were right – we did then go to Brisbane where we were thrashed 66–3 by Queensland.

During that defeat in Queensland, I broke my hand trying to tackle Test centre Jason Little. Afterwards, the Reds coach, John 'Knuckles' Connolly, complained about the ACT players' 'cheap shots' and suggested we needed to 'grow up' if we wanted to mix it with the big boys on a regular basis. Maybe it was true that a few of our players had taken the old-school view that if we weren't going to win the game, we'd try to win the fight, but the schoolmaster tone in Connolly's admonishment was a little condescending. I recall at one point the Reds driving more than half the field, with their halfback Peter Slattery counting the metres gained in lots of ten: 'Fifty . . . forty . . . thirty . . . twenty . . . ten . . . TRY!' We learned the true value of possession against Queensland; when we were under pressure and our running game was going nowhere, we'd kick the ball out, make a few metres, and then they'd march the ball down the field again. They controlled the ball, and thus the game. And when we ran the ball, it was as if they had twenty players out there. They had a presence about them, something I never forgot. In many respects, our loss was no disgrace. That Queensland team, featuring names such as Jason Little, Slattery, John Eales, Tim Horan, Michael Lynagh, Rod McCall and David Wilson, was an awesome combination that would go on to win the Super 10 provincial competition in 1994 and 1995, winning finals in South Africa on both occasions.

Within the Kookaburras group, we built up something of a renegade spirit, as if we were the younger siblings whom the elders looked down on. But the exposure we got in those games against the big provincial teams in 1993 and 1994, wins and losses, was so important, especially to young guys such as myself. There was still a long, long way to go before I could consider myself a top-grade footballer.

I wanted to reach the top in rugby, but at this stage of my life I had no timetable in mind, no specific match I wanted to play in, no tournament I set myself to be involved in. I did want to give myself the chance to 'make it' in rugby, so while my mates at uni and club rugby were having a good time, as twenty-year-olds do, I dedicated myself to my sport and my fitness. It wasn't as if I was living the life of a hermit – after competition, I'd enjoy having a night out with the boys – but I wasn't out and about in the middle of the week like most university students. I learned quickly that such activity would diminish any of the gains I was making at the AIS.

At the beginning of 1994, I had half an eye on the pinnacle of sevens rugby, the Hong Kong Sevens, but really I was more concerned with just playing well, enjoying the footy. The lucky break came when I was included in a young Barbarians development squad that played in the Fiji International Sevens tournament in early March. Also in the team was an eighteen-year-old Joe Roff and a seventeen-year-old Ben Tune. East Fiji knocked us out of the main competition, but we then beat Cook Islands in the Plate Final.

The great former Wallaby Greg Cornelsen, famous for scoring four tries in a Test against the All Blacks, was our coach. He told us to have some fun on the field, but he also ensured that we were prepared physically, because Polynesian teams are renowned for trying to intimidate opponents with big hits. 'Absorb it,' he said. 'You'll earn respect and you'll be in the contest. If you are in the contest, you have a good chance of winning.' Off the field, we were well looked after; all we had to do was grab our boots and mouth-guards, turn up and play. This certainly beat sitting in a university hall, trying to stay interested during lectures and tutorials.

Inevitably, there was plenty of talk about Hong Kong, as many of the people at this tournament were heading north. I kept thinking how good it would be, if only . . . and then Greg Cornelsen gave me the news, which I hardly believed. 'You're going to Honkers, mate,' he beamed. 'Well done.' The full squad was David Campese, Jim Fenwick, Tim Horan, Jason Little, Ilie Tabua, David Wilson, Brendan Fielke, Ryan Constable, Jim Williams and George Gregan.

The thing I remember most about the week before we left for Hong Kong was the training. It was an invaluable experience seeing how David Campese prepared. The intensity he brought to the process was revealing, and I sensed that all the young players lifted because of it. Before we left, Australian Sevens coach Glen Ella was quoted in the paper as saying that I could be in the Wallabies squad before the end of the year. Frankly, I didn't believe it. I do recall, however – it might have been at the airport – thanking Glen for taking the gamble and selecting me.

'We've given you an opportunity,' he replied. 'That's all you've been presented with.'

3

TEAM FIRST

1994

'I saw him [play for the Australian under-21s] last year and thought he tried to do too much. But I think he's got it . . .'
GLEN ELLA, AUSTRALIAN SEVENS COACH, 1994

In early March 1994, I flew to Sydney for a pre-tour camp before the Australian team headed to Hong Kong for the annual Sevens tournament. The Queensland boys on Super 10 duty – Tim Horan, Jason Little, David Wilson and Ilie Tabua – were joining us in Hong Kong; meanwhile, the rest of us worked hard at Coogee Oval. I quickly learned that coach Glen Ella was heavy on good skills, running, fitness, communication and 'making your first-up tackles' (themes I would hear often and embrace for the next fourteen years).

From day one, I was made to feel part of the team. This feeling that I was an important member of the side was accentuated when we landed in Hong Kong, largely because of the attitude of Horan, Little and Wilson, who were, of course, already famous players, men who I had been watching play Test rugby for the previous few years. From the first time I met them, I have always thought of Helmy, Litts and Bomber as a trio – they provided me with my first experience of what I call the Wallabies brotherhood. They introduced themselves to me with their full names (I was amazed that they would think they needed to do that – *I know who you are . . . you're bloody legends!*) and said it was great to see me in the side. The reality was that they might not have remembered seeing me play on the few occasions our paths had crossed, but they trusted the judgment of Ella and the selectors. The whole squad – coach and players – ventured out on the first night to a nice restaurant and then to an expat bar, where we proceeded to consume more than a few drinks. Timmy and Jason introduced me to Long Island Iced Tea, a concoction that has just about every bit of alcohol known to man in it, and after a few of these we were well and truly on our way to a big night.

Next morning, my room-mate, Ilie Tabua, was nowhere to be seen. He had caught up with his Fijian mates on the way back from our night out and ended up participating in a kava ceremony. I brought some fruit up for him just in case he returned while I was downstairs at breakfast and sure enough there he was, lying on his bed, sound asleep. We had to be on the bus in twenty minutes for training! Here I was, trying to wake up this big unit and the clock was ticking. I needed help and called on Bomber, Litts and Helmy to get him ready. With a few face slaps, splashes of cold water and cheap threats, we were able to get big Ilie downstairs, 'ready' to train. (Thirteen and a half years later, at the 2007 World Cup, I was at a function with the Fiji team, who obviously had enormous respect for their coach . . . Ilie Tabua – who, I found out, had been emphasising the need for strong discipline and dedication among his team. I'm not sure the coach enjoyed me recounting the story of his big night out in Hong Kong on my first Australian tour, but his players certainly seemed to!)

With the previous night's activities still working their way through our systems, our session in Hong Kong was always going to be a bit dodgy. Glen let everyone know that he enjoys a good time like everyone else, but you need to be able to switch on and off (another mantra I would live by for the next fourteen years), and now was a time to switch on. He had organised with Brendan Moon (the former great Wallabies winger who was coaching Papua New Guinea) for a practice match against the Puk-Puks, a contest that, when it was scheduled, I'm sure the coach would have seen as a good opportunity to rehearse some of our team tactics and general skills, as well as providing some match-play. But we proceeded to drop everything that was thrown our way, and were thumped by a side that was definitely a lower-tier sevens team. Glen was not amused and neither was David Campese. However, Helmy kept his sense of humour. He grabbed three balls, threw them all at Ilie and said, 'Catch the middle one.' Poor Ilie couldn't catch any of them – just like that miserable session we'd just had!

The next few days featured lots of shopping, Peking duck for lunch and dinner, plenty of noodles, and some training in the morning. On one of these shopping escapades with Helmy, Litts and Bomber, while down near the ferry terminal, I was tricked into going on a rickshaw ride. The rickshaw driver was an old Chinese man who must have been pushing eighty, and his mission was to carry me around the block, a journey of around 300 metres. Helmy was insistent, so I reluctantly jumped on and had the little ride, at the end of which I was obviously required to pay a fare. I had visions of handing over a small fee, but instead the driver was very aggressive and demanded two hundred Hong Kong dollars (about fifty Aussie dollars). Suddenly, everyone was looking at me, while my 'mates' had amazingly become invisible, only re-emerging after I'd paid up. They were pissing themselves with laughter, until eventually one of them regained enough composure to ask, 'How much?' When I told them, Helmy was ecstatic – I had smashed his record, which had stood at fifty Hong Kong dollars! As you can imagine, my achievement went down a treat with everyone, as did the purple suit I purchased from Sam's Tailor, 'famous worldwide for its unquestioned reputation for quality and discretion'. (Go to his website today, and the first thing you see is a photograph of Sam with former US President Bill Clinton.) I only wore it twice, maybe three times, but the legend lives on to this day. The flash colour looked terrific in the Wesley Snipes movie *New Jack City*, which had just come out, but not so good in real life. Even today, the boys occasionally bring up that sartorial misadventure.

I also bought some Ray-Ban sunglasses, bargaining the salesman down to around the equivalent of a hundred Aussie dollars. The guy made me feel like I'd robbed him after we finally settled on the deal, but I walked out proud of my haggling skills, even though it had taken forever. Bomber saw my new sunnies and stated emphatically, 'I want a pair of them.' I warned him about what he'd have to do, but Bomber just said, 'I'm not into bargaining.' He walked straight in, informed the salesman that he was happy to pay the same price I'd negotiated, and the deal was done. For me, it was a lesson about presence. Bomber had it; I didn't.

The boys also gave me the heads-up as to what it was like to tour with David Campese. 'This is the "Campo" if you are rooming with him,' they explained. 'If you shower in the morning, he will blow up because you've woken him. He'll make you get changed outside the door. Then if he can't sleep he'll get up in the middle of the night and turn the TV on. It doesn't matter if you're asleep.'

Ryan Constable was rooming with him on this trip, and sure enough there he was one morning, getting changed outside the room. Campo was still asleep. 'Not only can't I shower till I get back, I've got to get him some fruit,' he revealed sheepishly. Rooming with Campo was like the short straw. I only roomed with him once, and I can still remember him asking me to get him some fruit. 'Mate, I'll get you some fruit when you go down and get me some fruit,' I said.

Ricky Stuart had once advised me that if I was ever dealing with Campo not to get caught up in the master–servant game. 'Get on the front foot,' Ricky said. 'You'll get respect from him and after that he won't try it on you.' That's how it turned out.

I only played with Campo at the back end of his career, but based on that experience I wonder if he would have survived for long in the professional game, because he did have weaknesses in his game that the opposition would home in on. He was fragile in defence, and though he wasn't slow he wasn't lightning quick either. His awareness on the field was ahead of his time, his kicking game was excellent and his sense of anticipation was uncanny, but there are quite a few guys like that in twenty-first-century rugby. Only faster. Similarly, he was fantastic at creating space, but defensive strategies in modern rugby have evolved dramatically in the past fifteen years. In his day, for example, he'd cut back inside and be confronted by slow-footed forwards, but nowadays the forwards make those tackles eight times out of ten. For his time, he was a quality player with wonderful skills. But that was then . . .

In Hong Kong, Campo offered a great example of what it meant to turn up and train to improve yourself as a player. He worked tirelessly on most aspects of his attacking game and was always putting himself and his fellow players under pressure to execute an offensive skill perfectly. However, I began to realise that he was not so diligent when it came to defence, an attitude Glen and the boys warned me about well before the tournament started. 'You'll be making your tackles and his,' they said, 'especially when it comes to the big games.' Sure enough, from the quarter-final on, we suddenly had a fullback, something we had never trained for. The effect of such a strategy on the defensive line in sevens is massive because – with the open-side winger slightly back to cover any kicks – you are left with just five men in the frontline. This gives the opposing team a two-man overlap instead of one and stresses the players in the frontline because of the extra work they need to do. The fullback becomes another line of defence, but usually an ineffective one, as he'll be up against a line of attackers supporting the man who broke through. You can imagine how this self-appointed fullback stunt went down with the rest of us – particularly, as I said, because we'd never trained for it.

A great lesson I got out of this was that I saw how a team can cover a weakness and still play to its strengths. The way the coach and senior players made me aware of Campo's quirkiness was crucial in my preparation for the moment when it reared its head. Despite the fact that I was a young and inexperienced player, I was able to cope with this situation without getting the shits with Campo for not staying within the team structure. We weren't sure what he might do, but we expected something, and when it happened each of us just worked harder with the players on either side of us and did our best to overcome the problem. Because of the quality of the members of the team – men who would work themselves to the point of exhaustion – we were able to reach the final. For these guys, it was always team first.

When the tournament started, all the off-field activities finished; it was time to switch on and play. We cruised through the round-robin stages on day one and went into day two with some confidence. In the quarters, we played Samoa and won narrowly. Next was Fiji and it was in this match that I saw for the first time how important experience and attitude can be at the top level. All the boys spoke about how we needed to be very physical from the start and then let our skill follow, because if you win the physical battle the Fijian boys have a history of going quiet. For Ilie, this was a match made in heaven – belting his kava brothers for fourteen minutes! He was on fire and we won decisively, with everyone in the frontline doing their bit for the team.

We had to wait about an hour for the final, where we were to play New Zealand, who were a very good team and contained a young attacking powerhouse named Jonah Lomu. Two things from just before kick-off remain firmly entrenched in my memory. Firstly, there was the crowd of 40,000 who were singing and dancing to the Cathay Pacific and Coca-Cola advertisements; they made the stadium seem like a living thing. And secondly, there was the streaker who emerged from one end of the field and picked up the match ball on the halfway line and scored at the other end. Then he got up and converted his 'try', to the roar of the crowd, then bravely returned to the end of the field where his escapade had begun, only to be crash-tackled by bodyguards who were roundly booed for doing so!

In the end, New Zealand were too good for us and the world got their first real glimpse of how destructive Jonah would be. He was incredibly big, fast, agile and had a great time on the end of an experienced backline that included one of the great sevens players, Eric Rush, which provided him with plenty of space. We were always going to struggle to contain him, and with the final going for an extra six minutes the task became too much. They were crowned worthy champions, after which a great night was had by all the teams in a private function back at the hotel.

The tour was a fantastic experience, and I came home not just with a dud suit and two hundred Hong Kong dollars lighter but also having learned some important lessons that I would use throughout my career. I knew the value of laughter in the team environment, even at the highest level, of working and playing hard, being able to switch on and off and taking care of each other – and how important it is to make the effort to warmly welcome a new member to the Wallabies brotherhood.

4

THE TACKLE

1994

'*The tackle to save the Wilson try was the result of his working to involve himself as much as possible in the game . . .*'

DAVID KIRK, ALL BLACK CAPTAIN 1986–87,
AFTER THE BLEDISLOE CUP TEST OF 1994

The work players do off the ball can often be more important than the effort that everyone notices. There was some irony in the play that became known as 'the tackle', my hit on New Zealand's Jeff Wilson late in the Bledisloe Cup Test at the Sydney Football Stadium in 1994. The tackle put my face on the front page of the nation's newspapers and even onto morning television, giving me a prominence in the game that my then fledgling career hardly deserved. Yet I had only been in position to knock the ball loose because I'd come across in cover in case the All Blacks broke through the defenders in front of me. 'Plugging holes' in a defensive line is a big part of a halfback's job description. It's a high-energy position; a good half should always be working off the ball. In this case that was all I was doing, and I was fortunate to make the tackle. The result – in terms of public exposure – was drastic.

I was genuinely shocked when, in June 1994, I was first picked for the Test team, to be part of the bench for the two-game series against Ireland that was played ten weeks before the All Blacks Test. I was delighted with my Hong Kong experience, had played well for the Kookaburras (most notably when we beat NSW, with Roffy in dynamic form), and then, all of a sudden, I was among the Test reserves. Having been to Hong Kong, meeting my new team-mates when I was selected in the Test squad was not overly intimidating. I was still very much the rookie, but not a totally wide-eyed first-timer. Matt O'Connor was in the starting XV, the first Canberra player in four years to get a Wallabies starting role, and at fullback was Queensland's Matthew Pini, like me a St Edmund's old boy. I didn't get an opportunity in either Test, was surprised by how big the after-match celebrations were, and then in the week between the second Irish Test and the first Test against Italy, to be played at Ballymore in Brisbane, I received a phone call from the incumbent Australian halfback, Peter Slattery.

'George, you've been picked – good luck,' Peter told me. 'I'm really happy for you. Anything I can do to help . . .'

His calling was a massive gesture, and one that I never forgot. Slats had served a long apprenticeship under the recently retired Nick Farr-Jones and was entitled to treasure every minute as the first choice No. 9. Now the selectors had apparently decided to experiment with an untried rookie from Canberra. Yet he was brilliant about it.

'Slats, mate, I don't know what to say,' I said.

'Mate, don't worry about me,' he said. 'It's an opportunity for you. Take it.'

I promised to take him up on his offer to help. I knew there would be so much going through my head in the lead-up to the Test, and sure enough there was.

Slats, and others in the Wallabies set-up, were clever enough not to overwhelm me with too much information. There is only so much you can teach a new player; the trick is to offer him the right things. He advised me to focus on what I had to achieve to play my position well. Learn the calls, get the calls quickly from the right people, pass them on just as quickly. Effective communication with the back row, indeed with the entire pack, is important. Don't talk for the sake of talking. Be precise.

This Wallabies team included a number of men who had been part of the World Cup-winning side of 1991 and they had very high standards which they endeavoured and expected to meet every time they played. I fancied the challenge of trying to meet these standards, though at times over the next couple of years I'd be fully tested. The team also had an incredible self-belief and a strong culture of winning. If you didn't do your job, or forgot something, they would let you know. I remember Phil Kearns, the Wallabies hooker since 1989, now a great mate, getting into me at training a few times for not giving him a call. *Okay, fair enough*, I thought. I didn't mind him getting into me because I was at fault and I had to do better. This was one way the Wallabies psyche changed during my thirteen years in the squad. In my last couple of years, if someone went too hard at a team-mate, there was a fear that the criticised colleague might react badly. In 1994, you copped it and swore to yourself, *I won't do that again.*

I have no problem with this. It's a process that sorts out the weak from the strong.

My first Test was an ugly game, decided by a late penalty goal kicked by our replacement No. 10, Tim Wallace. My night was spoiled by an errant Italian finger, which poked my left eye, leaving my vision impaired and forcing me from the field. The Ballymore faithful roared their approval when Slats, the local hero, came on to replace me, but that didn't worry me. I would have expected nothing less. All up, I didn't feel as if the Test had gone too well, or too badly, so I was grateful to get another opportunity in the second Test against the Italians.

In the eyes of our coach, Bob Dwyer, our performance in the Test against Western Samoa played two weeks after the second Italy Test, was the high point of our season, principally because the team went out to do a job and did it clinically. We utilised just about every opportunity; it was one of those rare nights where everything clicks. It also showed that, even after two sub-par performances against Italy, the team had a certain confidence about it that was hard to break.

David Knox, into the side at No. 10 with Michael Lynagh injured, had a huge game. Knoxy was a very good player who, by standing up close to the defence, put himself under enormous pressure. But he had the most incredible pair of hands, catching and passing quickly, and by standing flat he created so much space for the men outside of him. As a halfback, it was easy to find him. If you were going forward, you could literally throw the ball parallel to the goal line and he was there. I remember when Stephen Larkham, who would become one of Australia's greatest No. 10s, took over from Knoxy at the Brumbies in 1999; we tried to get him to align himself as his predecessor had – flat, close to the defence – but at that time it proved difficult for him. Knoxy and I ended up playing a lot of rugby together, particularly with the Brumbies, and I was always amazed by his ability and understanding of how to create space for his outside backs.

From the moment we assembled in Sydney for the All Blacks Test of 1994 I noticed a difference in intensity between this and my previous Tests. The experienced guys' attitude to the game was different; every time we went on the training pitch, we went up another gear. I felt like I'd discovered Christmas, and couldn't wait to get out there, to see if I could handle it.

I guess, in a way, a young player observing the experienced team-mates is like a child watching grown-ups. You learn from what they do, and the things that matter stay with you. For me, this process started in Hong Kong, when I watched how the top players could relax and have a laugh, but when it came time to switch on to train or play, they did so straight away. It's not an easy mental skill but the great players do it every time. I can think of a number of talented players who were wired up all the time, as if they were playing the game beforehand. None of them lasted long.

Knowing when to switch on and when to have a laugh was second nature to Timmy Horan, as I was to discover when the phone in the hotel room rang a couple of days before the game. It was a 'New Zealand journalist', who began with a couple of straight up and down questions about the forthcoming match, and I answered them honestly. But something wasn't quite right, and I put my hand over the receiver and whispered to my roomie, Damian Smith, 'It's a gee-up.' I will admit I didn't know whom I was talking to, but I can recognise a dud Kiwi accent when I hear one.

The next question concerned the private lives of a couple of my team-mates, which I dismissed with a sharp 'no comment', and then the 'reporter' asked me about the rumours he'd been hearing about me being gay. 'Who the hell is this?' I asked.

It was Helmy.

The year of 1994 was a losing one for the All Blacks, but more than one of them told me at the '95 World Cup that one of the best things they took out of the season was the way the Test in Sydney panned out, because after it they knew they could beat Australia. The way the Wallabies played had changed very little since the 1991 World Cup, and the Kiwi camp now felt they had our measure, given that they had fought back from quite a deficit to take the lead at the Sydney Football Stadium, before losing so unluckily at the death. Though South Africa was the best team on the day of the 1995 Cup final, there's no doubt the Kiwis were the best team at that tournament.

The first try of the game came after sixteen seconds. David Knox put up a high ball, and Jason Little grabbed it out of the sky. Against the All Blacks, renowned as they are for fast starts, this was a phenomenal beginning, and it just got better, because after twenty-five minutes we led 17–3. We put pressure on them and created opportunities to score, almost like a carry-on from what we'd been doing against Samoa, but then they regrouped, took some chances of their own, and fought their way back.

Eighty minutes is a long time in a game of football, and it's inevitable when two good teams meet that each will get periods of time where they'll control possession. The team that best takes advantage of these periods of dominance and best absorbs the pressure when they are under attack is the one who'll end up winning on the day. Being fifteen or twenty points down doesn't mean you're out of it unless you think you are. It was very rare when playing against the top sides during my career that I felt comfortable even with a substantial lead. The All Blacks are renowned for putting two tries on you back to back.

The Wilson tackle was one of three I made during the Test that were highlighted after the game. Dropping front-rower Richard Loe, who had something of a reputation as a hit man, was nice. It happened at the back of a lineout, when he ran straight at me as if he was going to plough over the top of me, but I had good position on him. The thing with a tackle like that is that you can't dwell on it for an instant, because you have to get back in the line; another attack is coming. I also made a good hit on their big second-rower Mark Cooksley. In both instances, it was a case of the big guy thinking he could just run over the little guy.

There was a lot of luck in my tackle on Jeff Wilson. If, before he and I came together, other things had happened differently, no one would have noticed that I'd run across in cover. But things evolved the way they did. Wilson, who was playing on the right wing, actually did brilliantly, getting the ball more than 30 metres out, stepping inside Jason Little, evading David Wilson (who'd covered more ground than me in quicker time to be in a position to try to stop his namesake's run) and then brushing past David Campese. I was coming across as fast as I could, just about on the try line, and Wilson must have misjudged where the line was, because instead of sliding in as he could have done, he leaped for the line, reaching out to plant the ball with his right arm. I dived at him hard at about hip-height while he was in mid-air, and the ball was forced free.

There was no time for celebrations or recriminations. A 5-metre scrum, and my next task was to pass the ball to Knoxy's left foot so he could clear our line. Everyone in Wallaby gold was thinking the same thing: *Don't give them another chance.* Five minutes later – including an anxious final sixty seconds when the All Blacks mounted an extraordinary, desperate last stand – we were home, and I got my hands on the Bledisloe Cup for the first time in my life.

After the game, I was asked if, as the play unfolded, I thought I could get to Wilson. 'Yeah, I thought I could,' I replied. Unfortunately, my reply was twisted and some media reports claimed that I *knew* I was going to *stop the try*. When I saw that, I was horrified. I thought I could reach him, and when I did I hit him as hard as I could. That's what happened; the rest was luck.

A couple of the senior guys warned me that it was going to be crazy for a few days, and they weren't wrong. Everyone was interested in me, and I had no idea how to cope with the media attention. The Australian Rugby Union didn't have a media liaison officer at that time, and all the calls were going through to the Park Royal hotel room I was sharing with winger Damian Smith, who joked that he was now my personal assistant. One of those calls was from IMG, the global sports management company, who wanted to look after me. 'Life changing' is probably too strong a term to describe what was happening to me, but certainly there were moments when it felt that way. It really wasn't until I got back to university the following week that I felt that normal transmission could be resumed. But even then, I was conscious of the fact that I was being noticed *everywhere*. Whereas previously my name had featured once or twice on the back page and a few times on the inside back pages, now I'd made the lead on the television news and been prominent on the front pages, too. The women's magazines wanted to do stories on me, my family and my relationship with Erica, my girlfriend of a few months. The anonymity I'd taken for granted was gone and I'd lost it very quickly.

*

The final irony of this story is that over the course of my career, there were other tackles I made that meant more to me than any of those I made against New Zealand in 1994. I had actually made a very similar one on Western Samoa's Toa Samania near the left-hand corner post in the Test immediately before the All Blacks game, but we won that match 73–3 so it was hardly noticed. But if I had to nominate one tackle that meant the most to me it would be the one that stopped Lions winger Iain Balshaw near the end of the series-deciding Test at Stadium Australia in 2001. Again, in a sense, I was just doing my job, but the most logical response in this instance would have been for me to cover the open side, because that's the way it appeared the play was heading. But I sensed we were short on the short side, and when the play worked back that way, we were indeed in trouble. I rushed across behind the ruck, Balshaw got the ball, and I got to him, snuffing out their last attack of the game. If I hadn't made that tackle Balshaw would have been away with only Joe Roff in front of him. Roffy, for one, was over the moon that I was able to make that one.

5

DROPPED

1995

'The beauty of sport is you get to have a lot of experiences, some negative and some positive, but they are all very good in their own way.'

GEORGE GREGAN, 2007

Professionalism came to rugby at just about the perfect time for me. At the end of 1994, the IRB had relaxed the amateur rules slightly so players could receive income from sponsorships, but not from actually playing the game. As a consequence, we started to get rewarded for promoting the game, and Bob Dwyer's promotions company was heavily involved in assisting the ARU in finding such opportunities for us. After graduating from university, I went straight into a job as a trainee manager with Qantas, a major backer of Australian rugby. Further, the ARU came up with

45

a scheme that saw eleven Wallabies paid around $80,000 ('A' contracts) to 'ensure their endorsement of ARU sponsors and to make promotional appearances', while other players were offered second-tier (around $50,000) and third-tier (around $15,000–$20,000) deals. I was on the second tier, and with the addition of a sponsorship deal IMG had organised with Reebok and some speaking engagements, that for me was big money. I thought myself extremely fortunate, especially when I considered the calibre of many of the players who had been placed on lower levels.

What I found grating during this period (and in the years that followed) was the attitude of some people, including a few journalists, who became almost obsessed with the money we were making. A high-profile footballer such as Phil Kearns, who was inevitably a top-ranked player and also had a good job with Tooheys, was making well into six figures. There was some genuine bitterness about. One journo referred to the example of Kearnsy, and then said to me, 'There's no way I'd get near that sort of money.'

'Mate, you are not out there playing and making the tackles,' I said honestly, if a little naively. 'And it could end tomorrow.' The memory of severe knee injuries suffered by Tim Horan and Jason Little in 1994 was fresh in all the players' minds. Tim's injury had been especially horrific, and he was in the process of fighting back to make the upcoming World Cup. But the reporter didn't take too kindly to my logic. It was as if we were ruining the game. *How dare players earn this sort of money!* was his attitude.

John Eales and I took up Qantas traineeships at the start of 1995, three months before the 'Super League war' in rugby league sent rugby union hurtling towards a brave new world of its own. It was an opportunity to learn something of the business and a potential career path, which fitted in with our football schedule.

I was working largely at Canberra Airport, performing a wide range of tasks: checking people in at the Qantas Club, tagging bags, coordinating flight information, handling customer complaints . . . *what is the right thing to say when fog engulfs Canberra?* . . . a stint in the holidays department. I stayed with Qantas until the end of 1996, when the demands of a game that had become fully professional meant that my life as a halfback took precedence.

The spotlight from the Jeff Wilson tackle gradually faded as we reached the end of 1994, but occasionally there were moments when it flickered back to life, such as when I was named one of *Cleo* magazine's '50 Most Eligible Bachelors'. My mates laughed at my melon appearing in the pages of a publication like *Cleo*, I laughed, my girlfriend, Erica, certainly laughed. We weren't married yet, so I guess I was eligible for the 'award'.

I'd met Erica in Melbourne, after the second Test against Italy, and we'd clicked straight away. Originally a Sydney girl, Erica was living in Melbourne, setting up a business. In 1996, we would set up a home together in Paddington, in Sydney's eastern suburbs (which is why I turned out for Randwick in the Sydney club competition that year – my last, it turned out, because of my ever-increasing representative commitments). We would be married in 1998, in a wonderful, very personal, private ceremony on Fiji's Turtle Island.

In early 1995, the Qantas gig and the rugby contract meant that I could afford to move out of home, to a flat in Kingston. I was excited to be setting up on my own, but also keen, as I said in a magazine interview, to 'go home a few times a week to keep tabs on Mum's cooking, to make sure it doesn't slip'. (I still do that, though not as often as I'd like, with me living in Sydney and

Mum and Dad still at Kambah. And her cooking's never slipped. Never will.)

My football year started with the sevens, for what turned out to be my last year on the circuit. I was lucky enough to lead the Australian team to Hong Kong in 1995; the Super 10 clashed with the tournament, which meant the leading players from NSW and Queensland weren't available, so I suddenly became an 'old head'. We were belted by Fiji in the semis after beating England 26–0 in the quarters.

The year moved very quickly from this point on, with everything leading towards the World Cup. We played only two Test matches in Australia, against the Argentinians, and by late May we were flying to South Africa to start our World Cup defence.

I will never forget the bus ride from the airport to our hotel in the middle of town when we arrived in Cape Town for the start of the 1995 World Cup. It was impossible to miss the stark contrast between rich and poverty-stricken, the shanty towns and suburbia. We had ten days from when we landed to the Cup's opening game – Springboks versus Wallabies – and during that time, as well as settling in, attending functions and treating niggling injuries, we visited the township of Zwilde. In one sense, this was a PR exercise, though for me it was also a reminder of how lucky I was to be living the life I had. I remember the smiles on the kids' faces, but more than that I remember the bare and dusty field that they happily ran around, barefoot. All they wanted was the ball in their hands; there was no concern about grazes, cuts or a twisted ankle. They just loved their sport.

There had been a tiny bit of me wondering whether I'd be treated any differently to other Wallabies because of my African heritage. I'm not sure I ever was, though at the official pre-tournament function some prominent (white) South African players did make a point of coming over to shake my hand, which I assumed was part of a deliberate effort on their part to be seen to be welcoming a black man. The home team had a 'one team, one nation' slogan which was emblazoned on their team bus, and they took every opportunity to show they were fair dinkum about that. The most vivid illustration of this was during the final, when Nelson Mandela famously wore a Springbok jumper as he cheered the South Africans to victory.

I've travelled there a lot in the years since and I've come to accept that there is a part of white South Africa that is not going to lose the attitudes they grew up with until generational change is complete. The South African children of today will definitely be more open in the way they look at the world. It must be hard when a world view is ingrained in you and then, all of a sudden, you are told to 'mend your ways'. South Africa still needs a lot of work; it is an interesting place to experience for that very reason.

The hotel we were staying at in Cape Town was just a few blocks from Newlands, and it was evident on the morning of the opening game that there was a big match on. When we stepped from the hotel foyer to the team bus for the short drive to the stadium, the place was alive, with flags and whistles and Springbok jerseys everywhere, braais on the street and in the car park, people young and old getting their faces painted. It was a Thursday, but hardly a working day – for South Africans, who had been basically starved of international sport through the 1980s and early 1990s because of the international boycott of apartheid, this was an occasion to rival any sporting event in its history. I'd never played in an atmosphere like that. It was loud – not overly aggressive, just really, really loud and passionate. Nelson Mandela was there to open proceedings, and his presence and the unmistakable aura that surrounds him added to the feel that this was *their* day. Jet fighters roared overhead, tribesmen performed their war dances, the place was buzzing with anticipation, as if an emotional dam was about to burst.

We were confident going into the game, despite a number of guys being less than 100 per cent fit. (Four years later, Brett Robinson was left out of the World Cup team because he wasn't completely right. If the same measure had been applied in 1995, a few players would have missed the squad.)

We started really well. We had some nice rhythm and Michael Lynagh scored a good try that gave us a 13–9 lead eight minutes before half-time. But then we started to give a few penalties away, and they scored just before the interval – a critical momentum swing. After that, we seemed to lose our way in the second half, as their No. 10, Joel Stransky, started kicking goals from every-where.

I didn't play as competently as I wanted to in this tournament, and a moment that occurred served as a good lesson for me. I had gone into the tournament believing that a key part of my job was to communicate with the forwards, and part of that role was to call a lot of back-row moves . . . unless Michael Lynagh wanted the ball. If my captain asked for it, he got it. At one stage, I passed to Noddy, but I'd misinterpreted his call.

'Where's the back-row move?' he demanded.

'Hang on, mate,' I replied. 'I thought you wanted it.'

'No, I want back-row moves.'

'Okay, no problems.'

For the next few minutes, I called back-row moves, but then he was into me again, this time for not passing the ball.

'Okay,' I sighed. 'Let me know one way or the other.'

A halfback must be able to communicate with his team-mates;

if he can't, the machine can't function properly. Noddy and I just didn't gel as a combination during this World Cup, a fact which was more my fault than his. I think I matured as a footballer because of the problems I had during the '95 World Cup. The experience forced me to take on more responsibility and greater ownership of the role of directing the team. I resolved to never again give a fly-half a reason to get into me for being indecisive. If I was to make a call, other players would have to trust my judgment. If anyone didn't agree, they could discuss it at a break in the play or after the game, but had to commit to the move in the moment.

The quality of South Africa's performance didn't surprise us. The Wallabies had played them in 1993, when the Wallabies lost the first Test but fought back to win the three-game series. My experience against South African teams was restricted to games against their provincial teams, such as Northern Transvaal, but that was enough for me to know they were big strong guys, big on the set piece. In this game, they did put a lot of pressure on at the base of the scrum, but to be honest I didn't feel like they were specifically targeting me (though after the World Cup both South Africa and England claimed they had). You are always getting targeted at No. 9. However, the Springboks were very good at manipulating the scrum and while our scrum started very well, we struggled a little in the second half. A bit like a prizefighter not used to being knocked down, we lost a bit of confidence and, despite being an experienced side, we didn't deal with the situation well. I would learn over the ensuing seasons that when you find yourself in these situations, you need to come up with something that gets you back into the game, gets you a bit of momentum. We never did that. We just kept leaking oil. The Springboks actually beat us more emphatically than the 27–18 margin suggested.

*

This was my first Test loss. I had come into a winning culture; at times in my first four Tests we had not played well, but we had still won. And while I don't believe we handled the second half of the South Africa game well, in the days after that setback the senior guys, led by Noddy, were excellent. 'This wasn't the plan,' they said, 'but we have to move on.' The defeat meant the path to the final would be more difficult, with matches against England and New Zealand in prospect for the quarter-final and semifinal respectively. We handled Romania and Namibia comfortably, and the mood among the players was positive and upbeat, but the coach was growing more and more morose. I will never forget his address to the team at the meeting the night before the quarter-final. Bob thanked everyone for their efforts and, as he did so, he became very emotional, choking up and then crying. It was as if he was reading the eulogy at our funeral, and I couldn't believe he'd addressed the team in that way. It was like he had given up on us the night before we played. It is something that has stayed with me – a leader should never send that message.

Maybe Bob feared losing more than he hoped to win, and had resigned himself to defeat. He had clearly been a great rugby coach – his record, which includes leading the Wallabies to the 1991 World Cup, is proof of that – and I will always be grateful for the opportunity he gave me. He could quite easily have decided to give me more time before I was first picked to play for Australia, but he gambled on me.

After we lost that opening game in Cape Town, I had a one-on-one meeting with the coaches. There was discussion on the quality of my decision-making, and some valid criticism, and I conceded I'd taken some poor options and struggled at the set pieces. The video was revealing, as it showed their hooker, James

Dalton, running through our lineout. I wasn't blaming others for my problems, but I did point out that if we could tighten up at the set piece and at the breakdown, and improve our communication, we'd get cleaner ball which, of course, would have a flow-on effect to our backline play.

As a halfback, you throw your quickest pass when you get quick, clean ball. When it's an absolute dogfight at the break-down, it becomes hard work. I do agree that one of the greatest skills a halfback can have is to be able to compensate for a lack of team momentum at the set piece and the breakdown, but that isn't easy. As far as I could tell, there was no conscious effort to rectify these problems at the 1995 World Cup, and it was never brought up at a team meeting; instead, there was a blind faith that, because it had worked in the past, we'd keep going the way we were. Our campaign had been branded 'Mission: REPEAT' (short for 'Mission: Reach Ellis Park and Ensure Another Twickenham'), but to win this time we needed to do more than just mimic what had been achieved when the Wallabies won the Cup at Twicken-ham in 1991. There is always a danger in trying to be as good as last time, rather than better than last time. I learned some great lessons from this period of my rugby life in terms of what you need to do to recover from a poor performance, personally and as a team. And the most important thing is that you fight back as a team. It's a team sport. The softest and easiest thing for the leader-ship to do is deflect the blame down to a couple of people, which was what happened then. I was struggling, for sure, but I wasn't the only one.

Seventeen days after our World Cup started, it ended when we lost in the last minute to England in the quarter-finals. It was a wet day, totally different to the conditions in the game against South Africa, and the game became a 'set-piece fest'. Dewi Morris, their No. 9, made an absolute nuisance of himself at the back of our scrum, as for the first time I experienced a Northern Hemisphere halfback putting heaps of pressure on me. It was a scrappy game, and I got caught up in the arm wrestle at times. With four minutes to go, we were in front, but we crashed out. The end to that game was a terrible experience – one that would occur again for me at the same ground at the back end of my career, in 2007, when Francois Steyn kicked two late drop goals to win the day. In both cases, we knew the match-winning three-pointer was coming but there was nothing we could do to stop it. I remember the sound of the ball off the boot of Rob Andrew, the Poms' five-eighth – it was like a gunshot, and the ball just kept climbing through the posts. It was never going to miss and we were going home.

We flew back to Australia four days later, and the disappointment of our early exit was reinforced at Perth Airport, when we saw groups of Australian rugby fans in the check-in lounge, some wearing green and gold, waiting for their flights to South Africa to watch the semi-finals and final. When they'd paid their money many months before, they would have fully expected to be cheering the Wallabies in those matches. I couldn't help but feel that we'd let them down. Sometimes, giving your best just doesn't feel good enough. I didn't watch much of the final on television, maybe just the last few minutes and the presentation afterwards . . .

So it was back to Canberra, and club footy, while NSW played and beat Queensland twice in seven days, which gave the players from those two sides a chance to audition for a place in the Test team. As the ACT didn't play a game in this period, I didn't have that opportunity. In the Waratahs side, Steve Merrick, who worked in the mines at Singleton in the Hunter Valley was at No. 9. Merrick played very well, and suddenly the papers were pushing for his inclusion in the Test XV, declaring that he represented the 'fresh start' the team needed after our World Cup failure. Bob's position was tenuous, and while he wanted to stay loyal to the guys who had been good for him in the past, he knew he had to make changes, and I was one of them.

I was disappointed to lose my spot, but the memory of how Peter Slattery had responded when he was dropped for me was still crystal clear in my mind. I was on the bench for the two All Blacks Tests – one in Auckland, the other in Sydney. It was a new perspective for me, the first time I'd watched from the sideline while knowing from experience some of what was going on out in the middle, and I'd like to think I carried myself pretty well. But I do remember asking, as every player should when he is dropped, 'What are the areas I need to work on?' Bob Dwyer responded, 'You are playing really well, just keep going, your time will come.'

By contrast, a mate such as Dave Wilson, a sensible man and wonderful player who was twenty-five when he won his first Test cap, was fantastic, offering good advice about my technique and my communication on the field, and also giving tips on how to respond to the trauma of losing my place in the team. Bomber had a way of making you feel good about yourself, and he told me not to feel embarrassed about being dropped. Disappointed, sure, but not embarrassed. Tim Horan, Jason Little and Phil Kearns – three guys who had been brought into the side by Bob when they were very inexperienced – were also very helpful, assuring me that the coach had my best interests at heart. Maybe he thought I needed toughening up, or that the acclaim that went with 'the tackle' had come too quickly for me. As it turned out, being left out of the side at the end of 1995 helped me cope with what I would go through in 1996, when Sam Payne and I swapped the No. 9 jumper.

Soon after the second All Blacks Test of 1995, Steve Merrick announced he was retiring, to go back to his mining job. Early in

1996, Bob Dwyer was replaced as the Wallabies coach by Greg Smith. In between, the fallout from the 'rugby revolution', the stormy road to full professionalism that had rocked the sport to its core in the weeks after the World Cup, changed the face of rugby forever . . .

6

YESTERDAY'S MAN

1995

'To all Australian supporters here today, we thank you. It's been terrific, your support. And whatever happens in the future . . . we hope you and the Union support us.'
PHIL KEARNS, WALLABIES CAPTAIN, AFTER AUSTRALIA HAD LOST
TO THE ALL BLACKS, 29 JULY 1995

In the autumn of 1995, News Limited, the global media empire headed by Rupert Murdoch, launched their 'Super League war'. Rugby league's best players were being offered colossal money to either join News Limited's new league movement or stick with the traditional 'owners' of the game, the Australian Rugby League. This process had begun on 1 April, when a number of players agreed to Super League deals and the ARL responded with mega-offers of their own. It was only a matter of time before the best rugby players – with most eyes on Tim Horan and Jason Little – would be getting phone calls. Soon stories were spreading that some of the highest-profile Wallabies were going to switch to league, lured by contracts worth many hundreds of thousands of dollars. One *Daily Telegraph Mirror* article featured my photograph with a $400,000 price tag underneath. Elsewhere, I had people telling me I was worth this and that. I was thinking, *According to whom?* My bank balance hardly reflected that – and besides, in the eyes of many rugby people, I was a major reason why we'd lost the World Cup. In April 1995, I had been the rising star of Australian rugby. Three months later, after the World Cup, when all the talk was about rugby players receiving huge contracts, I was out of the Test XV, yesterday's man. Still, the *Sydney Morning Herald* listed 'The Wallabies Most Wanted' as Jason Little, Tim Horan, Matt Burke, Willie Ofahengaue, Tim Kelaher and me. Ironically, in the same article that had me signing a $400,000 rugby league deal, John Eales, the best player in Australian rugby at the time, was described as being 'unlikely to attract Super League offers'. This was 13 April 1995; on 10 April the board of the NSW Rugby Union had passed a resolution recognising that rugby was no longer an amateur sport, and during the same week Geoff Levy, a Sydney-based lawyer, went to the office of Ross Turnbull (a prominent figure in Australian rugby) and they came up with the concept of the World Rugby Corporation.

WRC was, in essence, a response to Super League. The idea was that rugby franchises would be established around the globe, with WRC owning the rights to the provincial and international tournaments that would be staged. Ideally, the existing unions would still administer the game, but if they chose not to under these circumstances, so be it. People spoke about WRC meaning the death of the Wallabies, but I frankly doubted that, though I guess it was possible that there might have been a period, as happened with cricket in the late 1970s, when there might have been 'rebel' Tests.

I wasn't really aware of WRC until after the World Cup. We had been warned that Ross Turnbull, a prominent and controversial figure in Australian rugby, was involved in some kind of rugby scheme, and we had been advised at a pre-tour meeting by ARU president Phil Harry to avoid him, but for me it wasn't until we returned home that things began to get interesting.

To my surprise, Bob Dwyer soon contacted me to talk about WRC. Bob seemed genuine in his belief that WRC was the best way to prevent the team from being taken over by Super League, but was vague when it came to whether the ARU would be involved. He told me that most of the team was already on board, but I had no idea if this was true, as I had been back in Canberra since the World Cup and had not been in contact with any of my Wallabies team-mates. I needed a player's point of view, and Bob said he'd get one of the guys to give me a call. I honestly can't recall who it was who rang me – it might have been Rod McCall or Ewen McKenzie or Phil Kearns (over the next three months I spoke to a lot of players at different times) – but it was Ewen who came down to Canberra to talk to a group of ACT players WRC was keen to sign up. It was only natural for me to be cautious – I was only twenty-two years old, with a lot of football left ahead of me and there was clearly a risk involved in taking on the establishment. But what got me in eventually was the fact that so many of the best players from around the world appeared to be committed to the plan, as were just about all my team-mates. On top of this, it would be a real boost for the non-international players who'd been playing at an amateur level for a long time – each team would have to have at least thirty players, so they'd need more than just international representatives. It was seriously

looking like a revolution, a genuine fast-tracking of rugby professionalism.

What I also saw in WRC – which didn't look likely in traditional rugby – was a chance for the Canberra boys to take their
football to the next level. WRC would be a vehicle for us staying
together as a group – maybe not playing in Canberra (there was
strong talk about us becoming part of a Melbourne franchise), but
at least we'd be involved in a level of football we thought we were
entitled to be a part of. In the end this happened anyway, when the
Brumbies were somewhat reluctantly invited into the Super 12 for
1996, but there was no guarantee of that at the time.

I didn't get my WRC contract checked by my lawyer before I
signed it – I decided to follow the guidance of WRC's legal team
because there was a high degree of confidentiality required, and a
high level of trust, too, on all sides. I don't think I was being naive,
but pragmatic. All involved knew instinctively that we couldn't
make the new rugby a reality if we acted as individuals; we had to
work collectively. If 100 or more players were committed, including the best in the world, then our unified voice would be a very
powerful one.

The Australian, New Zealand and South African unions
recognised this too, though initially, at least, the Australian rugby
administrators moved slowly to try to counter WRC. By the time
the ARU asked the players to sign contracts, weeks *after* the
governing bodies had committed themselves to their own $US555
million ten-year arrangement with News Limited, most of us had
signed contracts with WRC. The fact the rugby authorities signed
such a massive deal without at least keeping the players informed
that such negotiations were taking place was one of the things that
pushed the players to WRC.

The rugby authorities sought to divide and conquer. Jason Little and Pat Howard were convinced to sign with the ARU, then NSW forward Tim Gavin was too, while heavy pressure was put on elite players such as John Eales, who had signed a contract with WRC but was thought to be wavering.

The day after the All Blacks Test in Sydney, on 30 July, Phil Harry and NSW Rugby Union Chairman Ian Ferrier spoke at a team meeting and asked bluntly, 'Is there anyone here who cannot sign an ARU contract? If there is, leave the room; we don't want you.'

None of us knew quite what to do, until Tim Horan stood up slowly and said, 'I need a glass of water . . . I'm parched!' Everyone laughed, a little nervously, and the matter went no further, at that time.

A lot has been made of a meeting initiated by Rod McCall and Phil Kearns, held at the Parkroyal Hotel at Darling Harbour in Sydney, where the sports entrepreneur James Erskine was invited by Kearnsy to address the guys who had signed with WRC. As legend has it, Erskine promptly bagged WRC's commercial viability and, soon after the meeting, the movement collapsed. I don't remember it that way. I do recall Erskine's speech, and wondering why it was anti-WRC, seeing as he'd been invited by Kearnsy, but I really don't think that at that time Erskine swayed anyone who was genuinely committed to the cause. It wasn't long, however – within weeks – before it became apparent that WRC's backers were having second and third thoughts, and some people involved in the battle began to think Erskine's words were critical. Furthermore, in the preceding days a few more players had done the double-dip and signed contracts with the ARU; Josh Kronfeld and Jeff Wilson had returned to the NZRU; while the entire South African team had reneged on their agreement. When WRC's financial backing soon fell over, the rugby war was finished.

Our players jumping ship had an impact, but it was the South African team's decision en masse that was the death blow. The reticence of many players in the Northern Hemisphere to fully commit also didn't help. We went from being a strong unit to a fractured one in a matter of days, largely because WRC wasn't able to pay any money up front, while the ARU could.

What saved traditional rugby in the end was that WRC hadn't quite got their financial backing in place; they had to have the project up and running by 22 November; if they didn't manage that, the contracts we'd signed were invalid. The ARU, by contrast, were able to put News Limited-backed contracts on the table by early August, and players were faced with the choice of hoping that WRC would come good or signing with the cashed-up devil they knew. Enough players took the latter option and WRC was dead. It had to be one in, all in. We all knew that.

And so it was that in mid-August the ARU was able to announce an agreement by which the players would receive 95 per cent of the TV rights emanating from the News Limited deal, that no players would be discriminated against because of their links to WRC, and that the ARU would support the establishment of a players' association. At first glance the 95 per cent share of TV rights seemed generous, but whether that would turn out to be fair would depend on how much money was raised from other media rights, sponsorship and merchandise sales. The birth of a player's association was, in my eyes, the most positive and far-reaching thing to come out of the entire affair.

The fact that a number of players signed two conflicting contracts, effectively committing themselves to both sides of the fence, has never sat well with me. Some players were allegedly offered indemnity from potential WRC prosecution, others were told they'd never play for Australia again if they didn't align themselves quickly with the ARU, but my discussions never got that far.

At one stage, Phil Harry came down to Canberra, we chatted amicably about the issues and where the ARU was going, and then he put a contract in front of me. I'm sure he wanted me to autograph it on the spot, but I explained that I'd have to go away and think about it. The money in that deal was significantly less than the figure WRC had put on my table, but it wasn't the money differential that swayed me away from the ARU at that point. I'd signed one contract, with WRC, and felt bound to honour it. I wasn't going to bet each way.

Men such as Phil Kearns and Rod McCall were the main spokesmen for the guys who signed with WRC. Future Australian rugby players, at Test and provincial level, owe those two, especially Kearnsy, a massive pat on the back. He copped a lot of criticism – rumour has it that he would have lost the Wallabies captaincy (he was injured in 1996, so this was never tested) – but we wouldn't be where we are today without the leadership he offered at that time. Others who weren't so decisive and far-sighted signed conflicting contracts but escaped scrutiny. Kearnsy stood tough, and I was proud to be on his side.

If the Brumbies hadn't been invited into the Super 12 in the aftermath of the rugby war, I might have ended up in rugby league. As the end of the 1995 calendar year approached, I still hadn't signed an ARU contract. I had a strong view of what I was worth, based on what I'd heard other players had received, and the ARU offer was substantially below this figure. I'd also settled on a sum that was the minimum amount I'd accept, which was less than what a lot of players were on, and the ARU weren't even prepared to pay that. It was disappointing, to say the least.

One thing that had originally appealed to a lot of us was the fact that the WRC deal would see most of the top players getting paid in the same ballpark. There weren't the terrible discrepancies that were a feature of the ultimate ARU deals. It has never really been explained how the ARU calculated some of their offers, and when WRC collapsed there was no market force to get things right, unless you went to rugby league, as Matty O'Connor did. It is a fact that some promising guys from NSW who had never played Test football and who never did were offered amazing contracts while other players with much more to offer didn't get treated particularly well. Good luck to the guys who got the money, but it was unconscionably out of kilter. I know the ARU didn't offer me a great deal, even though I was still in the Test squad . . .

I came to look on the whole experience as a good lesson. Professional sport is about performance and consistency. The Test matches against Samoa and New Zealand in 1994 were now a distant memory, and I knew that I could never be satisfied with just getting back into the Test XV; I had to be consistent once I made it back. If I'd shown good form through 1995 the officials would have had no option but to pay me fairly, whatever my ties to WRC. However, the affair did put a slight wedge between me and rugby administrators, in the sense that I knew I had to be careful with them, and never assume they'd always be fair and reasonable.

Rod Macqueen, a former NSW breakaway, Waratahs coach and Australian selector, had been appointed the inaugural coach of the team that would be known as the Brumbies, and he was fantastic through this process. Rod was building an ACT Super 12 team from scratch, and he was quick to let me know he wanted me to be a key part of it. I explained my situation, and he committed to the Brumbies paying me a certain amount of money above the base salary I was being offered by the ARU, so that my total guaranteed pay reached that minimum amount I was seeking. I didn't like the idea of the Brumbies being out of pocket, because I knew their budget was tight, so I set myself the goal of playing enough Test football in 1996–97 so that the dollars the ARU would pay me per Test would be enough to get the Brumbies out of paying me a cent. It was nice, backing myself to do that; even better when I came through.

But before I finally signed that ARU deal, I caught up with Ricky Stuart, who was contracted to Super League. We talked generally, as mates do, but I definitely left him in no doubt that I was disappointed with my negotiations with the rugby union chiefs. Within days, I received an offer that involved seriously more money than I would earn if I stayed in rugby union.

I was approached to be the starting halfback for the new rugby league franchise in Adelaide, the Rams. Among the Super League men I talked to was the former union and league international Michael O'Connor, who would later come back to rugby as a Wallabies selector. For the first time in months, I felt I was dealing with officials who thought I could play and might be a positive influence. The league guys talked not just about where they thought their game was going, but how they could help me with opportunities off the field as well as on. They were extremely businesslike and professional in their dealings, whereas the rugby officials had been parochial and amateurish. I took a trip to Adelaide, where they demonstrated just how ambitious they were, how determined they were to build a modern league facility. They reminded me that Rupert Murdoch was an Adelaide boy, and that they wanted this franchise to be a showpiece.

If it was purely about money, I would have signed straight away, but I knew that I wasn't happy with what I'd achieved to that point as a rugby player. I'd started well, but now I was in a bit of a rut. I didn't want my rugby career to end this way, never knowing if I was good enough.

In the end it came down to three things: wanting to find out how good a rugby player I could be; validating my self-belief; and wanting to be a part of Rod Macqueen's Brumbies adventure. In the short term, at least, I cost myself a large sum of money, but I stuck with rugby. Even though the next twelve months wouldn't be easy for me as I battled to lock down the No. 9 Wallabies jumper, I never regretted my decision. Late in 1997, two years after the rugby war, it was time for many of those original ARU contracts to be renegotiated. A lot of players had their guaranteed money reduced, some by quite a bit. Mine went up substantially. I enjoyed that, because it reaffirmed what Ricky Stuart had told me in 1993: 'You get rewarded based on how you perform.'

7

TRUE PROFESSIONALS

1996–1997

'It was something Macqueen did very well. He involved his senior players in the decision-making to a degree which I hadn't seen before.'

DAVID LEWIS, ACT RUGBY UNION PRESIDENT IN 1996

Rod Macqueen was a different coach to any other I played under, before or since. It is true that with rugby tumbling into professionalism it was inevitable that the best coaches of the mid to late 1990s would bring to the game a whole new way of doing things, but even with this in mind Rod was ahead of his time. Way ahead. He introduced specialist coaches, as distinct from assistant coaches whose briefs covered a range of duties. He always talked about the 'big picture' and is still talking about it now. It's part of his character to do that. He brought a natural creativity to rugby, and blended that with an innate ability to get the best out of his men.

Whichever team he was coaching, Rod would look at his playing roster, and then come up with the best way for that team to play. He did this not by telling the players what to do, but by encouraging them to join the adventure, to help develop the means by which his side would win. He enjoyed surrounding himself with good operators, men who shared his vision and desire to be successful, whether they be players, coaches or support staff. He had a way of making you feel important, and encouraged us to think outside the box. At the Brumbies, when we played some of the higher-rated teams, he told us straight out that we couldn't play a traditional game against these fellows because we just didn't have the personnel to do that and prevail. We had to do things a bit differently, he told us. Of course, that was easy to say; what was much harder was coming up with the schemes that would work.

To try unconventional things and risk losing badly rather than merely conforming, to try hard and go down 'honourably', requires courage and a strong belief in yourself, as coach, and in your players. This kind of challenging approach can turn good into great, and it makes players confront their fear of failure, ensuring they go out hoping to win rather than fearing a loss. These were the traits that Rod instilled in the Brumbies culture when he was coach there in 1996 and 1997. He was more conservative as Wallabies coach from 1997 to 2001, because he could afford to be, given the quality of his squad. Rod never took risks for the sake of it.

Rod had a huge impact on Canberra rugby, but he wasn't the only one. Matt O'Connor was one of the first people I ever met who put a lot of time into studying tapes, seeing exactly how opposing teams performed, looking for things that could be exploited and things they did well, and Rodney Kafer thought along these lines as well. Consequently, we Canberra-based guys were ready for Rod Macqueen when he came to town with his analytical mind and preparedness to have every base covered.

We didn't see Rod as being so much a revolutionary as being one of us, someone who could take us much further along a journey we'd already begun. The members of the group that he eventually gathered together were all on the same page and had the same attitude. And we all had that point to prove, either because we were Canberra players who'd been neglected in the past, or guys who'd been flicked by NSW or Queensland. The vibe was brilliant, and Rod harnessed it beautifully.

At the Brumbies and then to the Wallabies, Rod's SWOT sessions became a thing of legend. Strengths. Weaknesses. Opportunities. Threats. It was his way of sorting through the issues facing us and identifying what had to be done to confront and overcome them. Players were required to study videos of past games involving our upcoming opponents, to determine what we'd be up against. We'd then tick off the various items under discussion, all of them written on butcher's paper or a whiteboard, until we felt we had all the likely scenarios covered. As the coach put it, he didn't want a thousand 'what ifs' running through our heads. It was about being prepared as best we could. Rod did enough of those SWOT analyses in my time that I eventually grew bored with them. When he recognised that, he turned the process on its head, asked us to SWOT ourselves.

Rod was no technical guru; the biggest thing he brought to the squad revolved around getting our positions right, whether we were defending, or carrying the ball, running a play, trying to create space. Whether it was second-, third- or fifth-phase ball, it didn't matter; it was about always making sure you were where you were supposed to be, where your team-mates expected you to be. One of his favourite expressions was *What happens next?* If we could predict that, and knew how to react or get ahead of the game, we'd win more often than not.

It was Rod who came up with the Brumbies nickname. Anxious to give us an identity to be proud of, he staged a 'workshop' in the high country at Thredbo, where he organised strategic planning sessions in the way businesses do. He was clearly very serious and it was our jobs as players to match his ambition. A lot of guys had been through the AIS program, which was very professional and certainly got you prepared for playing at the top level, and now this took the notion of superior preparation to a new level. There were plenty of questions asked: *How do we want to play? . . . How do we want to see ourselves? . . . And have others see us? . . . What are our strengths? . . . And weaknesses?* That first workshop, conducted over a weekend, was where what became the Brumbies philosophy was set in stone. We wanted to be a team who won games by using the ball, by scoring tries. We wanted to be intelligent in the way we played. Planning and preparation were going to be a big part of that. These things are now part of Brumbies DNA.

From day one, there was a united approach. Players, coaches – we were all in this together. It sounds clichéd, but that's how it was. It was a unique situation; we had no history, and were all starting on the same page. That was a massive point of difference from every other team in the competition. The level of player involvement was criticised by outsiders who really didn't have a clue about what we were doing, as if there were no leaders, no primary decision-makers, that we were being ruled by a mob. In fact, the leadership was well defined and a real strength for us was that we knew who was in charge. Yet everyone at the Brumbies had a stake in the endeavour, worked hard to support it, and believed in it.

Another thing Rod came up with was the idea of the players from Sydney and Brisbane staying in the same apartment complex. It jokingly came to be known as 'Melrose Place', but it helped build a kinship among the players who might otherwise have grown homesick, and it provided opportunities for the guys to work on game plans and study videos – as well as sharing pizzas and computer games. During the first year, when the ACT Rugby Union's finances were tight, the guys who were staying there had to pack up their gear every time the team went away on a long trip – such as to South Africa for three weeks – and store it in one or two apartments, leaving the rest to be rented out by the property's owners. That changed the following year, the first year I was a Melrose Place resident, but to this day it's a big, but worthwhile, expense for the Brumbies.

Even before a ball was kicked in Super 12, we were dismissed as a group of misfits with a few Canberra players thrown in. Yet as far as we were concerned, we had plenty to fight for. Our suspicion was that if we were hopeless, the rugby officials would quickly boot us out and set up another team in Perth, western Sydney or, more likely, in Melbourne. There was no siege mentality, because that's self-defeating, but there certainly was a strong sense of prove-them-wrong about us, at least for the first few years. Rod was excellent in channelling that feeling to our advantage, pushing the fact that while others didn't rate us, we *knew* we could play. We were definitely lucky with our timing. If Super 12 had started a couple of years earlier – before the Kookaburras had had a couple of big wins over other provincial sides and then reached the grand final of the 1995 'Sydney' first-grade premiership – I doubt Canberra would have got the call. The highlight was the day in July 1994 when we thrashed NSW 44–28 despite having a 16–5 penalty count go against us. 'Canberra played well,' NSW coach Greg Smith conceded. 'International sides haven't scored six tries against us, let alone a minor province.' The performance of the Kookas, made up almost entirely of Canberra products, was wonderful and I loved being a part of it. When it was time for the Brumbies to take over, and Rod recognised there was a need to bring guys in from Sydney and Brisbane, there was little objection from the locals. Had there been, it could have derailed the project before it began, but the Canberra guys, the players who missed out when at one point they might have thought they were going to be involved, were smarter than that. The spirit of the Brumbies went beyond just the playing group. It involved the whole city. Still does.

I was named vice-captain, supporting Brett Robinson, the inaugural skipper, and appreciated the recognition, especially after the events of the previous few months. It was like a new beginning. There were a number of guys in the squad with strong leadership credentials – 'Robbo', Ewen McKenzie, Troy Coker and the Argentinian Test prop Patricio Noriega – but with Matt O'Connor having gone to Super League, the backline, David Knox apart, was relatively inexperienced, so I was placed in a leadership role. When Robbo was injured in that first season, Ewen became captain and I remained vice-captain, which seemed eminently sensible to me. I kept that deputy role pretty much up until 2001, provincially and internationally, working under Rod, and it wasn't a bad place to be. A lot of the time I was probably the 'bad cop' as vice-captain to the 'good cop' captain. That was certainly my role with the Wallabies. With my nature – always questioning, always seeking to improve, always wanting the group to get things exactly right – it was a good role for me to play.

We were underrated right through that first season, as the press kept using the 'misfits' and 'rejects' descriptions without recognising that the players they were denigrating were actually very good footballers. The Reds, for example, had let a guy like David Giffin fall through the cracks, but that didn't mean Giff wasn't an outstanding lock – eventually playing fifty Tests. In my view, John Eales wouldn't have been the player he was without Giff, who called the lineouts in his first Test match as if he'd been doing so for a decade. He was one of the last guys picked by the Brumbies in 1996, and was my roommate during the Brumbies' tour of Japan prior to the 1996 Super 12 season.

Another key addition was Troy Coker, whom I would have been on the phone to for two or three weeks before he finally agreed to join us. Troy had been fantastic throughout the WRC saga, and I knew him as a straight up and down guy who would revel in the 'big picture' concepts that Rod was stressing to the team. The powers that be in Queensland had decided he was injury prone, but he was only thirty (he always said he was twenty-eight!) and presented as the No. 8 we desperately needed. I thought he was a must for us, and that's exactly what he proved to be.

We were a good team in 1996. We used the ball and it was just attractive footy to play and watch, which was handy, because Super 12 promoted positive rugby. Bonus points rewarded teams scoring tries, and the ball was in play more because the laws really encouraged players and coaches to use the ball. Before that, you could just hang on to it, knowing that if you were going forward you always got the feed. Now, if you were going forward but were held up, it was a turnover. We would often attack from our own half, and we scored forty or more points in a game four times in our first season, eight times in our second.

The manner in which our crowds at Bruce Stadium grew provided a barometer for our success. In the first season they were modest – not too shabby, but hardly full houses. We even played a game at Manuka Oval, which really was too small, but it had been the spiritual home of ACT rugby and the officials were loathe to desert it completely. In 1996, the Raiders rugby league team were coming to the end of the great run that had seen them win three premierships between 1989 and 1994. They were a dynamic team that had done much for Canberra's sporting identity, and had become so identified with Bruce Stadium that it was seen around town as the Raiders' ground. Initially, we were the poor cousins, but quicker than most expected we forged an identity of our own, to the point that our crowds, on average, were bigger than theirs.

The night we beat Auckland in 1996 remains one of the greatest in the history of ACT rugby. Auckland got off to a flying start, as Kiwi teams often do, but we reeled them in and ended up winning fairly comfortably. They did, though, end up scoring four tries and finishing within seven points of us, so they earned two bonus points. It was an incredible win and one that I really enjoyed – and not just because Auckland were undoubtedly the best provincial team in world rugby at that time.

The previous year, during the speeches at a function after the Bledisloe Cup Test in Auckland, Sean Fitzpatrick, the New Zealand captain, had looked straight at me and said, 'I thought the new Wallabies halfback, Steve Merrick, did really, really well. He has a bright future. I can see him being in that position for years to come.' It was classic 'Fitz'.

Andrew Mehrtens, who had been standing next to me, had whispered, 'What was that all about?' I could only think that it came back to 'the tackle' and how, in the aftermath of that game, Fitzpatrick had labeled me arrogant. This had been just another chance to chip at me Fitzpatrick-style.

Fast forward to that Super 12 game in Canberra against Fitzpatrick's team. In the second half, as we ran up a commanding lead, I couldn't resist. 'You are the Auckland Blues, the greatest provincial team in the world,' I commented during a break in play. 'Fitzy, what's going on?'

He copped it. I liked that about Fitzy, a champion forward whom I respect a lot. He knew when to cop it and when to give it. Near the end, when they scored that fourth try that gave them the bonus points, he said clearly, so the Brumbies could hear, 'Well done, boys, we got what we wanted tonight.'

'You came here looking for bonus points?' I cried out. 'For losing to us! C'mon, mate, that's embarrassing.'

He looked straight at me, but didn't say a word. We never entered into one-on-one dialogue on the field again, and off the field, from that moment, we were fine.

A rivalry quickly developed between the Blues and the Brumbies, one built on a mutual respect. Every time we played the Blues there was always a bit more in it, an attitude that was forged from day one. I remember Zinzan Brooke, the great Auckland No. 8 and captain, saying after that game, 'We will see you in the semis, so we can get one back on you.' The loss stung them, but they'd have to wait a while before we met in the finals.

In 1996, we ended up losing twice in South Africa in the third-last and second-last rounds, which meant we couldn't make the semifinals. Rather than moping, we ended our debut year with a 70–26, nine-tries-to-three romp at home against Otago.

The Brumbies' 1997 season was really just an extension of what we'd started in 1996. We had absolute faith in Rod, his methods and the way we played. Everyone knew their job, everyone knew what they were doing wherever they were on the field; whether we were attacking or defending, everyone knew exactly what was expected of them. Crucially, we had the confidence to express ourselves – on the training paddock and on the field. We became the first Super 12 team to score fifty tries in a season, and eight of those came against the Waratahs, whom we obliterated 56–9.

Only the unbeaten Blues were better than us, and that was simply because they had a fantastic group of players, including Zinzan Brooke, Sean Fitzpatrick, Michael Jones, Jonah Lomu and a young Carlos Spencer.

I had a good, consistent Super 12 season in 1997. New Zealand's *Rugby News* gave me their best-and-fairest award, ahead of the Hurricanes' Christian Cullen, the Blues' Eroni Clarke and the Reds' John Eales, and I thought my 'improved' play was largely a result of how well the Brumbies were going. The confidence of the group transferred itself to the individuals in it. The way the team was structured, the players in midfield were the key decision-makers, and those around us certainly made the options we took appear to be the right ones.

About the only downside of my entire 1997 Super 12 season came right at the death, when we played the Auckland Blues in the finals, at Eden Park. A late intercept try to the Blues' Michael Jones had made it 23–0, after we'd tried to attack from deep in our half and Jones had picked us off. It was all or nothing by then, and if that pass hadn't gone into the wrong hands we might have scored at the other end. Even though it was terribly wet, and the Blues had controlled the ball throughout, we still had the confidence to have a go, based on the belief that no cause is lost until the final whistle. We had gone into the final as long outsiders, but I still fancied our chances – I never went into a game thinking that we were going to lose, that a cause was lost before a ball was kicked. Never. Near the end of the match, we put on a tap move at a time when the Auckland crowd was already celebrating its impending victory. Zinzan Brooke read it, he smashed me, and our heads collided. We both had to go off with concussions, and when we caught up five weeks later in Christchurch, after the first Bledisloe Test of the season, Zinnie asked me, 'How did you go with that head injury?'

'Not too flash, was it?' I replied. 'I can't remember too much.'

I think it was three weeks before the fog lifted completely. He was the same, he told me. I remember one day, to amuse ourselves, my team-mates and I tried to come up with an 'Easter Island XV', made up of players we knew whose melons resembled the famous stone statues that inhabit the island. I was quite chuffed, in a macabre kind of way, that my head had been able to give the Easter Island No. 8 a headache that lasted for three weeks.

A lot of guys were coming off contract in 1997, as the two-year deals they signed in 1995 expired, but the Brumbies were solid. We all wanted to stay together, and we'd made a pact – players and officials – that we'd do all we could to see that happen. Guys who had played for NSW or Queensland didn't want to go back to that. The game might have gone professional in 1995, but for a couple of years, maybe longer in some cases, a number of players and administrators in Australian rugby struggled with exactly what that meant. There were players who still wanted to train just a couple of nights a week, despite being paid as professionls, at a time when 'amateur' track and field athletes, for example, were working a lot longer, a lot harder, just about every day of every week . . . and never complaining. The Brumbies were the first team in Australia to completely eliminate that attitude.

In the end, the one person who left was Rod Macqueen, who at the end of August 1997 would get the offer he couldn't refuse: the Wallabies coaching job. I will never forget what he did for me, and for the Brumbies, the lessons he taught us. One of the most important was to 'smell the roses' along the way. If you work hard and set goals as a group, and you achieve them, then you enjoy them, he taught us. I remember before the semifinal in 1997, he actually presented each player with a single rose, to emphasise the fact that by making the final four we'd reached a goal we'd set ourselves.

At the end of the 1997 Super 12 season, we celebrated in style. When we arrived back in Canberra from our defeat in Auckland, we were greeted by a big, happy crowd who almost made us feel as though we'd won. Then we all went up to Coolum, on Queensland's Sunshine Coast, for a three-day siesta (we pooled our bonus money from the finals series and spent it on this trip), after which it was back to the national capital for a civic reception. Finally, everyone connected with the Brumbies, including wives and partners, was invited to Rod and his wife Liz's home at Collaroy, on Sydney's northern beaches, where he laid everything on for us. The weather was perfect, mellow music in the background; we were celebrating what we'd accomplished, how we'd grown as a group, become true professionals. It was special. Rod was good at that.

8

TOUGH CALLS

1996–1997

'The name of the player wearing the Australian jumper doesn't matter to me. What does matter is that the player can justify his choice with consistent form.'

GREG SMITH, WALLABIES COACH, 1996–97

I knew very little of Greg Smith when he was selected to replace Bob Dwyer as Wallabies coach for the 1996 season. Matt Burke described Smith to me as a guy with a dry sense of humour, who would call a spade a spade but could also be hard to talk to. Phil Kearns said the new coach was one of the funniest men he had ever met. I would grow to enjoy my time playing for Greg, and grow to like him as a coach and as a man. He could be quite reclusive, though, and his communication and player-management skills weren't always effective. However, all this needs to be put in context: Greg died in 2002 after a long fight with a brain tumour, and my understanding is that his health was already beginning to fail him when he was in charge of the Australian team.

From the start, Greg stressed to the team that we were going to be doing things differently, his way, and that no one would be certain of his place in the starting XV. 'Not even the captain,' he stated at our first meeting, which we thought was a bit droll given that the new captain was John Eales, arguably the best forward in world rugby. Training was tough, long and with plenty of body contact, and Greg placed much emphasis on rehearsed plays, second-phase and third-phase plays, which we practised until he felt we had them right. Coming from the Brumbies, this kind of precision was appealing, but I sensed some players weren't quite so sure. A more modern, disciplined defence was coming into play; the days of pure 'off-the-cuff' rugby at the top level were over.

I started at halfback in the Wallabies opening Test of the 1996 home season, against Wales, which we won 56–25, but was then replaced by Sam Payne, from the Waratahs. I write 'replaced' deliberately – Greg would always say, 'You haven't been "dropped", just "replaced".' We quickly learned how the coach saw it. 'You are the best XXII in Australia . . . *this week*!' he would say after reading out the team for the upcoming Test. This was a sample of that dry sense of humour Burkey was talking about.

Greg saw something in keeping his players on edge, in reminding them that they were only as good as their last game, that there were plenty of players around Australia craving for the chance we'd been given. I'm a believer in continuity, in backing men and showing faith in them. In 1997, the Brumbies used the same XV for nine games straight, which helped build the momentum that took us all the way to the Super 12 final.

An early impression I had of Greg was that, like Bob Dwyer,

he seemed happier talking to the media about my strengths and weaknesses than talking to me face to face. I seemed to be reading a lot about Greg's view on me and my pass, and how I compared with Sam Payne. After I was left out of the second Welsh Test in June 1996 and Australia won 42–3, Greg told reporters, 'Sam has an edge as far as much quicker service is concerned. On the other hand, George's defence is outstanding – he's like an extra forward – and he's a very confident player.' Until this point in career, my pass had never been criticised. When I first came into the Test team, a number of journalists who later became among my hardest markers were lavish in their praise of my pass, but from 1996 on, the knockers rarely let up. For the rest of my career, my delivery was never good enough, just as in South Africa Joost van der Westhuizen's pass was never good enough and in New Zealand Justin Marshall's pass was never good enough.

Eventually I asked if we could actually sit down and talk about my pass. 'Let's go through the video,' I suggested. 'If you believe my timing is poor, let's find some examples so we can rectify the problem.' This proved to be an important discussion, and I wish we'd had it sooner. Until then, I think he was guided by long-held perceptions he had about the way I played, and our early relationship was distant, awkward and frustrating. But after our talk I felt that I was beginning to gain his trust and respect, and by 1997 we were working really closely – talking tactics, looking forward to the upcoming game. Never again would I make the mistake of stewing on a problem with a coach, rather than doing something about it.

Greg's earlier comment about my confidence was also interesting, because it was a part of me and my game that he really came to value. In 1997, especially when the team was playing without self-belief and Greg was growing less and less sure of his grip on the coaching job, he often complimented me on it.

'Whatever you've got,' he said to me one day, 'I want you to pass it on to the boys, because we need some of that in terms of the way we compete.'

With Phil Kearns injured, it wasn't a hard call making John Eales Australian captain in 1996. At the time, Tim Horan was the Queensland skipper and apparently there was some support for Matt Burke, but Ealesy was the outstanding candidate, with his quality as a footballer and stature in the game. However, while he did certainly evolve into one of Australia's finest sporting leaders, it wasn't so easy for him at the beginning, especially so given the situation in which he took over: a new team, he had little captaincy experience, and the captaincy was a much more consuming job than it had been in the amateur era. He was never overly keen to take players' concerns to management, which occasionally forced me and other senior players to take on the role of advocate. But he couldn't do everything – as I would observe then and learn first-hand later, the Wallabies captaincy is now a phenomenally demanding role, a whole different dynamic to anything you've faced before you get appointed. He always handled the media and on-field duties with aplomb.

If I had to pinpoint the moment when he became a good Wallabies captain, on the way to being a great one, it was in Sydney in 1998. The week before, we'd lost to South Africa in Johannesburg and now we were down again, this time to New Zealand. We had a penalty, 40 metres out and around five in from touch, and Ealesy looked at me and said, 'Whatdya'reckon? Do we go for the goal?'

'You're the skip, it's your call,' I replied. If I'd had a definite opinion I would have given it, but it was a tough kick, a tough call, so my reaction was valid.

Ealesy wavered.

'You know me,' I said. 'I'd go for the line. But it's your call. Whatever you decide, I'll back it.'

Suddenly, this great decisiveness seemed to come over him. 'I'll get us three points closer,' he muttered.

And then he knocked over this wonderful goal. That was a big moment for him, because he consulted, processed the information, and then was shrewd enough and brave enough to go with his gut instinct.

His captaincy had improved through that winter. After we beat the All Blacks in Christchurch, assistant Wallabies coach Jeff Miller was quoted as saying, '(Eales) has handled everything extremely well and his own game has not suffered. He has taken three or four steps up in his leadership.' That was true, but in my opinion it was in Sydney that Ealesy 'came of age' as a captain.

The two years when Greg Smith was coach are generally seen as a dark time for the Wallabies, and on the scoreboard that's partly true. We had some bad defeats – 43–6 in Wellington, 30–13 in Christchurch, 36–24 in Dunedin (after trailing 36–0 at half-time), 61–22 in Pretoria – but we did go through the twelve-game 1996 European tour undefeated and we won ten of twelve Tests played in Australia (losing twice to the All Blacks, in Brisbane, then Melbourne). Furthermore, many of the men who would form the basis for the successful 1999 World Cup squad came out of this period.

I can certainly remember some good times, and some excellent performances. I would always know when Tim Horan was nervous – he'd start talking a bit more – and he was really talking before the Test against South Africa in Sydney in July 1996. This was a week after we'd been thrashed at Athletic Park in Wellington, and for maybe the first time since he suffered his horrible knee injury in 1994 he really climbed into the physical contest. That sent a strong message to the team. He'd missed a couple of tackles the week before, but the way he recovered and applied himself against the Springboks was inspirational. It was fitting that he scored the try in the second half that sealed the Test for us. Daniel Manu also played out of his skin that night, as we managed to turn things around in a week, never an easy thing to do.

The way we played against the All Blacks in Brisbane in July 1996 was *almost* a great performance. We went into the game feeling inspired after watching Kieren Perkins win the 1500-metres Olympic Gold from lane eight in Atlanta, and after Burkey kicked an amazing goal from 54 metres out (it was still rising when it went through the posts) and scored a thrilling try (running 80 metres and beating any number of attempted tackles) we led by thirteen points with seventeen minutes to go. However, the Kiwis tied it up with seconds left, and then scored the winning try on the bell. We'd made the mistake of looking at the finish line too early, and forgot that great teams are never done. And that was a great New Zealand team, probably the best All Blacks team I faced.

I took a bad back away with me on the 1996 end-of-season tour to Italy, Scotland, Ireland and Wales. I'd damaged a facet joint playing for Randwick in the Sydney first-grade grand final, one of those injuries that needs rest, and maybe I shouldn't have gone to Europe at all. But I was fighting for my place and I didn't want to give anyone a head start – and this was to be my first Northern Hemisphere tour, an adventure no twenty-three-year-old would want to miss. I played in the first Test of the tour, against Italy in Padua, Campo's one hundreth Test, but I probably shouldn't have, and the game was a scratchy affair that we weren't sure of winning until the final twenty minutes. We hadn't played well, but it was still disappointing to hear that back in Australia, John Connolly, the Queensland coach who had been controversially beaten for the Wallabies job by Greg, was quoted as saying that the team was divided, with players living in fear of being dropped. Ironically, when Knuckles became Wallabies coach a decade later, he got himself into a public spat with his predecessor, Eddie Jones, after Eddie made some critical comments about the Australian coach.

Sam Payne played in the Scotland Test, but then I played well against Connacht, scoring a couple of tries, and was back in the side for the Test against the Irish.

As the tour continued we kept winning, and still we were criticised for the way we were playing. It was hard not to think that Greg was going overboard with his squad rotation, but there were some good things happening that went unreported, and I was disappointed by the lack of appreciation for the fact that this was a unique tour in one sense: the first of its kind for the Wallabies in the professional era. The Queensland, NSW and Brumbies camps had all been operating differently, and it was a challenge for us all to accommodate each other's philosophies and approaches. For example, the Brumbies players who worked with Rod Macqueen had seen the value of being involved in the team's preparation and craved a similar involvement at the national level, but others wanted to leave decision-making and game plans to the coaches. Greg preferred it that way, with his players concentrating on the playing.

And it wasn't just in tactics that we differed. There was also a variety of views as to how hard we should be going on the training ground and what we should be doing to recover after matches. We were also frustrated sometimes when Greg would make statements in the press that seemed out of kilter with what he was saying privately to the team. He once tagged David Knox a 'non-tackler' who wasn't up to international football, yet a week later picked him at No. 10 for a Test against South Africa. And before the Test against Italy in 1996, he said that vice-captain Tim Horan was a 'centre not a winger' . . . then put him on the wing. Communication between coach and team could have been better – it would have helped everyone – but it was never the case that the team was bitterly divided in the way some journalists reported it.

The team had certainly improved from the previous season, and there were many new players becoming Wallabies – a healthy sign within the team that seemed to go unnoticed by the media.

With Ealesy out with a fractured eye-socket, Tim Horan captained us against Wales, and made himself famous by following to the letter Greg Smith's directive not to go for penalty goals. We copped a lot of stick for that, especially after we conceded an intercept try (off a pass from me that was meant for Timmy) at a crucial time, when we put on a set play after getting a penalty within kicking distance. But we wanted to break the tempo of these games, which too often in the mid 1990s and beyond developed into arm wrestles where teams were content to trade penalty goals. Further, at that crucial stage of the game, we took the attitude that if we could score back-to-back tries we'd blow the game wide open. I thought it was a really courageous decision by Tim and Greg, a real Australian way to go. And we recovered to win 28–19, so it was hardly a calamitous strategy.

Campo had been out of the Test team since the Test in Italy, but he came back here for what proved to be his farewell. On this tour, when he was out of the first XV, he became more bearable, as if the experience of not being the team star showed him the worth of thinking 'team first'. We all knew he was on the way out, and his parting words to the squad stayed with me: 'When I retire, boys, I'm not going to be one of those people who bags the team, because I think that's wrong . . .'

Six days after the Wales Test, we played the Barbarians at Twickenham. In between, we went to Buckingham Palace for afternoon tea with members of the royal family, which could have led to an international incident. At the beginning of that year, Joe Roff had moved into a new apartment he had bought in Canberra, and at various stages of the tour he had seen opportunities to add to his cutlery collection. 'Mate, you can't do that,' I'd say to him, to which he'd reply, 'I'm just a poor university student, they won't miss the odd dessert spoon.' It reached the stage where it became a mission for him to pick up another item for his kitchen.

The function at Buckingham Palace was a tea-and-cucumber-sandwiches affair, with plenty of sterling silver on show. I was amazed by the way the Queen went around the whole group, engaging in interesting small talk – I'm a republican, but I couldn't help but be impressed with the warmth and hospitality she showed us. I was so taken by her good humour that I forgot to keep an eye on my Brumbies team-mate. But afterwards, as we hopped on the buses to go back to our hotel, and I looked over at Roffy and inquired, 'Afternoon tea, did you enjoy that?'

'Yes I did, thanks, George.'

'Did you notice the spoons?'

'Yes, I did notice the spoons.' Now he was wearing a smirk.

'You took one, didn't you?' I didn't so much ask as state a fact.

'No mate, no mate,' he cried.

I went straight for his inside pocket and out it came – one very shiny teaspoon. His only explanation was that the spoon had his grandmother Elizabeth's initials on it, 'ER'.

I remember Greg Smith as a funny man. Near the end of the 1996 tour, we played a drinking game in which everyone had to come up with a 'Greg Smithism'. It might be a phrase, an expression, a word, a response Greg came up with to emphasise the point he was making. Often it would reflect that he was a well-read, well-educated man. If you couldn't come up with a 'Greg Smithism' of your own, then you had to skol. We went around the room and everyone had a different one. One day, for example, Greg was trying to explain something to hooker Michael Foley, basically saying that the method Michael was trying wouldn't work, but this alternative would. 'What you're doing, Foles,' the coach said, 'that's alluvial gold. This is what you should be doing . . . Did you get that, Foles? Alluvial gold . . . [long pause] . . . fool's gold!' At the time, none of us had the slightest clue exactly what 'alluvial gold' was, but we did after that meeting. Another time, to stress the point about the way he wanted us to defend as a unit, he shouted, 'I don't care if your head is falling off, don't leave the line.'

I had an entertaining meeting with him one day. John McKay, the Wallabies team manager, who was good mates with Greg, was, in a sense, our conduit to the coach, occasionally leaking information to us on his foibles, his likes and dislikes. So before I went to his room, I grabbed a handful of the complimentary soaps you get at hotels, and after we'd greeted each other, I said, 'Smithy, before you start telling me how I can't pass, I can't do this, can't do that, I want to give you a gift. I heard you like these . . .'

The coach looked at the soaps, there was a bit of a grin, and then he went very serious. 'Yeah, nice,' he said. 'My family loves these. We don't get many things as coaches, and I've always thought you blokes just take, take, take. You never give. But maybe you are a giving bloke. It's not lost on me, George.'

Then we laughed, and got down to business.

Family meant so much to him. As coach, he said it was fine for us to spend time with members of our families, but we had to be back at the hotel in time for any team commitment. Wives and partners couldn't stay at our hotel, but they weren't made to feel like villains because they wanted to keep in contact, which brought a human element to the squad – not a bad thing. I know there are some who don't agree with me, who claim that the Wallabies set-up is not a place for families, but I believe that thinking comes from a long-gone era when there was supposedly no place for a man in the kitchen or changing nappies either. Keeping players apart from their wives makes them hungrier, more likely to rip a few arms off, these people argue. But that's rubbish. It's old-school thinking. In John Feinstein's superb golf book, *A Good Walk Spoiled*, he quotes the American professional Tom Kite as saying, 'When you're home, you feel like you ought to be on tour; when you're on tour, you feel like you're missing something important at home.' That happens in rugby, and the emotional swings that can come with such a mindset can harm not just the player concerned but also damage the psyche of the entire squad. Negativity can be contagious. Getting the balance right between family and rugby is important, and Greg Smith was good at recognising this fact.

Another area where Greg made a lasting impact concerned the way members of the Wallabies squad were being paid. When rugby started paying its players for appearing in Test matches, there was a difference between what a starting XV player received and what a bench player was given. This was the case whether a substitute played two minutes or twenty, but there were times when a player came on, changed the game, maybe even won us the game, but he still didn't get paid what the starting guys received. One night in 1997, Mitch Hardy came on as a blood-bin replacement at the Sydney Football Stadium, scored two tries in nine minutes, and turned a Test match against France. Afterwards, Greg said, 'Boys, I'm not going to tell you how to divvy up your money, but you've got a bloke like Mitchell Hardy playing his first Test match for Australia, he comes on and wins us the game, two tries, fourteen points – you put a price on that, boys. You tell me.' It didn't happen immediately, but certainly by 1998 the money was being pooled evenly between all the players in the squad. To me, that was an excellent initiative.

A sadder memory for me is of how Greg often opted to remain remote from the playing group. A running joke was to ask him, 'When are you going out for your toasted sandwich, coach?' We knew he enjoyed a good toasted sandwich, usually ham and cheese, occasionally with tomato thrown in, but he would rarely join us for meals. Later, he would reveal that for much of his time as coach he suffered from severe headaches, and sometimes had 'no motivation', which could be blamed on the tumour that had started to invade his brain.

Our Test results in the winter of 1997, on paper at least, don't look that terrible: two wins over France, two losses in New Zealand, a win over England, a bad loss to the All Blacks at the MCG, and a win over the Springboks in Brisbane. Before the Test in South Africa, which would prove to be his last, Greg announced that we were going to 'create history' by being the first Wallabies team since 1963 to beat South Africa at altitude. To achieve this, we were going to run them off their feet, and in the lead-up we did some intensive training sessions at our base in Durban. With hindsight, I think that the extra work flattened us, and going from a Test in Dunedin to a Test in Pretoria in seven days didn't help either. The result, in so many ways, was a disaster, yet at half-time, when the score was 18–15 to the Springboks, we were fairly confident. We'd fought back from 13–0 down to take the lead in the thirty-ninth minute. I was thinking, *Gosh, we've got them. Let's keep doing what we've been doing and we'll win this game.* They were looking tired.

However, the try South Africa had scored right on half-time – one that had a little bit of magic about it: flick pass, kick, five-pointer to James Dalton – turned out to be a prelude for an amazing forty minutes where everything went right for them and we disintegrated. One try came after we made a break, kicked through, and their fullback Andre Joubert instigated an incredible counterattack that led to the home crowd going crazy. When it gets away from you like this, it can get ugly, and we became the first Wallabies team to concede more than fifty points in a Test. When we were on the right side of these times where everything sticks we'd call it 'show time'. It was definitely show time for the Springboks that night. A few days later, the new CEO of the ARU John O'Neill convinced the coach that it was best if he resigned. The Greg Smith era was over.

RIGHT THOUGHT, RIGHT ACTION

1997–1999

'Me, We.'

Muhammad Ali

It was August 1999, more than a week out from the final Bledis-loe Cup Test of the season, our final Test before the '99 World Cup. I was a little worried about the way we were going; a few of us were. We'd lost our last two matches – badly in Auckland, narrowly in Cape Town. My biggest concern was that we hadn't really evolved from 1998, a year in which we'd reasserted our-selves as a rugby power. Our opponents were on to us, as is the way in rugby if you try to do the same thing for too long. We needed some variety, something new, and after the loss to South Africa I'd had a discussion along these lines with Rodney Kafer, who had come into the team earlier in the season, after Stephen

Larkham was injured, and assistant coach Jeff Miller. When Rod Macqueen, the head coach, found out what we'd been talking about, he was upset.

'Why do you talk to these people about this?' he asked me, annoyed. 'Why didn't you speak directly to me?'

He was a great mentor and a great man, Rod Macqueen, but he could get a little paranoid and jumpy if things weren't going right. I think a lot of creative people are like that. In this instance, it was clear he felt betrayed. I looked at him straight and said, 'When have I ever not come to see you face to face? If I've had a beef with you, we have always sat down, like we are doing now. If you are suggesting I'm trying to damage the team, that's just ridiculous.'

I was genuinely disappointed that he would insinuate that I was ever about anything other than trying to improve the team. He should have known me better than that, having made me vice-captain at the Brumbies, and then vice-captain of the Wallabies when he became the national coach in late 1997.

'Oh, sorry, mate,' he said, suddenly quiet. For me, it was ridiculous, but Rod's discontent also captured the pressure he was under, we were all under, after two consecutive losses. It was always the way with the Wallabies – if we got on a winning run, the expectations quickly became colossal, out of proportion, especially from outside the team.

This was probably as angry as Rod and I ever got with each other. It was also just about the last time we had such a heated discussion. After the success he had had at the Brumbies, and because he quickly turned the Wallabies into a winning team again, he had something of an aura about him which meant that many people would automatically agree with him, tell him that everything was fine. That wasn't me. But I wouldn't speak up just for the sake of it, and I'd always propose a solution. 'No, I don't think that's right,' I might say, either in a team meeting or privately, depending on the circumstances. 'I reckon we could do this, this and this. What do you think?' I am a questioning type of person; if there could be a better way, let's explore it.

'What's he like?' I lost count of the number of times I was asked this question after Rod was given the Wallabies coaching job. It must be awkward for the coach of a provincial team to walk into the national job, because immediately he is trying to win the confidence of players he's previously been plotting against. There are fears the coach will be biased towards those he knows best, and little things can accentuate this. This occurred when Rod became coach, and soon the media was quoting unnamed sources complaining about cliques in the squad, of Brumbies receiving preferential treatment.

In October 1997 we had a new coach, some new players, it had only been a few weeks since Greg Smith had lost his job, and we were starting an overseas tour in Argentina. It wasn't going to be easy, not right at the start, given Rod had so little time to settle into his new role, and touring Argentina is never easy. In this case, we made the mistake of starting the trip by winning 76–15 at Tucumán, creating a false impression that we were going to romp through South America. Instead, as everyone had expected, the Tests were hard work, Rod and the team were still getting used to each other, and the press pounced. Instead of a mature analysis of our situation and how things might improve, they went for this clique rubbish. The Brumbies players and their ex-coach were tagged the 'Cappuccino Club'. It was hard not to believe they were trying to destabilise the team. All they needed was a source, reliable or otherwise, and away they'd go. It never ended.

Rod copped a lot of flak for picking an all-Brumbies back row

(Troy Coker, Brett Robinson, Owen Finegan) for the Tests against Argentina, but he did so because he felt, given the short timeframe he'd had to work with, that it was best to start with people who knew his system. But this meant leaving Willie Ofahengaue and Dave Wilson on the sideline, and when the Pumas won the second Test, the press reaction was savage. I was one player in their sights, tagged as 'hot-headed' after I reacted badly to being spat at, but that is something, up there with gouging, that I can't cop. Still, there was a lesson to be learned: I had to control my emotions, whatever the provocation. Players were also criticised for lying on the ground immediately after the second Test, something Rod doesn't like, going back to his surf-lifesaving days, where the mantra is always 'stand tall, be proud', whatever the result. The guys were disappointed after the loss, and some reacted as many have done over the years, by lying or sitting on the turf, but Rod told the group forcefully that he didn't want it to happen again. There were certain standards he was going to insist the team met, and this was a good place to start. If that's what the coach wants, fine, but when the press heard about it, it was twisted to suggest that the guys on the ground didn't really care about the loss. That was so wrong. The guys were devastated.

Still, I have a few terrific memories of that tour, most notably a day out we enjoyed just after the first Test. We were split into two groups, on two planes, but one flight (not mine) didn't land, just circled for eight hours, because of the bad weather. We were lucky that a rare break in the clouds came at the right time, so we were able to end the day at the remarkable Iguaçú Falls. They showed us where the Robert de Niro film *The Mission* was made, offered us some extraordinary stats on the volume of water that flows over the 270 different falls that are spread over nearly 3 kilometres of the Iguaçú River on the border of Argentina and Brazil, and offered us the chance to really enjoy ourselves, until all of us were soaked and looking for a change of clothes. I remember Tim Horan and his group, who had spent the day in the air with glorious views of the clouds, were especially filthy at me for describing the beautiful banquet lunch that was put on for us. All they could do was ignore me and walk away. Maybe that was the 'split' in the team the journos were writing about.

One story that had gained plenty of prominence over the years concerns a conversation John Eales and I had with Rod Macqueen at the after-match function following that Test loss to Argentina. It has been widely reported that, at a time when we should have been focused on analysing the defeat and looking for solutions, we sidled up to Rod and asked if it would be possible to change the accommodation we'd be staying at when the tour continued to Britain, from a hotel in Windsor to one closer to the bright lights of London. (We'd found the hotel we'd stayed at in Kensington in 1996 to be terrific, especially because its location gave the players a chance to get away, occasionally, from the sense of 'being in each other's pockets' that can sometimes afflict a large touring group. Later, Rod sat down and explained why he'd chosen the hotel at Windsor – being away from the city spotlight would help us gel as a group, he argued, and that was something he saw as vital given that he was so new to many in the squad.) While we were at it, we also raised the matter of six members of the thirty-four-man squad being sent home, rather than travelling with the rest of us to the Northern Hemisphere.

It amazes me how this incident has been twisted over the years. One, we didn't approach Rod out of the blue – it was a meeting between coach, captain and vice-captain that had been scheduled in advance. We had tried to bring these matters up with Rod before the Test, and had agreed to discuss it straight after the game. Two, it was that second matter that was easily our greatest concern, and it wasn't about the six missing out on the best part of the tour. We had been under the impression that everyone was sticking around for the duration of the tour. Brendan Cannon, one of the guys now going home, had even postponed his wedding. Others had booked European holidays for *after* the games in Britain. It had not been decided until midway through the Argentina leg that these guys were going home, and while we conceded management had the right to make that decision, it didn't seem fair that these guys were going to be out of pocket because the powers that be had changed their minds at the last minute. Our feeling was they were entitled to be paid for the entire tour, as they made a commitment to the entire tour, and we wanted to tell Rod and the tour managers that. Let's be fair and reasonable.

To Rod, that was a matter for management, and he suggested we go and see John O'Neill and ARU chairman Dick McGruther, who were travelling with the team. As for the matter of where the team would be based in England, Rod was clearly exasperated that we'd brought it up, and told us to go talk to O'Neill and McGruther about that, too. They were also at the function, so it was just a short walk across the room . . . to discover they were appalled by our 'frivolous' request, coming as it did so soon after the game. Here, they said, was proof that our attitude was poor, our commitment blurred. That we didn't care.

It meant none of those things. The timing wasn't great, but unavoidable. The issue of the players losing out because their tours had been curtailed early had to be resolved. Ealesy and I, as team leaders, had an obligation to do that. If an employer shuts down this line of communication, or the employee is too intimidated or accommodating to speak up, then minor issues can fester into major sticking points. That has certainly been my experience.

It wasn't going to be the end of the world if we didn't change hotels, but it would have been a *major* problem if those players who were being sent home continued to feel misled and be out of pocket. That's why we had to address that issue promptly; I was surprised the ARU bosses couldn't see that.

In future years, Ealesy never really approached management with these types of issues. Instead he allowed me and other senior members of the team to resolve them with management. I always put a lot of thought into it before I approached Rod or management to voice players' concerns. If someone came to me with an issue, and it happened plenty of times, and I didn't think it was in the team's best interests to pursue it, I said so. I was never going to table something for the sake of tabling it, to make a point or to cause unnecessary trouble. I must stress that we were looked after very well – Rod was fantastic in this way, and John O'Neill and his team were committed to giving the Wallabies every chance to be successful. However, for me, the concept of 'team' is all about preserving and enhancing the group dynamic. If it's broken, you've got to make it right. The key is that all parties must have respect for each other, and where negotiations can break down is if one or more of the people involved is a political dealer, prepared to lie or exaggerate to try to win a short-term advantage. If everyone is honest, the respect that comes from that will lead to even the toughest of issues being solved quickly and amicably.

The tour that began so slowly in Argentina ended positively three weeks later when we ran away from Scotland in the second half at Murrayfield to win 37–8, five tries to one. Before that, there had been positive signs in a 15–all draw with England, and in the process Rod won everyone over. I can remember Michael Foley saying to me, 'Mate, this is fantastic, the way we're playing. The team's needed direction, and now we've got it.' I'm not sure if

I ever met a player who didn't like Rod's planning sessions, the way he encouraged us to get involved in the way we went about our business and, flowing on from that, the way he insisted we knew what we were doing, as best we could, before we ran out on the field. (It was little wonder that he called his autobiography *One Step Ahead*.) 'I finally feel as though I know exactly what I need to do when I'm out there on the field,' Foles continued. 'I can see why you guys love it so much.'

Rod introduced a series of innovations to the Wallabies set-up throughout 1998, and just about every one of them helped the team. One was the appointment of Steve Nance, who had been working with the Brisbane Broncos rugby league team, as our fitness coach. There were some reservations, because most of us had pretty firm views on this aspect of our preparation – stretching, flexibility, speed drills, strength exercises, aerobic work – and in many cases were already working with highly credentialled trainers. I had been something of a student on fitness since my days at the AIS. It took some time, but Rod and Steve worked with the players, conceded different players might need different programs, and eventually we were able to improve the team's overall fitness.

Another new face was John Muggleton, another 'leaguie', a man whose involvement in rugby dated back to the very first Brumbies camps at Thredbo, back in 1996. He was working then as an assistant coach with the North Sydney Bears league team, and they, like us, were preparing for the upcoming season. As like minds are wont to do, we started talking shop, and at one point Rod Kafer turned the subject to similarities and differences between league and union defensive styles. Kafe made the obvious point that league had been professional for a lot longer than union, so there had to be things we could adopt, and Muggo pointed to league's 'slide defence' as an obvious example. In the 1990s, there were no weak links in an elite league defensive line, with forwards and backs both having the mobility and awareness to be effective anywhere from sideline to sideline, or in cover if needed. First, Muggo became a consultant for the Brumbies, and then the Wallabies; then, just before the World Cup, he came on full time and stayed with us until 2007. Muggo was a very good coach who made all the Wallabies teams I played with defend as a unit. He always made his sessions informative and enjoyable. After we won the World Cup in 1999, it became fashionable across the rugby world to have former rugby league players as part of your coaching staff. That process started in the Snowy Mountains over a decade ago.

Another innovation of Rod's was the establishment of a 'Camp Wallaby' at Caloundra in June 1998, though it was not enthusiastically embraced when Rod first raised the idea. For the Brumbies players, the idea wasn't that far removed from 'Melrose Place', but some guys weren't happy with the thought of being kept away from their families for extended periods. We were due to play eleven Tests in less than four months – one against England, two against Scotland, four Tri Nations, a third versus New Zealand for the Bledisloe Cup, three World Cup qualifiers, then there'd be a short European tour – so to take even more home time away from the players seemed to some like overkill. Further, while the Queensland players could duck home from time to time, the guys from Sydney and Canberra couldn't.

Rod compensated for this by saying wives, partners and children would be welcome at Camp Wallaby. He was certainly keen for his wife Liz to come up as much as possible. Players shared units (I was with prop Andrew Blades); those with kids were given slightly larger places. As it turned out, we probably saw more of our families than we would have if we'd been living out of suitcases in five-star hotels, and soon everyone was won over. This was a wondeful time, when friendships and family were cherished and we often all got together in large groups. Many of my strongest friendships have come from this era of rugby, and to this day many of us live in the same suburb of Sydney and our families catch up regularly.

Caloundra was a pretty modest facility. The local authorities had redone the ground for us, but it was quite hard a lot of the time – when it didn't rain. And when it rained, it turned boggy pretty rapidly. But the community really embraced the team, and we revelled in the beachside atmosphere, the fact everything was nearby – even little things like cooking and cleaning for ourselves and riding pushbikes to the training ground, became fun. It only had a short shelf-life, however; by 2000 we'd grown too comfortable with it, which is one of the reasons the ARU relocated Camp Wallaby to Coffs Harbour, halfway between Sydney and Brisbane. The new camp was better than Caloundra – it had a superior training ground, good meeting rooms, a wonderful gym and decent recovery facilities. The set-up was better for families too; the only people who didn't like it were the press, who occasionally complained that the place was too much like a creche and it was too hard to get access to the players. Caloundra was good, but Coffs gave us everything we needed.

Back in 1997, we'd played New Zealand at the Melbourne Cricket Ground in front of a crowd of 90,000, but it was hardly a good night. We were down 23–6 after half an hour and never recovered. The MCG Test in 1998 was so much better, with Burkey scoring all our points in a 24–16 victory. It was an important game for the team in terms of growth and self-belief. It was our first win over the All Blacks since 1994.

A week later, we were in Perth, where South Africa – who were in the middle of an unbeaten run that would extend to sixteen games – beat us by a point, and were lucky to do so. Burkey missed a goal that to this day he maintains went through, but most of the controversy concerned a late play near their posts when from a centre-field scrum we went for the winning try, instead of a field goal.

I'll never forget Rod's reaction to that. During the post-game media conference, he'd expressed his disappointment in how we'd played, and stressed the fact that there had been a call for a field goal near the end. This was news to the players who'd been out on the field, because we'd never received such a call. Even today we still have a laugh about the 'phantom' call at Subicao!

In hindsight, we *should* have called the field goal. But the question of who is responsible for a specific call is never as cut and dried as it might appear. At different times, the No. 9, No. 10 or No. 12 might take responsibility. Inevitably, there will be different views as to which way to go. I would go into games with firm views of what I wanted to play, but Stephen Larkham, if he was five-eighth (which he was quite magnificently throughout this 1998 season, after Rod surprised many by handing him the No. 10 jumper), might have equally firm views and his preferences might not have matched mine. We'd go into the game with a fair knowledge of what we'd do at the start, but the dynamics of the game change things. There is always flexibility in calling. I could have made the call if I had to, but it was funny how, when you're part of a good team, you get a sense for which guy has the best idea in a particular situation.

A characteristic that separates a good team from a not-so-good team and a shrewd footballer from a not-so-shrewd footballer is the ability to know when you have to push hard for your call, and when you should give way to your team-mate. Of

course, your call might prove to be wrong, but in such circumstances the response should be – after the player who made the
call has acknowledged his error – 'No problems, mate, we'll look
at it later'. What is *very* important in such a situation is to support
each other afterwards.

We had a good discussion about what Rod had said in that
media conference, which began with him stating again that a call
had been made but been ignored. Whether there was a call or not
wasn't the point; the decision had been made on the field and we
had to back it, even if it had been the wrong one. Learn from it
and do it better next time. That was all the team needed to take
from this experience in order to move forward.

In Christchurch, we won a Test that was most notable for a
try that the Kiwis still talk about, one where we held the ball for
eighteen phases and I handled it fourteen times. The way it's often
written up, we were like chess players as we systematically
moved down and across the field, but in truth we weren't sure
what we were doing for much of it – we knew we were hanging
onto the ball and we were determined not to turn it over, but we
were really just hoping a hole would materialise. Eventually, we
worked down to the corner, near their try line, and Burkey went
over.

That was the day when it was my turn to come up with an
inspiring quote. This was another of Rod's innovations, and
players would spend days, weeks even, researching books of
quotations and the internet to try to find a few words of motivation, ideally from a renowned orator, world leader or sporting
legend. I came up with 'Me, We,', which Muhammad Ali said to a
group of Harvard students in America in the late 1960s, after he
was asked to recite a poem. (As the late iconic sportswriter George
Plimpton told the story, this was the shortest-ever poem, beating
the previous record, entitled 'Fleas': 'Adam 'ad 'em.')

I love selflessness as a character trait, being aware of what you need to do for the team. Forget your personal stats. You could have the best possible year, but if the team is performing poorly, what does that prove? In some ways, purely on a personal level, my 1997 was better than 1998, as I took great pride in solidifying my place in the side and then stepping up into a leadership role when Rod became coach. But we lost nearly as many Tests as we won. In 1998, we improved dramatically as a unit, so this is the year I remember best.

The Bledisloe Cup component of '98 ended in Sydney, where the key moment came when Burkey scored a brilliant seventy-third-minute try and wrecked his shoulder in the process. Four weeks earlier, in Christchurch, the vastly outnumbered Australians in the crowd had started singing 'Waltzing Matilda' late in the second half, as we closed in on a famous victory, but I was so focused on the game I never heard it. I loved hearing about it afterwards, but in the moment it passed me by. Now we were in Sydney, in front of a full house, home crowd, an opportunity for an historic clean sweep that had been feverishly talked about all week, but again all I was thinking about was the game. There was half a chance down the short side and the All Blacks held off me . . . I took the space and then Burkey switched inside to take the pass . . . hurdled a fallen player and scored! The crowd was thunderous, I sensed that, and the adrenalin was pumping, but I still had to remain calm. I was focused on what we had to do next, and tried to remind others to think the same: *We've got to catch the kick off, we've got to play the game out.*

The concept of 'right thought, right action' is something I have tried to apply to my life. You have to be disciplined to get the process right, otherwise you can get distracted by outside influences. *Next play, next task: what do we have to do?* Focusing on that simple mantra was a skill I had to learn. I worked hard at it,

Rod was keen on the whole team thinking this way, and I really enjoyed the challenge of making it work for me and for the team.

The Christchurch test had been a big game for Toutai Kefu, our Tongan-born, Queensland-raised No. 8. He had made his Test debut in Pretoria the previous year as a replacement centre, not the ideal place to start, and through his first full season in the Wallabies squad had been sharing time with Willie O. But in the second All Blacks Test, he stayed on for most of the game, simply because he was playing too well to be subbed. From then on, all the way to the World Cup final, he was first choice.

On our relatively brief end-of-season tour to Europe, which involved only two Tests in a week, big 'Kef' scored an extraordinary try, when he took off from the back of the scrum, about 45 metres out, and just kept running. 'The only problem I had when scoring,' he said later, 'was trying to get out of George Gregan's headlock.' I was only trying to let him know I was happy! On that blockbusting run, it was as if he knew where the French line was from the moment he grabbed the ball, and nothing was going to stop him.

Unfortunately, I wasn't quite as aware of the whereabouts of the try line in our game against a 'France A' combination at Lille. In 1996, we'd played a Scottish Districts Select XV in a midweek game at Perth, Scotland, on a really wet ground and Joe Roff had scored an excellent try where he actually dived in from a few metres out and slid over the line. Now, Roffy ran a lot faster than I did, and was at least 20 kilos heavier, and I failed to take that into account as I raced away to score. I also made the mistake of decelerating as I began my 'Roff dive', so instead of sliding in I landed as softly as a Tiger Woods lob wedge. Basically, I plugged, and had to commando roll the last metre or two to get across the line. It looked silly, I felt stupid, and never put the ball down like that again.

In the Test against England at Twickenham, we put in what Dave Wilson described as our 'second-worst performance of the season'. We still won, only by a point and without scoring a try, but we had lost the skill of 'winning ugly' and it was nice to get it back. Only a few months earlier, against South Africa in Perth, we'd managed to lose a tight one we should have won, but there was another tight match to be played with the Springboks the following year, one where the stakes were so much higher . . .

Throughout the 1999 Southern Hemisphere season, David Wilson was captain because Ealesy had done some very serious damage to his shoulder. Even though I was vice-captain, it never occurred to me that I would automatically get the top gig. In fact, when I looked at the more experienced guys in the squad – Wilson, Kearns and Horan, all past Australian captains, to name three – I thought it would have been a mistake to put me in charge. I had plenty of responsibility already, a set role in the team. Don't get me wrong; if I been named captain then, I would have loved giving it my best shot, and been extremely honoured. But the captaincy was never something I chased. I have often found myself in leadership roles, in part because it's in my nature to be at the front of the pack, and also because I was the halfback, which meant I was usually at the scene of the crime.

When I'd first became vice-captain in October 1997, Timmy Horan must have been gutted. He had been John Eales's deputy, and had captained the team when Ealesy was out, but now he'd been superseded by a younger player. 'No worries, mate,' he'd said to me. 'Obviously, I'm disappointed, but team first. I'll always be there to support you.'

Like Ealesy, Steve Larkham was out for much of the '99 season, after he badly injured his knee in a Super 12 game against the Crusaders, but we still did pretty well. With Tim looking good in the No. 10 jumper, we took our unbeaten run to ten Tests before we hit a speed hump in late July, when we lost to the All Blacks in Auckland and then to the Springboks in Cape Town. The loss at Eden Park was particularly disconcerting – even though we scored two tries to one, we were outplayed at the scrum and lineout, and had trouble controlling the ball at the breakdown. The Kiwis seemed to have a pretty good read on most things we were trying to do.

The 1999 Tri Nations title had already crossed the Tasman, but the Bledisloe Cup was still at stake. Further, whichever side came out on top in the second Wallabies–All Blacks Test of the season would be able to claim a definite psychological advantage going into the World Cup. When the teams were announced we had made a major change, with Tim Horan moving out to No. 12 and Rodney Kafer set to make his Test debut at fly-half.

Even before he was chosen in the starting XV, Kafe had been working on a strategy to change the way we played. This process had been the subject of that meeting with Jeff Miller and me after Cape Town, the one that so upset Rod because he hadn't been in on it. The new ideas weren't too drastic, and were as much about communication and having more options as they were about the way we engaged the All Blacks defence at the lineout and changing a little of the way we reacted at the breakdown. Kafe was smart in that, when he presented his thoughts to Rod, he came armed with sheets of paper on which he'd drafted his proposals. The coach always liked that sort of detail, and he looked at and listened to the presentation and then said, 'How good is this?' Full credit must go to him for first empowering his players to have a shot at this type of strategic planning, and then having the humility, courage and vision to put Kafe's plan to the Test.

Rod, Kafe, David Giffin (who was always our primary lineout caller during this period, even when Ealesy was in the side) and I had a meeting with Jeff Miller, along with Tim Horan and David Wilson. It was agreed that we would use these tactics in the Test and train accordingly. I've rarely enjoyed the lead-up to a Test more. Kafe would have been in the side anyway, but when his plan was adopted so enthusiastically it meant he went into the game full of confidence. We all did. Kearnsy later compared the atmosphere on the team bus to that before the 1991 World Cup semifinal victory and the 1992 Test at Cape Town, when the Wallabies won 26–3.

The final score was 28–7, a record winning margin for Australia in a Bledisloe Cup Test, achieved in front of a crowd of 107,042 at the new Stadium Australia in Sydney. Bomber had a brilliant game, Kef might have been better, the scrum was rock solid, Giff and Mark Connors had a great time in the lineout. An hour after the game, we were still singing 'Waltzing Matilda', 'King of the Road' and 'True Blue' in the dressing room, savouring one of the sweetest victories of our careers. Next stop was the World Cup, our chance to bring back the Webb Ellis Cup.

10

DESTINY

1999

'In the last few months, we have watched you every step of the way from here in East Timor. We think we know of your sacrifice and dedication and the unrivalled teamwork you have achieved to get you to this point . . .'

MAJOR-GENERAL PETER COSGROVE, HEAD OF THE AUSTRALIAN PEACE-KEEPING FORCE IN EAST TIMOR, IN A FAX TO THE WALLABIES WRITTEN BEFORE THE 1999 WORLD CUP FINAL

I first had my head shaved at the end of 1996, after the Wallabies' long European tour, while Erica and I were holidaying in New Orleans. I remember the guy who did it, with his big American accent, asking, 'Have you ever shaved your head, boy?'

'No I haven't, mate,' I replied. 'I've just been clippering it.'

'Where are you from?'

'I'm from Australia, mate.'

'Once you shave it,' he said. 'I'm telling you, you will never go back.'

'Why's that?'

'It's low-maintenance, man,' he said. 'It feels good.'

Nearly three years later, before the World Cup, the boys were into me. 'If we win,' a few of them said one night, as we were enjoying a Guinness in Ireland a few days before the tournament began, 'you'll grow your hair back, won't you?'

'We are going to win it,' I responded. 'But I ain't growing it back.'

About the only negative I can think of concerning our 1999 World Cup campaign is that the great attacking prowess of that side has been forgotten. The lead is always about the defence, about the fact we only conceded one try in six games – against the United States in Jason Little's only game as Australian captain, something we often rib him about. But we were an offensive force, too. It is true that there wasn't a try scored in the semifinal, but if you watch the game you will see that we played some superb rugby. So I remember that Wallabies unit as a great *all-round* side, full of outstanding talent from 1 to 30.

We were also one of the best-prepared teams in rugby history. Rod Macqueen, John O'Neill and team manager John McKay went to enormous lengths to give us every chance of victory. The establishment of a base at Portmarnock Hotel and Golf Links, about twenty minutes by cab from the centre of Dublin, was a masterstroke, and the planning detail that went into getting that facility right for us was far more extensive than anything undertaken by our opponents.

In a story in the Melbourne *Herald Sun* before the World Cup final, I said that my funniest moment of the Cup came when we crossed the Welsh border into England for the semifinal, and Jeremy Paul asked where we had to go to change our Welsh pounds into English. Now, with the benefit of ten years' hindsight, I think the funniest time came right at the start, on our first night at Portmarnock.

Guinness were the chief sponsor of the World Cup. Our backs coach, Tim Lane, was well acquainted with a senior figure at Guinness, and had arranged for a few kegs to be provided for the team for the duration of our stay in Ireland. The first of these was to be opened immediately after we played nine holes of 'ambrose' on the Bernhard Langer–designed layout, which had been deliberately scheduled to give us a chance to rediscover our 'land legs' after the long flight. As it turned out, these 'couple of pints' at the nineteenth hole turned into a few more than that and we blew our whole supply in a single night.

I can remember different players sitting on either side of Rod Macqueen, beers in hand, getting into him about anything. Rod was looking quite serene, at one point being serenaded by Joe Roff on guitar, and I couldn't help thinking, *After all the planning and all the talk over the last eighteen months about our intricate World Cup planning, did you really intend for us to be here, full of Guinness on the very first day?* Every single player was there.

So this is how we are going to go about winning the Cup . . .

It was good fun, and it was funny. Toutai Kefu still calls that night the best preparation for a tour ever. I would imagine that just about everyone who was there would agree with him.

Rod, who'd checked out the place at the end of our 1998 European tour, was always happy if a facility had a golf course (and I was always delighted, too, because it gave me another chance to take some money off him; I saw him as my 'personal ATM' whenever we hit the fairways). A four-star boutique hotel looked out over the course, and at the back end of the course the hotel owners had flattened out an area of spare ground and converted it into a training field. Not too far away was Malahide, a quaint maritime village, while the Irish Sea was a hooked tee shot to the east. There were no distractions. Most of the media focus was back in London, on England, New Zealand and South Africa. It was perfect.

For the first few days, we were very much in 'switch on, switch off' mode. In the team room, a banner had been hung that read: *Our Destiny is in our Hands*. Rod had always referred to our path to the World Cup as a 'journey', and had given us thick manuals that mapped out our preparation in businesslike fashion. Now we were at the 'pointy end' of the adventure. There was no work at all on our first full day there, but after that it was definitely 'switch on' when we hit the training ground, especially when Steve Nance was in charge. At other times, though, we were encouraged to relax. It was almost a ritual that every night we'd have a Guinness as a nightcap, before we went to bed. It was always possible to go into Malahide, or even Dublin, for a beer and a meal, but it was too easy at our hotel. I've never been a big drinker, so that didn't appeal to me anyway; during the day, if I had some time off, I could have a putt, hit some wedges or go and play a few holes. A physio or masseuse was always available, so getting treatment was never an issue, and the team meals were terrific.

Even narky comments by David Campese that were widely reported in Australian newspapers – that we were boring . . . crap . . . paid too much . . . couldn't win – were turned into a positive. 'Normally we ignore his comments,' wrote Phil Kearns (who sadly was about to pull out of the squad because of an injured foot) in a newspaper column, 'But there comes a point when you have to say enough is enough.' Such criticism made us just that fraction more determined, brought us together just that little bit more.

As far as our three pool games went, the second one, against Ireland, was the one that mattered. In the other fixtures, Romania was defeated 57–9 and USA 55–19. We sensed that the Irish were confident, but we handled them quite comfortably, 23–3, to go through to the quarter-finals. The only downside came when we lost Toutai Kefu, who was cited and then suspended for two games after he squared up to Ireland's back-rower Trevor Brennan, their alleged hard man, who was threatening to do something (I'm really not sure exactly what). Kef would be out till the semis, but we weren't upset with him. The way Brennan was carrying on needed fixing. It was something like the fourth time he had had done something stupid, and sooner or later he was going to hit the wrong guy. Kef was the wrong guy, and while discipline is crucial, there is also a point where you have to say, *We're not going to cop that*. 'We believe he was in the right,' Rod Macqueen said after the game. 'He was just defending himself,' reckoned David Wilson. I guess the powers that be had to be seen to be doing something, which is why Kef was suspended, but I wondered if they should have looked at the extenuating circumstances and focused on punishing the man who started it all.

The noise at Cardiff's Millennium Stadium for the quarter-final against Wales was much, much noisier than for any other game I ever played there. At one point, we were defending our line, and I was yelling at Tim Horan, our No. 12, and he couldn't hear me. I can also remember Erica and other players' wives, who'd watched the match from the grandstand, commenting on the ringing in their ears hours after the game. The atmosphere was electric, fantastic.

The day before that quarter-final, we were at Millennium

Stadium (which would also be hosting the Cup final in two weeks' time), just having a look at the place – a few kicks, a bit of passing – when one of the groundstaff gave me a wave, beckoned me over, and then said in a thick Welsh brogue, 'Take a good look at the place, because it will be the last time you see it this year.'

'Is that right?' I said.

Normally I would have let it go; he seemed like a good guy, and after looking all serious he now had a big grin on his face.

'Are you here every day before a game?' I inquired.

'Yes I am,' he replied.

'I bet we'll be having this same conversation and you are eating humble pie in two weeks' time,' I challenged him.

'We'll see,' he muttered, then repeated, 'I won't be seeing you in two weeks.'

He was a good guy, typical of Welsh rugby – loved his football, loved his team. Best of all, he was full of rugby spirit, the sort of character you love meeting on your football travels.

We were edgy before the game – maybe a carryover from 1995 in that no one involved in the quarter-final loss then wanted to feel like that again – but we started well. Then it rained and they'd left the roof open, and the match became a scrappy affair, but a key for us was our discipline: we didn't concede any second-half penalties within kicking range. The quarter-final was one of those games where I always felt we were in front but never by enough to feel safe, at least not until right at the end when I scored a lucky try that put us 24–9 clear. That gave us the chance to play South Africa in the semifinal at Twickenham. This was a big game – the kind you cannot wait to start – and the South Africans were their usual confident selves in the lead-up to the match.

*

Back in June, the Aussie cricketers had won their World Cup. In the final, they had beaten Pakistan comfortably, but to get there they had to overcome South Africa twice, first in a Super Six match, in which captain Steve Waugh scored an inspiring century, then by forcing a tie in the semifinal, which was just enough to get them into the final because of their superior record in the earlier games. Now, on the eve of our World Cup semi against South Africa, Ealesy walked into our team room with a sheet of fax paper in his hand . . .

Attention: The Wallabies, John Eales

To the team:

The momentum is building, you can see it and feel it and so can the opposition. The whole country is behind you guys, so just get out there and back yourselves because we all are. There's only one thing better than beating the Springboks and that's tying with them and then beating them on a countback. Don't make it too easy, tease them and then nail them in the dying moments just to show them who the greatest country in the world is.

Play well. Trust yourself.
Steve Waugh

As it turned out, we played most of the attacking rugby in the semifinal at Twickenham, but South Africa showed how the mood and pressure of a World Cup suits them. They've always come armed with a good set piece, genuine scrambling ability and a good goal kicker and drop-goal kicker. Because the stakes are so high, so many knockout Cup matches become 'arm wrestles', games that are won not by short periods of flashy football, but by

117

wearing your opponent down, hanging in there, showing guts and character. There was never more than six points between the two teams, and late in normal time, after we'd held the ball for eight phases, I almost scored the match-winner when I dashed down the short side, and thought it had all opened up for me. In hindsight, I should have passed to Jason Little, because he would have scored for sure, but just as my instincts said *go for it* their winger, Pieter Rossouw, came in and closed me down. Even worse, I was then penalised for holding the ball. All I could do was run back and then get into the next play.

Time was almost up, into the sixth minute of injury time, and we were three points clear, 18–15. A ruck formed, and we were shouting 'no hands, no hands' but Owen Finegan took one last bite at the cherry and was pinged. It was a tough kick, into a stiff breeze – some might say a gale – 35 metres out, near the sideline, a crowd of 70,000, millions more watching back home . . . but Jannie de Beer was always going to kick it. I was certainly thinking, *This is going to extra time.* The good thing was – and this comes back to Rod and the way he sets up his team – after the kick was successful we went into the dressing room and immediately went into a routine. We had spoken about the possibility of extra time, and planned for it. The backs and forwards separated, we talked briefly, then we got together. John Eales stood up and explained how we were going to treat this new period of play as a new game. Then we strode back out there.

Perhaps the South Africans were less prepared. Who knows if that was the difference? They did kick the first penalty after play resumed, so maybe it didn't really matter, but there was always a sense in extra time that we were more assured, more likely to come through. We knew, for example, that there was going to be a very short break at half-time in extra time; the Springboks didn't, and seemed ruffled as a result. A few of our guys came up with some big plays at critical moments, such as when Jason Little kicked long and then made a big tackle on Rossouw, giving us excellent field position in a game where field position was everything. That led to the penalty that levelled things once more. And then came the moment, with seven minutes left, when Stephen Larkham found himself with the ball in his hands, 48 metres out, wind behind him . . .

From my perspective, there was nothing too complicated about the field goal. Replacement centre Nathan Grey charged forward from midfield, Steve called for it, I passed it to him, and he decided to have a crack. He had no record of kicking field goals, admitted later that when he'd attempted a few at training before the semi he'd missed most of them, but he hit this one sweetly and it sailed through. Apparently, Tim Lane had mentioned the idea as we walked out at the start of extra time; I think it was just a case of a gifted footballer rising to the occasion, as the best ones can. There were players celebrating, and I was certainly happy, but there was still time left for the game to be won or lost. As it turned out, the only further scoring was a 40-metre Matt Burke penalty (jeez, Burkey kicked well this game), which meant South Africa had lost a World Cup match for the first time. I was going back to Cardiff to see my mate on the groundstaff.

After the game, John Eales gathered us in a huddle on the field, and his message was straight to the point: one more game to go. Normally, we'd do that sort of thing in the change room, but here our captain seized the moment, shrewdly tapping into the truckload of emotion we were riding. Equally shrewdly, we didn't overdo it. 'Advance Australia Fair' was sung with much fervour in the change rooms, Rod was as emotional as I've ever seen him, and I remember being concerned for Tim Horan, who had been unbelievable, ignoring a severe gastric complaint to play brilliantly for seventy-four minutes. He was everyone's man of the match.

I knew he'd been a bit crook, and he'd been quieter than usual on the 45-minute bus trip from our hotel to the ground (we always sat next to each other on the team bus, though we never said a lot; often I'd have my earpieces in, listening to music). In fact, I think he might have spent a fair a bit of that journey down the back of the bus, in the toilet. Then, just before we went out at the start of the game, one of our medical staff whispered, 'Keep an eye on him, he might not last the game.' I did keep a close watch on him, mainly to admire his line breaks and big tackles. He was massive.

Games don't come bigger than the World Cup final. I guess that's stating the obvious, but the challenge is not to let this reality spoil the experience, because there is a real danger that the game can just pass you by. If you get caught up in the hype, one minute you can be thinking about the week and how exciting it's going to all be and the next you're in the change room with only forty minutes left to play. It hasn't turned out the way you dreamed it would and there's nothing you can do about it. You're thinking, *Where did it all go?*

Rod recognised this, emphasised the need for us to keep to our regular routine, and deliberately kept things low-key in the build-up. We found a nice little Italian restaurant in the centre of Cardiff – good pizza, pasta salad, cold Peroni – that became a regular haunt and finally the site of the closest thing we had to a team dinner before the game.

We had expected to play New Zealand, and the backroom boys had accumulated a lot of footage in readiness for the analysis the coach, his assistants and the players would apply to the preparation for the final. But then France stunningly knocked the All Blacks out, and a new collection of tapes had to be prepared. Our reaction to this shock victory was: the task is different, not easier;

the physical preparation is, in essence, the same. It was stressed, though, that no one was to make a comment to the media that we were glad New Zealand were beaten, or that the Frenchmen would be an easier target. There was no need to give them any extra ammunition, and the reality was that they'd beaten the Kiwis on their merits. France were a very good side.

There had been a connection between Australia and France for much of the tournament through a French journo who had been assigned to cover Australia throughout the World Cup. I'm dirty on myself that I can't remember this fellow's name, because he was a good guy and an excellent rugby writer, with a real feel for the game and an ability to ask perceptive questions. Before the final, Rod was a little anxious about having a French journalist so close to the team, but I trusted him completely and he didn't betray that trust. The day of the World Cup final, he presented me with a couple of really nice cigars, and he'd even done his research here, as they were ones I liked. 'Good on you, mate, for doing your homework,' I said. 'I'll smoke these tonight.'

A feature of the week leading into the final was the fact that back home a referendum was scheduled for 6 November, the same day as the final, to decide whether Australia would become a republic. We had actually voted earlier, when we were in Ireland, and the issue wasn't one that was discussed at great length; some players were more heavily into the subject than others. I was a committed republican, but didn't feel it was my job to push my view on others in the team. Another journalist, former Wallaby Peter FitzSimons, knew which way I was leaning and he asked me to have a photograph taken in my World Cup final jersey specifically to promote the republican cause, but I wasn't comfortable with the idea. If I did that, my views would have been interpreted in some quarters as being representative of the team. I did wear a republican badge at a media conference, but I wasn't in the

Wallabies jumper – that, to me, is a big difference. John Eales knocked back a similar request, for precisely the same reason. For Australian rugby players that gold jersey is akin to the Australian cricketers' baggy green cap. It's sacred. It may have changed a little bit in design during my career, and not always for the better, but its impact on me never changed. I always loved wearing the Aussie coat-of-arms over my heart – even more so when it was explained to me that those two great animals on it, the kangaroo and the emu, can only be found in Australia and neither of them can take a backward step. That's Australian.

The final was a day game, with a 3 o'clock kick-off, and by mid-morning I had my game-day face on. I have a vague memory of the winning captain from 1995, South Africa's Francois Pienaar, walking out of a lift as I waited to enter and saying, 'Good luck, this is the big day,' but I was so focused I just responded, 'Thanks.' I wasn't trying to be rude, but even this early my mind was on what I had to do, which in this case was get to the team room, where others were waiting for me. We were due to go for a brief walk, as we always did on game morning, just to get out of the hotel. In the foyer, a supporter was playing 'Waltzing Matilda', over and over – badly! – on his bagpipes. There was a nervous energy about us this day, a positive vibe that reflected a quiet confidence. I've never looked forward to a game as much.

Another of Rod's innovations had been the 'Classic Wallaby', where he would invite a former Australian player to speak to the team about what it meant to wear the Wallabies jumper, to present the jerseys for the upcoming Test, and then travel to the match on the team bus. We had thus been introduced to a number of past champions, all of whom enjoyed the experience as much as we did. For the final, the former Queensland and Australian prop, TV commentator and raconteur Chris 'Buddha' Handy, had the job – in part because he had always been a strong supporter of the team, in good times and bad – and he performed it beautifully, bringing a bottle of 1991 Penfolds Grange with him. He also helped out when we were ready to begin our brief bus journey from the hotel to the stadium but found our way blocked by two illegally parked cars. Together with a few of our reserves, he picked the offending vehicles up and moved them out of the way.

It's funny how sport can work. At the end of normal time of the semifinal, Owen Finegan had made the mistake that pushed the game into extra time, a desperately unfortunate mistake by one of the smartest footballers I ever played with. I think while the rest of us were thrilled with our ultimate semifinal victory, at least a little bit of Owen was just mighty relieved. Proving that a week can be a lifetime in sport, during injury time in the second half of the final, it was Owen who changed the game again, this time crashing his way over after a rehearsed move worked beautifully. That play was set up for a mobile back rower such as my big Brumbies team-mate, going off the back of the lineout, and he just kept running, brushing off at least four French defenders and in the process fulfilling a promise he'd made to his family that he was going to score a try in the final. The celebrations that try set off were wonderful, if a bit loopy. How are you supposed to react when you've achieved a life's ambition?

After the game, there were media reports about some on-field discussions between me and France's flanker, Olivier Magne, who had been a star of their semifinal win. To me, it was just a little gamesmanship that was more noticeable this time because Magne was such a standout player. He stood around 193 centimetres and weighed 100 kilos and had a thick strap of plaster across his nose.

Much was expected of him, and he was having a hard day at the office. We had a deliberate policy to run at him, make him work, tire him out. After referee Andre Watson awarded us the penalty that would lead to Burkey's third penalty goal, I turned to Magne and said, 'We spoke about you in the team meeting, how you're always good for nine or twelve points . . . That's nine already.'

He might have pretended he didn't understand English, but he knew.

Those penalties, and a few others, meant we had our noses in front for much of the game, but never comfortably. It was 12–6 at half-time, four Burke penalties against two from their No. 10, Christophe Lamaison, and it remained reasonably tight until the last twenty minutes, when we surged away. Burkey's seventh penalty pushed our advantage to nine points, and then Ben Tune forced his way over in the right-hand corner after a sharp blind-side work from Horan and Finegan. The final score was 35–12, still the biggest winning margin in a World Cup final.

After the game, French forwards were strongly criticised for gouging and squeezing testicles, but they left me alone in this regard. I did get a scratch in my eye but that was just an accident, and I got rucked at one point. But you should get rucked if you're on the ground and on the wrong side – I've never had a problem with that.

Some of my strongest memories of the Cup final are actually of the after-match festivities. In the dressing room, we drank Chris Handy's '91 Grange out of paper cups and it tasted beautiful. Rod Kafer and his fellow members of the team's social committee had organised a private function at Brannigan's nightclub. The location was supposed to be top secret, and it was only for the team, close friends and family. First, though, we were required at a big dinner at Cardiff Convention Centre with players from all of the top four sides in attendance. It was an event for many speeches and a few drinks, before eventually we said, 'Let's go to our own party.' But when we got there every man and his proverbial dog had got in. There were queues for everything, so we quickly decided, *Stuff this!* We trudged back to our hotel and ordered drinks at the team bar, smoked a few cigars, including those beauties from my French journalist mate, and had a really memorable night.

It was a small bar, though, and the staff struggled to keep up. Justin 'Goog' Harrison, a lock for the Brumbies who would actually play in his own World Cup final before his career was over, was travelling with a 'Classic Wallabies' supporters tour and had followed us back to the hotel. He had his face painted, was wearing an outlandish green-and-gold wig, and was loud and just about unrecognisable. Meanwhile, Ben Tune and his family were parked in a corner; they had ordered toasted sandwiches but had been obliged to wait the best part of an hour for their tucker. Finally, the sandwiches arrived and it was obvious the Tunes were delighted by this development. Unfortunately, so was Goog, who saw or smelled the food tray coming out, flew across the room, dived over a sofa and lunged for his share.

Those of us who trained with him knew that Ben had a nice knockout punch, and when this lout he didn't know tried to steal his dinner, he had it loaded in an instant. For me, watching, it was like watching a car crash in slow motion. I made it just in time, grabbed Tuney, and pleaded, 'Mate, don't do it. It's Googie! It's Googie!'

Tuney looked at him and said, 'Is that really you, Goog?'

'Yeah mate,' the big second rower said sheepishly. 'I just want a sandwich, mate.'

'Mate, we've been waiting for a while . . . but I'm happy to order you one.'

Poor Justin suddenly looked miserable and embarrassed.

'Mate,' said Ben Tune, world champion, 'I tell you what. You can have some chips.'

Erica and I had booked an early-morning flight from Gatwick to spend five days on the Amalfi coast, so we left the team hotel the morning after the Cup final at about 6 am. At a point when our celebrations started to tone down, Erica said she would go up to the room and have a sleep for an hour; I decided to stay at the bar. I had a kip in the car, and then we were on the plane to Italy. Just like that, it was over.

We had a tiny window to have a total break and I had to be back in Sydney within a week to be part of the celebrations that would include a series of ticker-tape parades in Sydney, Brisbane, Melbourne and Canberra. I knew, too, that I'd be seeing everyone again soon enough in a football setting – Brumbies pre-season training was due to begin in early January – and also socially, because a few of the guys were getting married. We'd been together for nearly two months, two of the best months of my life. And we'd soon be in each other's pockets again.

SO YOU WANT TO BE
A HALFBACK

'The people who write that stuff should probably do their homework. I know that for the last four or five years that I'm off the ground the quickest halfback in the world in terms of throwing the ball from halfback to the pivot receiver.'

GEORGE GREGAN ON HIS CRITICS, 2003

Most No. 9s across the rugby world get on well – maybe not on the field when we'll get into each other and try to provoke a reaction, but definitely afterwards. From the time the first whistle goes to the final bell, we're competitive players who talk a lot (a South African would say we're 'quite chirpy'); off the park, we're often much quieter. I'm not a massive talker except for the eighty minutes that matter, but I am transformed when I slip into game mode. Chris Whitaker, the Waratahs halfback who was my Wallabies team-mate from 1999 to 2005, is similar – laidback, really quiet away from the spotlight, but put a rugby jumper on him and he is super competitive, and a non-stop talker.

Of course, we're all little guys – I'm 173 centimetres – and because our place of work is the back of the scrum, we're mixing in a world where most people are bigger than us. I was around 75 or 76 kilos at the start of my Test career, and got up to maybe 81 kilos at the end, but only when I drank as much water as I could before I stepped on the scales. I'm not sure why I did that, because I never felt disadvantaged by my weight, but there are some people in the game who are almost obsessed by these sort of measures, even though a player's weight is not a great reference point for his strength.

The modern halfback has to be a good defender, prepared to plug a hole in the line if one appears. This could mean that one minute I was confronting a big forward and the next I was one-on-one with a fleet-footed or big-stepping outside back. This never worried me – it meant that occasionally I was run over or left grasping at straws, but it also gave me the chance to make some important tackles. I think my tackling ability might have come from my early days playing rugby league in the Midgets, when everyone was huge and I had to adapt. When a big guy was running at me, either with the ball or to tackle me, I never thought that I was about to get hurt, which gave me a good head start over many kids who were wary, either upfront or subconsciously. My time in judo showed me ways to position myself so that I could throw guys to the ground even though they were much bigger than me, and it also taught me that there are more legal ways to bring down the big guy than just those outlined in the rugby coaching manual. Whatever your size, to be a good defender you need self-belief and a positive attitude. It is in most halfbacks' DNA to have these characteristics.

Most top-level No. 9s are naturally competitive. I know I

was whenever I walked onto a football field, whether for a game or training. I was the kid who would never walk in backyard cricket; from the day I discovered there was no lbw in those games I got hit on the legs a lot. We No. 9s are also cunning – we have to be, in a world where only the strong survive. I always liked to think of myself as half back, half forward, so at training I'd share my time with the forwards and the backs and, if I had any say in it, organise for the scrum-feed practice with the forwards to coincide with a heavy running session for the backs! When I was going to go out and have a few drinks with my buddies, there was never a delineation between forwards and backs. I enjoy good company, and would happily initiate a prank in which someone else became the focus of attention and I could stay in the background. It was a bit like setting up an important try – the scorer could have the glory, I was just happy with the satisfaction of doing my job well, of keeping the engine running. Back at training, during scrimmaging practice, only a halfback among the backs could get away with shouting all the rhetoric the forward coaches love to say . . . 'Get your right shoulder up . . . push . . . engage . . . chase your feet . . .' A winger could never say that. I could.

When I broke into the Wallabies team, the role of the halfback was still pretty 'traditional'. I can remember Bob Dwyer and his coaching staff used to teach the forwards to hold the ball at the breakdown, close to your body, until you saw the green and gold socks going over and then you placed it for the halfback to spin it away to the No. 10. Times moved on. First, counter-rucking became brutal, which necessitated a rule change. If you waited for your cavalry to arrive at the 1999 World Cup, you were pinged for 'not releasing'. Into the twenty-first century, prowlers such as

Georgie Smith, Phil Waugh and Richie McCaw emerged, men adept at ripping the ball out of your grasp and into the hands of their own halfback in a second. After that, in the blink of an eye, the ball was 30 metres down the field. The players waiting for socks had been left behind.

From 1998 on, Tana Umaga had made it fashionable for centres to be as good at the scrimmage as back rowers; he became known as the Predator. Tim Horan and Jason Little were also good at getting into the breakdown, making a mess of it and sometimes turning the ball over. The team that could control the ball at the breakdown, who could facilitate multi-phase play despite these terriers being about, had the advantage. The breakdown became fiercely contested, and many coaches opted to send more numbers to it, to create a form of organised chaos. In these circumstances, it was rare for the ball to be placed at arm's length, ready for the halfback to sweep it off the ground to his five-eighth.

My pass has been criticised – I thought often unfairly. It is true that I sometimes took a couple of paces before I passed the ball, but as John Hipwell, one of the greatest of all Wallabies halfbacks, pointed out to the Sydney Morning Herald's *Philip Derriman in 2003, 'It's not necessarily his fault. He's trying to get clear of the mayhem . . . he's stepping over players or stepping away, and guys are leaning over the ruck and maul, trying to grab an arm or whatever while he's trying to clear it.' Ideally, a halfback wants his pass to be quick and accurate, but of the two accuracy counts more. 'Repeatability' is crucial. If you throw a bad pass, what tools do you have to correct it straight away? If one bad pass evolves into three or four in a row, a bad spell can become a disastrous game. In professional sport, the ability to recover, physically and mentally, is important. I don't think I played a game where I didn't throw a bad pass, and there were some games where I threw more than I would have liked, but I always backed myself to get back in the groove before it was too late. That was important to me.*

Many was the time – especially from 2002 on, when changes in rule interpretations meant defenders seemed to be coming from all directions – when I could see the ball at the breakdown but couldn't get at it. But you had to go digging, because if you waited for it to be presented on a platter the likelihood was that a teammate would be shoved back on top of you. Getting the damn thing out of that melee and then passing it became a skill that had to be practised.

In a typical ruck in the late 1990s, there might have been four defenders with eyes on where the ball was going. The third and fourth defenders were focused on the No. 10, while the first and second defenders were out to stifle the halfback. In this situation, we used to have a field day at the Brumbies with the inside ball to Owen Finegan; often, the first two defenders would chase that halfback really hard and leave that space inside gaping. It was money for jam, an easy way to break the line, gain ground and score tries. Even when other teams finally woke up to it, it was still important for us to ask questions of those first two defenders, because otherwise they'd feel liberated to pursue the 10 and 12. Part of John Muggleton's defensive scheme, where the emphasis was on the defensive line keeping its formation to stop not just the ball-carrier but also the support players if they received the ball, was to stop that inside ball. Until opposing teams started to mimic that plan, Owen and I used to have a lot of fun. We called that area we attacked the 'transition zone', and thought of it as the joint between the forwards and the backs that could be exploited, torn apart, especially late in the game when weariness might set in. To do this effectively, a No. 9 needs to run towards the second defender to force the defensive line to make a decision.

The twenty-first-century halfback needs to be very fit, because he is on the ball all the time and the pace of the game has increased so much in the past fifteen years. He rarely dive passes, because then, no matter how good it looks, he's on the ground, out of the game. A big responsibility is to 'coordinate' the defence during a match, to organise the width of the defensive line and ensure defenders were in the right places. I spent heaps of time with Muggo and other defensive coaches planning that.

By 2004, the game at the breakdown had become so cluttered that Wallabies coach Eddie Jones decided to build all our plays around the No. 10 and No. 12, because to try to do so closer to the breakdown was becoming self-defeating. Initially, this change brought some dividends, and I fully understood and supported Eddie's reasons for doing it, but because we weren't working those defenders at the edge of the ruck, they shifted their attention a bit wider, and the advantage was lost. We needed to find a balance, which we eventually did, and once again I started testing out those prime defenders every once in a while. That was good, though for the fans, because the interpretation of the rules at the breakdown had changed, it made for some boring rugby. For the last three or four years of my international career I was frustrated at how the game had evolved to the point where teams could win Test matches by being negative at the breakdown. There was no reward for trying to use the ball.

Back in 2000 and 2001, with the Wallabies and the Brumbies, unless we were close to our line, we weren't going to kick the ball away. We were prepared to back our skills to get the ball positioned in the parts of the field where we could exploit weaknesses in our opponents. The momentum built by this style of rugby was irresistible, and the laws of the game as they were interpreted at that time allowed us to do it. It was also exhausting to defend against, and often was the time that we'd blow opponents away in the final twenty minutes. The Super 12 final of 2001 was a case in point, when we played the Sharks, who we knew were a fast-starting team. It was 6–all at half-time, and in the dressing rooms we reminded ourselves that this was where we wanted to be, and they weren't where they needed to be. The final score was 36–6. It took a lot of skill and planning to do that.

At that time, the attacking team only got one crack at the breakdown: it was use it or lose it. But defenders couldn't enter the breakdown from the side and the onus was on the tackler to get out of the way, so it was possible to use that ball. Things changed from 2002 on, when the point of entry for defenders at the breakdown broadened, referees seemed more concerned with policing the attacking team, and the breakdown became a messy, chaotic and unattractive part of the sport. Some teams were happy not to play the ball at all, just wait for the penalty. The results of some important matches were determined by how obsessive the referee was on the day.

The crucial try in the Test at Auckland in 2003 demonstrated just how messy the breakdown had become. Midway through the first half, at a time when we had our noses in front 9–7, the referee, Jonathan Kaplan, was shouting, 'Hands away, black, it's a ruck, it's a ruck. Hands away, it's a ruck.' And then the All Blacks' Jerry Collins picked up the ball, passed it to five-eighth Carlos Spencer, who kicked through for winger Doug Howlett to score. Afterwards, I was criticised for being too slow to react. At the time, all I could do was ask Kaplan, 'Mate, didn't you say "it's a ruck"? Didn't you just say, "Hands away, black"?' Despite losing Glenn Panoho, Wendell Sailor and Toutai Kefu to injury in the first forty-five minutes, we ended up losing the Bledisloe Cup, which we'd held since 1998, by just four lousy points. To this day, I don't know how Kaplan allowed Collins to get away with it.

*

Defensive lines grew more aggressive the longer my career went. They were also faster, as a unit, focusing on reducing the time and space of the attacking team. However, there were still means for the side with the football to overcome the best of defences. Whereas in the good old days, a halfback's bread-and-butter was the pass to his five-eighth, now a No. 9 needs a wider variety of attacking methods, and the subtleties of his short-passing game are really important. Scott Johnson, the Wallabies attacking coach in 2006–07, was big on players carrying the ball in two hands, 'staying loaded' as he liked to put it, and like many coaches he always emphasised the value of guys working off the ball. Those players can make a halfback look good.

One of the best football lessons I ever received came at a training session back in 1998, at Caloundra. Rod Macqueen had organised for the accomplished league coach Wayne Bennett to come along. Wayne watched all the session with Rod, and afterwards we were expecting to hear some words of wisdom, but he was silent. 'Wayne, thanks for coming,' Rod said eventually. 'Is there anything you would like to say to the team?'

'Oh no,' said the master league coach, 'everything looks pretty good.'

Then, almost as if it was an afterthought, he added, 'I would just mention, when you run your routes, you've got to run them like you are going to get the ball, like you've got a job to do. Don't just go through the motions when you run your routes.'

We would have said 'lines' instead of 'routes' but it didn't matter. Suddenly we were transfixed.

'If you are running as a decoy,' Wayne continued, 'you're not necessarily a decoy if your defensive counterpart doesn't defend the way he should. Always understand what your role is, but if that defender moves off you, then you call for the ball.'

Wayne Bennett could have said a lot that day, and it might have all blurred together. Instead, I never forgot what he said, and stressed it often to our attackers in the years that followed. Watch the way decoy runners are used in league and union today and you can see how Wayne was ahead of his time. If players are working off the ball and running their lines, doing their job, then opportunities arise and the result of the game will come down to whether we have the ability to take those opportunities. Because he has the ball in his hands so often, the No. 9 plays a key role in determining that outcome.

South Africa's Joost van der Westhuizen was not the best halfback I played against, but he was very good. Joost's 'X factor' was his speed, but that diminished a little towards the tail-end of his career because of a chronic knee injury. In his prime he was very dangerous, but he was something of an individualist. He was such a dominant personality within a team, there were times when we felt that if we could nullify his opportunities and frustrate him out of the game, then we were a long way down the road to a win. But his unpredictability was often difficult to counter, and his pace and strength around the edge of the ruck meant that if we were loose around there he'd hammer us. He could tackle well, kick off both feet; he was special.

Van der Westhuizen was certainly a different style of halfback to New Zealand's Justin Marshall. Marshy always worked really hard around the edge of the ruck, and was very good in a team structure. He was never going to make many errors in a really tight game, and I always respected his grit and consistency. We played against each other at under-19 level in 1992, Tests from 1996, Super 12 finals and a World Cup semifinal, and early on we'd go out there and try to bash each other, until one day we stopped doing that and tried to beat each other by playing football. It wasn't as if anyone called a truce; maybe we just matured. Marshy and I have always been mates off the field – I think because of the respect we had for each other on the field.

Of the Northern Hemisphere guys, I'd probably put Wales's Rob Howley, a well-balanced scrum-half with a really good kicking game, on top. He could pass and run, too; until he injured his shoulder in 2001 he was keeping England's Matt Dawson out of the Lions top XV, a good indicator of his quality.

Chris Whitaker was a great player because he was so consistent in his performances and he was such a good team man. I really missed him when he finished up with the Wallabies in 2005. You take it for granted when you have great guys like him around your team, and it's not until they're gone that you really appreciate what they brought to the set-up. Whits has a good running game, great pass and excellent short-kicking skills. And he's super courageous, would tackle anything.

11

WORLD'S BEST

2000–2001

'I'll buy Toutai Kefu a drink anytime and anywhere.'
JOHN EALES, AFTER HIS FINAL TEST, SYDNEY 2001

We played two fantastic Tests against New Zealand in 2000. The Test in Sydney is considered by many to be the best game of rugby ever played. The game in Wellington wasn't far behind it. The manner in which the laws at the breakdown were interpreted was excellent, both teams had a great deal of talent right across the park, and the attitude was terrific, too. For much of the game, neither team was going to kick the ball away. We were going to use it and attempt to score tries.

We got off to the perfect start at Wellington's Westpac Stadium: try to winger Stirling Mortlock, a try to Joe Roff, 12–nil after fifteen minutes. However, they reeled us in, and then after an exchange of penalty goals it was 20–18 at the break. The second half was much different, incredibly tight, tense rugby, until with only a couple of minutes left on the clock the home team led 23–21. We were deep in our 22, but with both John Eales and David Giffin in imperious form and Mark Connors having just come on at half time to make things worse for them, their lineout was a mess. Anton Oliver, their hooker, had nowhere to throw the ball. So rather than try to run the ball, which is what they expected, Stephen Larkham kicked for the line.

At that point, Justin Marshall quipped to me, 'You can't keep doing that! You're just giving the ball back to us.'

'Are we?' I replied. 'With that lineout?'

Giff stole the ball again, it went back to Larkham, and he found the line again. 'We'll just keep kicking it out all day, Marshy,' I said loudly.

Ten weeks earlier, the Brumbies had lost the Super 12 final on a controversial call when Roffy was unlucky to get pinged in the last play of the game for not releasing the ball in the ruck. When South African referee Andre Watson blew the whistle on that occasion, I really thought he was going to nail the Crusaders' Dallas Seymour for hands in the ruck, but instead he gave the penalty to the New Zealanders. Seconds later, the game was over. Here at the Stadium, the ref was a different South African, Jonathan Kaplan. Another lineout, more brilliant work from Giff, and then Kaplan penalised All Blacks prop Craig Dowd for hands in the ruck. There was a moment of confusion, when Ealesy looked around for Stirling, our regular goal kicker, to give him the ball for the vital kick, not realising he had gone off with cramp minutes earlier.

'Stirlo's off,' hooker Jeremy Paul told him. 'You're up.'

'Once he heard that, he was all over it,' Jeremy told reporters afterwards. 'The eyes lit up, he wanted to take it.'

Our hooker was standing near me, Roffy and Giff as Ealesy

lined it up. If he kicked it, we'd retain the Bledisloe, and be in pole position to win the Tri Nations trophy for the first time, too. 'What d'ya reckon?' Jeremy asked. 'He'll knock it over,' I smiled back. Which he surely did, starting a mad scramble to see who could embrace him first. Soon after, I was back with Roffy, and I said simply, 'What goes around comes around.' The Kiwi crowd was filthy on the penalty, but we thought it was sweet, in more ways than one.

That night, both teams got together at a nice location on the waterfront, where we shared a meal and a few beers. I spent most of the time with Marshy and their No. 8, Scott Robertson, and then on the way home, in quite a ridiculous fashion, I banged my head on a park bench. There were lots of people about – Australian and New Zealand supporters – and I was walking right on the edge of a footpath when I slipped on, of all things, a Junior Burger wrapper, and went down harder than I'd fallen at any stage during the Test. I clipped the corner of the bench, bounced straight up, felt the red stuff and thought, *That's no good*. Giff was with me, looked at the nick, and said, 'Mate, you've done some serious damage.' Eighty minutes against the All Blacks couldn't hurt me, but the combination of a McDonald's wrapper and an old wooden bench was too much for me.

As is reflected in my response to Jeremy Paul's inquiry, I wasn't surprised that John Eales booted that goal home. He was always very calm under pressure, and he was an excellent goal kicker who used to practise a lot and trusted his technique. His kicking had been similarly rock-solid at Twickenham in 1998, when we beat England without scoring a try, while his decision-making in stressful situations in matches had become unflappable. The only time I ever saw his goal-kicking deteriorate was at Bruce Stadium, where he had a couple of bad days when the Brumbies fans got into him. But just about every kicker I saw, Andrew Mehrtens apart, struggled there. Bruce could be a very daunting place for visiting teams.

Eales's captaincy had been just as assured in the Sydney Test three weeks before the game in Wellington; indeed, even though we lost 39–35, it was in many ways one of his, and our, greatest triumphs. The crowd at Stadium Australia was a rugby world record 109,874, everyone was pumped, and then the All Blacks charged out to a 24–0 lead. The game was only eight minutes old! We were entitled to be shellshocked, but the message from the coach's box was simple: 'Forget the scoreboard, hold onto the ball.' Ealesy insisted we stay calm, be patient, and the mood changed when Stephen Larkham put Stirling Mortlock over. The game's first lineout occurred soon after, with thirty-one points already on the board, and then Stirlo scored again. The converted try to Chris Latham, then a try to Joe Roff and it was 24–all . . . after half an hour. Test rugby had never seen anything like it.

Just before half-time, Jonah Lomu made a break, pushed off a few people and suddenly it was me against him. It was one of those tackles that I was expected to make, and I did so in a slightly unconventional way, grabbing his fend and then using his body weight to throw him to the ground. It was all instinctive on my part, and while everyone wanted to tell me how good it looked, I couldn't help thinking of the many other times when the big man had made me look silly. This one was important, though, because it gave us the chance to go into half-time on level terms, and then take the lead briefly early in the second half. But Justin Marshall went over almost immediately, and the All Blacks stayed in front until the seventy-third minute, when I made a bust and Jeremy Paul backed up to put us a point in front. David Giffin snared a couple of lineouts on the All Blacks' throw-in, and it seemed he was going to be the hero of the night, but then Taine Randell put Lomu away for the final score of the night.

Afterwards, I had a few minutes with Wayne Smith, the New Zealand coach, and – maybe this says a little about both of us – we started discussing the way the breakdown laws were being interpreted. 'We've got to fight hard to keep the game the way it is going,' Wayne said, 'because that was just an awesome game of rugby.' I was loving the way rugby was being played. The ball was in play more – teams with the skills to use the ball in hand and who practised those skills hard were getting rewarded. This was why, according to legend, William Webb Ellis picked it up and ran with it. I can understand why he did that – everyone at Rugby School in the 1820s was kicking it the whole time and he wanted to improve things. Wayne and I agreed that it was the best game we'd been a part of, him as a coach and me as a player. That still rings true for me. We weren't on the right side of the scoreboard but it was a special Test.

Three weeks after the Wellington game, we were in Durban, and this time Stirling Mortlock kicked the last-minute goal that won us the Tri Nations. My father-in-law, Joe, has been one of my keenest supporters in rugby and has seen a number of my games, in Australia and overseas, and I recall him telling me that he was taken by the way Stirling grabbed the ball and walked towards where the penalty was given. 'I knew he was going to kick it,' Joe said. 'You could just see it through his body language.'

Again, I have to go back to the Super 12 final. After that game, there was a feeling in rugby circles that Stirlo struggled with his kicking under pressure, but this time he coolly knocked it over, never looked like missing. Ironically, when Paul Honiss, the referee, began holding his hand out, giving us the advantage, he was right in front of the posts. We could have thrown the penalty goal over and won the game. Honiss kept saying, 'Let's play the attack,' but we were shouting, 'We'll take the penalty, sir.' When he finally blew play up, he was out near the touch line. I'm not sure why he did that, but after Stirlo's mighty kick, we didn't care.

That Test in Durban was the last for three great warriors: Jason Little, Richard Harry and David Wilson. A fourth, Tim Horan, had finished up earlier in the season, after suffering a foot injury against Argentina, but he came over with his wife Katrina for the game, and filled the Classic Wallaby role before the game. That was an emotional experience for all of us, especially when Tim started sobbing as he told us exactly what being a Wallaby meant to him. After the game, Bomber was also choking up, saying, 'You don't know how much I'm going to miss you blokes.' I sat in the corner, contemplating what was happening. For me, this was the end of an era – the Wallabies brotherhood that I'd first tasted in Hong Kong six and half years earlier was breaking up. Good men would take their place, but for me playing for Australia would never quite have the same pure sense of joy that it had between 1994 and 2000.

Out of the dressing room, the emotion of the guys' farewells merged into the celebration to mark the end of a long Southern Hemisphere season and a sequence of extraordinary success. We had won twenty-three of our last twenty-six Tests, and were now Tri Nations winners, Bledisloe Cup holders and world champions. We had been staying about half an hour out of Durban, at a resort with a very good golf course (who'd have thought Rod would have found a place with a few greens and fairways?), and while some of the boys went into the city for a while, with a bus provided to get everyone back safely, many of us were happy to stay at the hotel and have a few quiet drinks and the odd cigar.

Eventually, the lads returned and they were in a playful mood. Two of the retirees, Jason Little and Dick Harry, got into a debate about something that didn't matter and eventually they decided a little Greco-Roman wrestling would be necessary to resolve the matter. This led to the guys' number one team shirts, those required for official functions, being shredded, and just as they shook hands and started laughing loudly who should stride in but Phil Harry, ARU chairman, a man with an extraordinary ability to appear whenever a good cigar or some nice wine is about. Phil is also, of course, Richard's father. Litts was okay, in the sense that he and I were leaving the next morning for a few days in Botswana, so he didn't need the team shirt for his flight home. Richard wasn't so lucky; all he could do was duck up to his room, find his other (well-worn) team shirt and then try to convince the hotel's outstanding laundry service to help him out before the team left for the flight home the following morning. The chairman of the Australian Rugby Union was insistent.

In one area of the hotel was a water display that featured maybe a dozen flamingos. The first time we saw them we expressed amazement at seeing these live birds inside the hotel, and soon a challenge was put out to anyone who could get themselves photographed with one of them. Front rower Bill Young had not been in our XXII for the Test, but he was about to become one of the stars of the tour.

'Youngy, see those flamingos,' I whispered. 'Remember how we've talked about them all week?'

Bill looked up, but didn't say a word. Then he smiled.

'Go get it, Youngy.'

A good forward always does what his halfback tells him. Quickly, Bill was wading through the waterhole, and he gently grabbed a flamingo by the neck and brought it back. The bird just went limp, played dead. Days later, when we prepared to snap some magnificent photographs of lions, cheetahs and zebras on our safari, we discovered there'd been no film in the camera. After Bill introduced the flamingo to Phil Harry, he returned it to its home, and no harm was done, but I wonder what might have happened if a photograph of the moment had made it into the papers. It was all good fun. When I think of South Africa in 2000, I think of the Tri Nations, of Stirling Mortlock, of my best Wallabies mates retiring. And I think of the pink flamingo.

Leading into the 2001 season, there was some conjecture about Rod Macqueen's future. The general consensus in the media was that he would retire at the end of the Australian season, after the Tri Nations, but I wasn't so sure. He had asked me a few times at the end of 2000 if I was going to play on, which intrigued me. 'Yeah,' I kept saying, 'I'll keep playing.' Truth was, with Little, Horan and Wilson having retired, I had thought briefly about giving it away.

Rod kept saying, 'I just want to win the Lions series.'

The coach, as we know, used to love planning, and it wasn't unusual to be having strategy meetings at the start of the year to discuss the footy ahead. We would go around to his beach house at Collaroy, on Sydney's northern beaches, and we'd beat him at golf, take his money. As usual, he was really positive, but in 2001 I sensed that this would be his last hurrah. The pressure kept building and a constant thought nagged away at him: *How much longer can I do this?* World Cup . . . Tri Nations . . . Lions series . . . that was his trifecta; after that, we'd be going for repeats, and I'm not sure innovators such as Rod Macqueen are ever content chasing more of the same. He had the energy for one more *big* campaign. The British and Irish Lions was that big one.

Much was made of the fact that we had only one lead-up game before the first Lions Test, but I didn't think it was such a problem. The nature of the program for that season, with the Lions series fitted in between the Super 12 and the Tri Nations, meant that we were never going to have too much time together, but we had enough meetings to plan how we were going to approach the challenge. There were three Tests in three weeks – Brisbane, Melbourne, Sydney – and one of the biggest things we talked about was recovering better than our opponents. It was logical to believe that the team that 'backed up' best was going to win, and a short preparation, given that we'd all played in the Super 12, might help in that regard.

Further, the beauty of that Australian squad was that we had played a lot together. Guys such as Nathan Grey, Andrew Walker, Elton Flatley, George Smith, Justin Harrison, Nick Stiles and Rod Moore (who'd been on the fringes of the team for at least the past year), came into the starting team during the series. Matt Burke, who'd missed the 2000 Tri Nations and the Wallabies' end-of-season European tour, also returned. We knew each other very well and I felt we could come together again at fairly short notice. I've always thought good teams could do that – and that was an outstanding team.

Our coach was very agitated after the first Lions Test, not just because we lost 29–13 but also because he felt he'd lost some control of our preparation (due to the cramped schedule) and the huge expectations on the team were unrelenting – even the massive support the Lions were getting from their army of singing and chanting supporters was getting to him. A few days after the game, he quietly told Ealesy and me he was finishing up, that he'd reveal this at the media conference after the second Test, regardless of the result.

The series turned on a Joe Roff intercept try in Melbourne. We were hanging on as half-time approached, down 11–3 because they had the ball and the momentum, but Burkey kicked a penalty before the break and we still had that confidence – even though it had been a really good first forty minutes for them, and we hadn't played well, we still believed we could get it done during the second half. I'm not saying we were super-confident, but we certainly hadn't written ourselves off. Thirty-two seconds after play resumed, the Lions' Jonny Wilkinson tried to push a pass down the short side, Roffy nabbed it, and dived over in the corner. Eight minutes later, after another Burke penalty, Ealesy grabbed the ball after a Lions scrum shattered, and after a rush of green-and-gold passes, Roffy was over again. Suddenly, we were ten points clear, and any self-doubt had been obliterated. Our back rowers – Smith, Finegan and Kefu – were making an impact every time they touched the ball. Test matches where you've got the game won at the sixty-five-minute mark are invariably fun, and that's where we found ourselves after Burkey went over. The silence of the British component of the big crowd was palpable.

Stephen Larkham, who'd been smashed a couple of times in Melbourne, and David Giffin were out of the third Test, and Harrison and Flatley came in. Justin would be making his Test debut, and he'd be doing so knowing that the Lions' Austin Healey had labelled him a 'plod', a 'plank' and an 'ape' in a news-paper column. We weren't quite sure what Healey was trying to achieve, and it didn't change the way we prepared or the content of any pre-game speeches, but it might have been in the back of Goog's mind after the Test, when he reflected on his great effort, especially his key play right at the death, when he stole a Lions lineout from their captain, Martin Johnson, on our line as the visitors were mounting a desperate last assault.

Before the first Test, we had come up with a game plan that was intended to have them chasing the ball. We'd get the ball wide, outrun them. But our execution was sloppy. This time, we got it right, though the big moment we were seeking didn't eventuate until the fiftieth minute. By this time, the score was 20–16 to the Lions, two tries to one, but the game hadn't quite opened up. We were still looking for that hole in their defensive line . . . and there it was . . . off a seven-man lineout. We played Nathan Grey in the back row, to take out their flanker Neil Back, then we attacked the channel outside Wilkinson at No. 10. We needed a quick ball, and sure enough Kef set it up so we could go back down the short side. That's where the weakness was. We'd created a three-on-one situation, and Daniel Herbert waltzed over the line. You practise a lot, put hours in and when you get it right on the night, when the pressure was extreme, it's a beautiful feeling.

Everyone remembers Googie knocking off that Lions lineout in the last minute – and that was a great and bold play; I still think of him as the 'Lion Tamer' – but to me that try we scored ten minutes after half-time was the one that encapsulated our quality as a team. A Wilkinson penalty brought them back to 23–all, but they didn't score another point, while we added two more penalties to win 29–23.

Much was made of some gestures we made after we scored and at the end of the game, how we formed a 'gun' with our thumb and forefinger and blew smoke as if we were duelling sharpshooters in the Wild West. People outside the team had no idea what we were doing. It came back to our tradition of smoking cigars after important victories. Kef was one who would always bring a quality cigar to a big game; if we won, he'd smoke it, if we didn't, he'd wait until next time. Before this Test, I saw Kef's cigar in his bag and I said to him, 'We're smoking that tonight.'

A funny postscript is that when that cigar was done, Kef threw the stub in the urinal. Seven weeks later, just before we were due to run out on the field for John Eales's last Test, against the All Blacks, Kef and I were in the toilet, having a nervous pee before we ran out, when I said to my great mate, 'There is no way we are going to lose this Test – there's the cigar, mate.' The stub was still there! Sure enough, Kef went out and scored the match-winning try.

Initially at least, with Rod leaving, it was hard to shake the feeling: *We've done it all*. Given this mood, the fact that we went on to win the Tri Nations and retain the Bledisloe Cup has to be seen as a great triumph, a credit to the players, the captain and especially the new coach, Eddie Jones. We knew the Springboks and the All Blacks would be queuing up to knock us off, and we managed to accept it as a new challenge, a great challenge, and rise to it.

We did, though, lose our first game against South Africa, in Pretoria, and afterwards much was made of a comment by Tim Lane, who was now the Springboks backs coach, who stated that it was part of their game plan to 'put pressure on George Gregan at the breakdown'. The media reacted as if they'd discovered gold. To me, it had been happening since 1995, since the World Cup when the English were at me for the entire quarter-final. During the Lions series, Neil Back had been relentless; every time I played against him he'd be tackling me and trying to hold me down. That was in his job description. I was always a 'marked man', but so too were the other top No. 9s in world rugby. It's part of the game.

To survive, I had to be technically good. I had to be strong over the ball and I had to be adept at moving it quickly and accurately, because if that ball stewed at the breakdown it would stifle our momentum, create a chain reaction in which the entire backline would look out of sync. I guess Tim's comments gained prominence because of his past work with the Wallabies, so the journos thought they were getting inside information – and there was also the matter of Giff copping a two-match suspension after he clocked the Springboks' Robbie Fleck. All my big mate was doing was looking after his halfback, after he saw me being rudely dragged away from a ruck.

We retained the Bledisloe in Dunedin, the first win there by the Wallabies, dating back to the first Australia–New Zealand Test at Carisbrook in 1905. The first thing I think of from that day is not a specific football moment, but of Justin Harrison crowd surfing after the game, like Rod Tidwell in *Jerry Maguire*, looking for his mum. I also fondly remember walking around the ground with Phil Waugh after the match. It was his first Test against the All Blacks; he'd won at his first crack, had seen us win the trophy for four years straight. 'Mate, don't forget this,' I said to him, keen for him to be aware that beating New Zealand is always a mighty tough task. 'Enjoy it. What we have done here today is special.'

Nathan Grey was big for us this day. We planned to attack the short side, and use a short kicking game to turn them around. If we could run it, we would; otherwise, we would kick and chase and play to their corners – a simple game plan, sure, but never a bad way to play a pressure game. It was, in many ways, similar to how we'd played in the World Cup semi-final. For Eddie Jones, the transition to the national coaching job was an almost seamless one, just as it had been when he took over at the Brumbies back in 1998. Of course, attention to detail and organisation had been two of Rod's virtues, and Eddie is cut from the same cloth.

A draw against South Africa in Perth set up Ealesy's farewell, against New Zealand in Sydney. After a decade at the height of his sport, the big man was retiring. But then, in the eleven minutes after half-time, the All Blacks piled on seventeen unanswered points to take a 23–19 lead. The next eighteen minutes produced a stalemate – just a penalty goal per side – but after that we were pretty much camped in their half, looking for the try that would send our skipper out in style. Ealesy declined a chance to kick a penalty to get us within one, and then, with time almost up, Larkham passed inside to Kef, who rampaged past or through four defenders to plant the ball next to the post. I know it sounds really arrogant to say, *I knew we were going to win*. Truth is, we didn't know that – but we did know that if we were given an opportunity we'd give it everything to make the dream come true. That was the never-surrender culture that was a feature of this team.

I have never played a perfect game of rugby in my life. There were periods in games where the team I was playing for got close to perfection, but in eighty minutes mistakes are going to be made. The key is to minimise the consequences of those mistakes. Great teams and great players recover very quickly; all of a sudden, they are back in a winning position. And they don't make that error again. You see it in elite sport all the time – a participant makes an error and follows up with a handful more. These guys might be gifted, but that's not enough. The great players follow up an error with a great play. As if to stress the point, they are also ruthless in their ability to exploit the mistakes of their opponents. It might not have always been apparent when he was deep in the middle of a ruck or maul, but John Eales had that ability. So did the Wallabies team of 1998–2001 that he led so successfully. It was these qualities that I wanted to maintain and grow within the Wallabies.

12

EDDIE AND THE BRUMBIES

1998–2001

'I would like to thank you Australians for your wonderful sportsmanship. It is always a pleasure to play here.'

SHARKS CAPTAIN MARK ANDREWS AFTER THE
2001 SUPER 12 FINAL IN CANBERRA

After the 1999 World Cup, I was at the wedding of Michelle and Owen Finegan, and I found myself sharing a beer with Eddie Jones, coach of the Brumbies since Rod Macqueen replaced Greg Smith at the Wallabies. Eddie was talking about the upcoming season, and he was so excited. 'Mate, we're going to change the way rugby is being played,' he said with a real sense of certainty in the voice. 'There is a way our game is going to be played and we're going to be the first ones to play it.'

He was so insistent, I had to agree with him. By the end of

pre-season training everyone in the Brumbies squad believed it. It's powerful when your boss is so emphatic about something and he truly believes in it.

Eddie wanted us to play with a greater width and variety to our attack than other teams, and at the same time we would become quicker and more aggressive at the breakdown. We'd move the ball into space, and do it time and again, ball in hand, negating the defensive strategies of teams who tried to jam the game up tight. He had recognised that the way the breakdown was being interpreted promoted the value of retaining the ball and being positive. If we could be technically sound with the ball in hand, then as the attacking team we'd be entitled to all the 'rights' in terms of keeping and using it. If we were good enough, it would be to our advantage to retain the ball even near our own line, and then we could just wear teams down with relentless attacking football.

A former Randwick hooker and coach, Eddie Jones had been coaching in Japan in 1997 when Ewen McKenzie recommended him to the Brumbies board. A group of us met him at the Qantas lounge in September, his appointment was announced soon after, and I quickly discovered that he is the most tireless and meticulous planner I'll ever come across. In terms of life skills, he had a wonderful effect on me. We'd turn up for a meeting with our diaries ready and the agenda organised, and whatever was decided was in action the next day. He was also passionate about rugby, with an incredible knowledge of the game.

I went on the Brumbies pre-season tour to Japan in 1998, but didn't play as I was rehabilitating after both a shoulder and knee arthroscopy. At half-time of our first game, Eddie really blew his top over the way we were playing, and when he finally finished I stopped to watch how the boys reacted. They weren't happy.

'I can understand your frustrations, Eddie,' Brett Robinson said to him after the game, 'but maybe they need more specific stuff at half-time.' This was the first time I saw a trait that I really came to admire about our new coach. He has the ability to take advice; if it's important and makes sense, he will make the change. He still got agitated, made sure people realised he wasn't happy, but with the team he was always in control, at half-time and at other times.

We had a terrible run with injuries in his first season in Canberra, but by the time 1999 came around he had matured and gained confidence as a coach, much like a player does. He'd come to grips with the expectations and the pressures of the job, and knew how to motivate footballers. One of the things I loved about Eddie was how he occasionally enjoyed having a beer with the boys. In those times you would see how an 80 kilogram man survived so many years on the front row. He was very quick with his dialogue and astute with his sense of humour. He was a lot of fun, but he always commanded the respect of his men. He earned that through his knowledge of the game and the way he got to know and challenge his players. He didn't always press the right buttons, and sometimes he pushed some players too hard, but overall he was very good at challenging footballers and getting the best out of them. Jim Williams went from being a first-grade winger to a Brumbies No. 8 to starting Test matches for the Wallabies. That was just Eddie confronting him, and Eddie loved it when you responded. Billy Young was an experienced prop from Eastwood with a bit of potential; Eddie told him he shouldn't be satisfied with that, showed him what he needed to do, and Billy went on to play forty-six Tests for Australia. The important thing was that when Eddie challenged someone, he did so knowing that the player could do what was being asked of him. If that person then responded and took himself to a new level, then the respect between the coach and player was enormous – the player for the coach because he believed in him; the coach for the player because you can't help but admire someone who's prepared to take advice and have a real go.

The best example of this is Troy Jaques. When Troy came to the Brumbies in 1998 he was a big strong guy who'd done a lot of rowing at Waverley College in Sydney, made the Australian Schoolboys and under-21 representative teams, and played some good club rugby. But Eddie rode Troy hard. I can remember Troy at one stage pleading, 'Mate, talk to me like a man, treat me like a man.' Eddie took that on board; in response Troy really applied himself and he became a polished footballer with a few key subtleties in his game. In 2000, Troy Jaques became a Wallaby, a credit to him for all the work he'd put in. That he'd achieved a life's ambition was also a sign of a great coach.

In the last round of the 1999 Super 12, we played Auckland at Eden Park. We needed to win, get a bonus point and also hope that a couple of teams above us on the ladder fell over if we were to make the semifinals. It didn't quite happen, because NSW couldn't beat the Crusaders for us, but we did our bit – scoring four tries in the second half on a wet night. That was a sign things were moving in the right direction, as was the fact we'd scored the second-highest number of tries in the competition, and conceded the second least. Little wonder that Eddie was in a good mood at Owen Finegan's wedding. As it turned out, we earned the right to host the final in 2000, but lost by a point to the Crusaders. Andrew Mehrtens came up to me after that game and said, 'We won tonight, mate, but I just want to say well done for the way you've played this year – you have changed the way the game is played.' That was one of the very few times in two years that our method didn't work, as Mehrts and his team-mates produced a remarkable defensive effort, the rugby equivalent of Muhammad Ali staying on the ropes to absorb the best George Foreman could throw at him. The following year, however, we were dominant, and we smashed the Sharks from Durban in the decider.

When I was interviewed for Michael McKernan's history of the Brumbies, he asked me to describe my best moment as a Brumby. I went for our first win in South Africa: 29–15 over the Stormers in Cape Town in our third game of 2000. It was an amazing team performance. I passed the ball more than 150 times, we were patient when we needed to be and controlled the ball magnificently, in front of a full house at Newlands. The big downer was that this performance occurred at the start of one of the toughest weeks in Brumbies history.

We had a good 'happy hour' at the team hotel that evening. I had been lucky to be named man of the match and had received a big bottle of Moët, which we were sharing around the group. After a while, the party separated; some players were happy to stay at the hotel while a few others decided to head out to a bar just down the road. But it was crowded – Cape Town is a big rugby town, they love their rugby – so we didn't stay there too long.

I remember when we left. Stormers supporters had been into us since the day we arrived in the city. At the game and in the bar afterwards many of them were armed with signs that carried slogans such as *Percy Percy Show No Mercy* (after fullback Percy Montgomery) or *Breyton Breyton The Try Line is Waitin'* (after winger Breyton Paulse). Their digs at us were all good-natured, but they were relentless, too, so it was very nice to put them in their place. After a while, though, it did start to get a bit nasty, and one woman began to show some aggro towards Brett Robinson. 'Let's get out of here,' someone said. I was thinking straight away, *We don't need an incident here.* This was a precursor to the real trouble to come.

We woke up on Sunday, our day off, and headed out as a group to Camps Bay, a beautiful beachfront area with stunning views back to Table Mountain, where we hoped to enjoy a few beers and a steak on the barbecue. Most of the guys went there; I was doing the driving. Everything was sweet, and most of us left not long after sunset, when I suggested we stop off at a Thai restaurant called Wang Thai on the way home. We'd had a good day, there'd be stories to be told, and from first thing in the morning it'd be back to business. Unfortunately, a few of the guys opted to stay at Camps Bay. These were the players who later found themselves in the spotlight.

Next morning, there was a knock on my door. It was Phil Thomson, the team manager, who was looking worried, and tugging at his shirt. (Whenever Thommo was nervous, he'd pull at his shirt.) 'We've had a few incidents last night,' he told me.

'What went down?' I asked.

Later, Thommo explained it this way: 'They had drunk too much, far too late into the night, taken a taxi, first for food and then for their hotel, had become alarmed at the size of the fare, insisted that the driver take them to a police station, and sought to detach the taxi meter to prove to the police that they were being overcharged. You've got to realise that a taxi meter in South Africa is not much bigger than a pager and plugs into the cigarette-lighter socket . . .'

By the time some commentators were finished with the story, however, the players' mistakes were a hell of a lot worse than that. I am not shying away from the fact that the guys shouldn't have been drinking excessively two days in a row, and they hurt the game with the mistakes that they made, but how some reporters (and a few rugby officials) back in Australia added 'colour' to their versions of the affair was really quite extraordinary. It left a nasty aftertaste with me and others that took a long time to heal.

Because of the time difference, with Australia nine hours ahead, the story was already breaking back home before the guys could get up the next morning to put their side of the story. One person in the media who was fantastic was Alan Jones, the former Wallabies coach turned broadcaster, who actually made contact with Thommo and me to find out exactly what had happened *before* he made a comment on his top-rating radio show. Not everyone was fair like that. We were wrong, we'd made some errors, but the way we were portrayed was so over the top – 'Wallabies running wild' . . . 'drunken rampage' . . . 'police reinforcements' . . . and so on – that it became almost impossible for us to discuss the matter sensibly in public.

Even now, there are some prominent rugby officials who want to paint this incident as one of the worst examples of player misbehaviour in living memory – yes it was bad, but not *that* bad. A spokesman for the South African police later agreed that 'the entire incident had been grossly exaggerated'. No player had been arrested, and the damage to the taxi was 'not too serious'. 'It is a professional game so we have to be answerable,' commented Joe Roff. 'It would just be preferable if we were only answerable to things that actually happened.' The players were fined amounts ranging from $500 to $1500 and given suspended two-match bans, which wasn't enough for some who hadn't heard the evidence. The entire episode provided a good lesson, the kind of lesson you don't want to learn, but one the Brumbies took on board. In the modern world of rugby, especially in South Africa, you are right under the microscope so you can't put yourself in a position where you can let yourself, your team-mates and rugby down.

I couldn't help but think that there were some people who'd been waiting for an opportunity to cut the Brumbies down, and because we'd been so successful *on* the field this off-field incident was their chance. We'd been an experimental team that was only supposed to last a year, then we made the final in our second season, dropped back for a year, but now we were beginning to establish ourselves as the most accomplished provincial team in Australia. That was always going to get a few people's noses out of joint.

Five years later, the Wallabies were in South Africa for two very important Test matches. Not long after we arrived, we discussed as a group the fact that we were in Cape Town, and how the city has a history of beating up off-field controversies, so it was important we didn't put ourselves in a position where that could occur. We were there chasing history, trying to win two Tests at altitude, something that no Australian team had done. I thought everyone was ready to go, that we were in good shape, confident. We had won our first four Tests of the year, building some nice momentum.

Everyone was asked to make a massive commitment for the fortnight. Part of that was that we wouldn't go out. There was no curfew as such, but there was no reason to be out having a big drink. Or so I thought . . .

As I understand it, some of the guys were out at an hour when things can go wrong. They weren't drinking but something had sparked some push and shove, and a few players were told to pull their heads in. When word got out, there were headlines about the Wallabies getting themselves in a blue again, which we didn't need, and Matt Henjak was sent home.

Some people argued that Matt shouldn't have been sent home. Thommo, now the Wallabies manager, was under a heap of pressure to be hard but fair. There were two other guys out with Matt, both of whom were likely to be in our starting XV, but in the end the decisions made were based not on who was in and out of the Test side but on the fact that Matt had been warned over a few previous incidents. That was a critical factor in the decision not just one particularly grievous incident in its own right, and that's why this affair was treated differently to the taxi incident.

I missed the Wallabies' European tour in 2000, because I'd been carrying a damaged nerve in my neck which had weakened the shoulder. A nerve injury is strange – it's not like a strained hamstring or a dislocated shoulder; you just slowly lose power. My problem had emerged during the Tri Nations and worsened from there. It affected my pass, especially my ability to throw left to right, and if I had continued playing I would have probably needed a reconstruction. Instead, I let the area regenerate, and felt as sharp as I had in a while in the lead-up to the 2001 season.

During this break, the Brumbies had a joint training session with the Essendon AFL club, who'd won the flag in 2000. It was a really interesting couple of days, especially when the players spoke about their experience in 1999, where they were the best performing team through the season but lost in the preliminary final and thus missed the grand final. Rather than bemoan their misfortune, they were inspired to set things straight the following year. What also impressed us was the way they trained smart – they weren't running heaps and heaps of miles but instead were looking at players' running styles, making them work more efficiently. The logic was that they would get more out of the distance they did run, and there would be fewer injuries and less fatigue. This was a period where AFL clubs such as Essendon, Brisbane and Sydney were taking fitness training, and especially preparation and recovery, to a new level. This experience was part of a very smart and productive pre-season that had us feeling very positive about the upcoming year.

The only games the Brumbies lost in 2001 were at Durban, Wellington and Dunedin. Against the Hurricanes, we played twenty minutes of excellent football, but then – as they could do with guys such as Tana Umaga and Christian Cullen in their line-up – they killed us by taking advantage of turnovers, and ran away with the game. We kept fighting, trying to salvage a bonus point, but as full-time approached guys were forgetting calls, which was really unlike us. Afterwards, we did extra work to make sure everyone knew exactly what they had to do and re-inforced the notion that, no matter what the game situation, we had to be able to trust everyone from 1 to 22 to know their role. The Highlanders overmatched us physically on a wet night, so we had to make sure that in future games, whomever the opposition, we could 'muscle' up. We had a bye after that game, then, in what were our last two games before the finals, we thrashed the Blues and the Waikato Chiefs.

In the semifinal, we handled the Reds comfortably, which meant for the second year in a row the people of Canberra would be watching the final, this time against the Sharks from South Africa. But before I could focus 100 per cent on the big day I had an important appointment in Sydney, for on the Tuesday before the final our son Max was born. I was in Canberra for training on the Wednesday, returned to the hospital on the Thursday, and was back in Canberra to prepare for the game on the Friday. Easy. I guess someone could have complained about my time away from the group in such an important week, but that is not the Brumbies way. Everything was possible, provided the travel didn't hurt me, which it never did. In terms of preparation, the big days were Monday and Wednesday, and I was there and switched on for both of those. I remember the exhilaration I felt flying north on the Monday night, knowing the next day Erica and I would become parents for the first time, and a pride I'd never known as I flew back first thing on the Wednesday morning, having seen my wife and new son so healthy and beautiful. I felt overjoyed and so damn lucky.

On the Saturday night, the Sharks came out to play a very physical game. That's the South African mentality; you match them there and you're a big chance to beat them. Their strength is their weakness. Now I reckon a lot of statistics are irrelevant, but some are revealing and by studying the stats we came up with some important 'team targets'. We'd established by analysing the score sequences of matches that the ten minutes before half-time and the twenty minutes after were critical times in games. We felt that if we were the best team in the competition over those thirty minutes in matches, we would win and win well.

We put a name on them: the 'championship minutes'. On the field, we'd shout 'championship minutes' and increase our focus – we were tired and fatigued, but every player on the field was the same, and if we could fight harder the advantage would be ours. We worked at it in training, too, to be really clinical during this part of the game. In 2001, we were clearly the best team in the competition in the championship minutes, so if we were even close to our opponents as half-time approached we knew we were in the box seat. We knew we were the best finishing team, too; we were always highly confident we would finish every game better than anyone else in the competition.

We went into half-time against the Sharks at 6–all. In such a situation, with the game apparently in the balance, many teams might not be as calm or as focused as they could be. Perhaps not enough is said in the dressing room? Or too much? We knew we were just where we wanted to be. The Sharks were the fastest start-ing team in the competition, so they couldn't have been happy to be all tied up. We ran away with it and finished up winning 36–6. The way Canberra celebrated that victory, on the night and in the days that followed, is a memory that will stay with me forever.

A GAME INSIDE
THE GAME

'I've played, mate. I don't need to ref.'

GEORGE GREGAN

I'd be surprised if some referees don't profile players. And then they probably talk about those players when they get together. I have no direct evidence of that, but I've seen the way some refs have operated over the years, pinging certain players for specific infringements while letting others get away with the same 'crime'. But we profile them, too, so it's a bit hard for me to complain about the practice.

Eddie Jones was a classic. Before each game, we'd receive a two- or three-page dossier on the referee which described their strengths and weaknesses, how many penalties they'd give in a game, when and where they'd be most stringent. Rodney Kafer loved it. If a ref started blowing his whistle a lot, Kafe would mutter, 'This is what we expected, sir. You are going to blow thirty penalties today and it's going to be a stop-start affair.' Then he'd add, 'But that's okay with us, because we've prepared for it.'

The ref had to start thinking, What? Then, maybe, we might start to see the game flow a little bit because he was not going to behave the way he thought we expected him to. Occasionally, we could even predict the way he'd change course. To us, this was just another of those little things we could do that might give us an edge, but at the same time we realised we couldn't be too disrespectful. Unfortunately, I did sometimes overstep the mark, but more often I believe I helped my team. It's a game inside the game and I loved it. If I could get a few penalties out of them, or help them identify something they might otherwise have missed . . .

In the Test at Durban in 2000, the one that ended with Stirling Mortlock's sideline penalty that won the Tri Nations title for Australia, referee Paul Honiss ruled against us very early in the game for coming in from the side. Late in the second half, with South Africa in front and the crowd bellowing, something similar happened, only this time with a home player at fault, and I shouted on the run, 'Coming in on the side! You gave a penalty for that in the first minute, don't be afraid to penalise them now.' He didn't blow anything then, but soon after he did give a penalty our way and Stirlo took his kick. I probably didn't influence Honiss one bit, but maybe it made him think.

However, in a Super 12 game against the Highlanders at Dunedin in 2001, the South African referee Andre Watson snarled at me, 'You'll never talk to me like that again.'

I can't remember exactly what I said, but I did speak to him without much respect. I didn't call him a cheat. In a newspaper article a few weeks later, an unnamed ARU official suggested I abused Watson in the vilest way, which was untrue, but the manner in which I spoke to him was out of line, he pointed that out, *and I never spoke to him like that again. It was a dumb way for me to direct my energy, and there is a point where you can push a referee so that it becomes a personal battle between the two of you, and a player won't win that one. In this case, I let the frustration of a poor team and individual performance get the better of me, but that was no excuse.*

The Brumbies' form over the following four weeks was sensational as we ran to the Super 12 title – but, foolishly, I gave my detractors some more ammunition a few weeks later in the Test against South Africa in Perth when, after Springbok captain, Bobby Skinstad, gave a penalty away, I threw the ball in his face. It was a really stupid thing for me to do, the penalty was reversed, and I had to find another three points for the team. In the moment the reality of what I'd done hit home, I felt lousy; but it was done. I do, however, try to learn from my mistakes.

As soon as the refs were 'miked up' it had a big effect on the game. Suddenly captains weren't able to have a sensible conversation with them about an incident on the field; it was if we were disempowering them when we questioned a decision. There are occasions when a captain needs clarity, and Test-match captains are pretty up to speed on the rules of the game, but in the last few years refs have taken to waving the skippers away, because they don't want conversations that might highlight a mistake to be heard through the commentary box. It's a Test match, though, so you are going to get tested, and that's true of everyone on the field. The players are tested physically, everyone is tested mentally, and if you are not up to it, I don't think you should be on the field.

I think my talking to referees got more attention than it deserved. Before his last Test, Watson was asked about the reputed animosity between us and replied, 'It was total BS and blown out of all proportion. Somehow Georgie and I are tagged as having this sour relationship but nothing could be further from the truth. I admire the man . . . we had one problem in one game. I dealt with it and he dealt with it.' However, I reckon I received the ultimate rap from Jonathan Kaplan – though he shouldn't have brought it up – before the Tri Nations Test at Cape Town in 2007, when he publicly advised the twenty-seven-year-old English referee Wayne Barnes that I would be putting him under a lot of pressure.

'[Gregan has] won plenty of 50–50 calls for his team and he'll have done his homework for Saturday,' Kaplan was quoted as saying. 'He'll know he's up against a bloke who is new to the international game.

'The Aussies will know that value when it comes to targeting the inexperience of the referee and there is no one better qualified to do it than George.'

Ten or twelve years years before Kaplan made his remarks, I was on the other end of such escapades, watching and hearing opponents such as Sean Fitzpatrick and Zinzan Brooke 'working' the referee – telling them, for example, that there'd been a bit of 'coming in from the side' on the blindside of a ruck. When they said this, I had sympathy for the ref, thinking to myself, It's not his fault, he can't see everything. *Then, at the very next ruck, came the shrill sound of the whistle and we'd been caught 'coming in from the side'.* Bloody unbelievable! *When you are on the wrong side of it you don't like it, but when you are getting a bit of love, it's good, it's really good. Who wouldn't want a bit of love for his team?*

It always amused me the way a referee changed the day he was identified by the powers that be as a prospective international referee. Now he was being assessed by the IRB judges, and it seemed that in his mind he was auditioning for a job, trying to get all the boxes on his application ticked rather than just adjudicating what was in front of them. That's so frustrating. I've seen plenty of good referees become just like the rest of them.

Oh, I love refs!

I mean that in a loving way. Many of them are good fun and we wouldn't have a game without them. Most of all, I want them to be consistent. Even if I didn't agree with them, if they were consistent I could accept it. It is possible to adapt in such circumstances. But if a ref is changing his tune during the night, that leads to frustration and even suspicions of bias and incompetence. There are so many laws and there are so many variables in a game of rugby, it's a tough game to interpret. So the game has to help them, make their life bearable rather than more complicated or less forgiving.

In all my years playing I can only remember one or two officials asking me to change the way I approached referees, and in these cases it was as if they were half-heartedly responding to something they'd read in the paper, rather than being seriously concerned. Indeed, I believe most of the good refs actually enjoyed the way I spoke to them. I might be wrong in a few cases, but on the whole they appreciated the banter.

I remember Jonathan Kaplan, who is a very good ref, apologising to me before we played the Chiefs in Rotorua in 2002. He had made a blue in our Super 12 game against the Crusaders. This came at a time when my relationship with the referees was under the microscope after Waratahs coach Bob Dwyer described me as 'arrogant' in the way I talked to them. Maybe Bob was thinking that if he raised this matter in such a provocative fashion, he'd get the refs to come down hard on me in future matches.

'I know you are under a bit of pressure,' Kaplan said to me.

'This is my life, Jonathan,' I replied. 'I'm used to it. You're under a bit of pressure, too.'

And he was under a bit of pressure, having been criticised for a few recent decisions. I didn't pursue any of those, as they weren't relevant to our discussion. 'I looked at that game [against the Crusaders] and I got it wrong,' he then said. 'I know you guys are in this position [of needing to keep winning to make the semi-finals] because of that decision and I don't feel good about it.'

I suddenly felt a big chunk of respect for the man for saying that.

Kaplan was responsible for the best refereeing decision I ever saw. It was the penalty given against All Blacks prop Craig Dowd at Wellington in 2000, the one that led to John Eales's penalty goal that won us the Bledisloe Cup. It would have been easier for Kaplan, a South African in New Zealand, to let that go, but he had been consistent in his interpretation of the breakdown all day and, even though it was the last minute and the penalty was against the home team, he still gave it. Not too many refs would have.

It's funny how some things that are said on the sporting field can get to you while others go through to the keeper. A funny crack might read well in a joke book or a newspaper column, but a good sledge is one that gets an opponent thinking or changes the way they go about their business. I'm sure there have been instances where an opponent has said something to me that they thought was a piece of sledging genius, but I didn't pay any attention. My background in junior representative cricket, where the banter could be genuinely biting, might have thickened my skin a little.

I remember before the under-17s cricket carnival in 1990, the ACT played NSW in a warm-up game at Kingston in Canberra, and I was opening the batting. The Kingston track in those days was a very flat one, and you expected to get a big score when you batted, and our coach came up with the strategy of batting all day and keeping our opponents in the field, to show them we were a *serious outfit. I took this tactic to excess and for two sessions was the most boring batsman in the world. They weren't happy, and their keeper Corey Pearson, who went on to play for NSW Colts and also some first-grade rugby league, was keen to let me know about this. Even after tea, they still had three slips in for me, that's how flamboyant I was, but I was under instructions so I just kept playing straight, or nudging singles around the corner.*

Then, suddenly, I got one on leg stump and flicked it off my pads for four. All they did was slow clap. 'Well done, Webster,' Pearson said through gritted teeth. 'It's a good feeling to hit one off the square, isn't it?'

When they brought a spinner on, as he was crouching behind the stumps, he said, 'Gee, I never realised you're wearing harrow [junior] pads. You need to grow into men's pads, Webster.'

I'd been copping it since the first ball of the day, but for some reason that one got me. 'Mate, that wasn't bad,' I smiled.

A good sledge will stop and make you think. In rugby, if you can stop an opponent focusing on his football even for a moment, it's worked. While I talked a lot on the field, I didn't sledge too often, and when I did it didn't always hit the mark, but I'd like to think that from time to time my words had an impact. And, of course, there are some players who bring sledging upon themselves, by their manner, the way they carry themselves, or maybe they just need to be brought down a rung or two.

In 2004, we played the Chiefs on a dirt track in a pre-season game and they thrashed us by fifty points. During the game, they were really into us, which we found a bit weird given that it was a trial in which the most important thing for us was getting some match fitness. However, at one point, their lock Mark Robinson described us as the 'weakest and softest pack' he had ever played against. But our wheels hadn't fallen off, and we ended up beating Auckland in the first Super 12 game of the season.

It was early May when we played the Chiefs again in the final round at Waikato. It's funny how sport has its way; this 're-match' was a close contest but we were always in control and ended up winning 15–12. Even before full-time, despite the impending result of the game, the local fans were cheering because it was the first time the Chiefs would play in the semifinals. But if they had won the game they would have had a home semi, so we had a shot at them for their lack of ambition. They were celebrating a loss! We were also kind enough to tell them about what it would be like the following week, playing in a sudden-death match in Canberra. We had experience of that; they didn't.

What goes around comes around. Our friend, Mr Robinson, had been particularly critical of David Giffin during that trial game in summer. In contrast, throughout the semifinal, he was awfully quiet, as Giff kept reminding him that the Super 12 competition is a bit like the Melbourne spring racing. It's not about being primed for a first-up run in August; more about being at your best on Melbourne Cup day. 'What's happened?' We asked him at a lineout. 'Have you been scratched from today's race?' Robinson didn't say anything, not then and never again in a match against the Brumbies.

Three seasons later, against the All Blacks in Melbourne, I had a bit of fun with Carl Hayman, a good guy, the premier tight head in world rugby and a player more than capable of causing some trouble in the scrums. From the start, I was into him, asking if he could keep up his side of the scrum. Normally, Carl would ignore this sort of chat, but here it seemed I was pressing the right buttons.

'Mate,' he snarled at a scrum, 'are you going to feed the ball tonight?'

'Here is the deal, Carly,' I replied. 'I'll feed the scrum if you can just keep it square and steady. Can you do that?'

Three weeks later, we were in Auckland and I was into Carl again about keeping his side of the scrum up. 'Carl, you've got to keep it square,' I said with the referee standing next to me. 'You've been illegally scrimmaging your whole career.'

This time he just smiled. I was getting nothing out of him. But then, out of the blue, from out in the backline, their No. 10, Dan Carter, shouted out, 'Come on, mate, are you going to feed the scrum?'

I spun around, totally stunned. 'Was that you?' I asked. 'I haven't heard a word from you your whole career, and now you're starting to get into the fun.' And it is good fun. 'But Dan,' I added, 'you've got to be prepared!'

He had a laugh, we winked at each other, and the games went on.

During the Lions series in Australia in 2001, Rob Howley was the tourists' starting halfback with Matt Dawson playing the mid-week games. Then Howley injured his shoulder during the Melbourne Test and Dawson had to come off the bench, but at a time when we had the Test sewn up. He was about to feed a scrum when I looked at him and did a double take.

'Daws,' I quipped, 'what the hell are you doing out here?'

He gave me a look that said what do you mean?

'It's Saturday, Daws. You shouldn't be here. You play Wednesdays.'

I thought it was harmless enough, but on the night of the third Test, after we'd won the series, I actually caught up with Matt's parents. 'I heard you boys had a bit to say,' his dad said to me. 'And that it got a bit personal.'

I didn't think it was that bad, but I was happy to know that my jibe had landed. But then, during the World Cup final in 2003, Matt lipped me back. I was down injured at one point, and he called out, 'What's the matter, George? Not tough enough to get up and play?' *Although I was hurting, I sort of bounced back to my feet. For a few seconds all I could think was* Get up and don't give him the satisfaction, *and while the fact I was temporarily sidetracked didn't cost us, it could have.*

That's a good sledge.

13

AUSTRALIAN CAPTAIN

2001–2002

'I'm a halfback, so I'm not going to stop talking. But I'm aware of my responsibilities.'

GEORGE GREGAN, SEPTEMBER 2001

I was at a function at the Hunter Valley, two hours north of Sydney, when I received a phone call from my manager. 'It's true,' he said, 'they're going to announce it at a press conference on Monday.' I can't remember what day of the week it was when I received that call, but I remember the Monday. It was 10 September 2001.

From my experience, you don't get invited to be captain, you don't sit through a formal job interview or get asked what you might require before you'd accept the job. You just get appointed. If you don't want it, I guess you just tell them when they contact you. In my case, if they'd wanted someone else, it wouldn't have been the end of the world; it is not, in my opinion, a job you can aspire to. It is a great and wonderful honour, and at that stage of my life, as a footballer and as a person, I felt I was ready for it. I was captain of the Brumbies and we'd won the Super 12, I'd been vice-captain of the national team for almost four years, and I was comfortable with the machinations of the position, the off-field requirements, and the fact you were much more 'on call'. Certainly, if I was ever going to be ready, this was the time.

I knew it wouldn't all be roses. There are certain parts of the job that didn't appeal to me, such as the fact that I'd be giving up a fair bit of myself. I knew that questions were going to be asked at media conferences which I wouldn't like – about off-field issues that might not concern me directly, but which did concern the team or members of the team. Sporting controversies might come up, or even issues not related to sport but to Australia, and because I was an *Australian* captain someone would consider my opinion relevant or worthwhile. I knew I'd have to careful about what I said, knowing there were reporters out there praying for me to say the right thing in the wrong way, so they could twist it to suit themselves. There would be inquiries about my family, and press photographers and TV cameramen out the front of my house, or following me as I went about a 'normal' day. I didn't have to like it, but I did have to be prepared for such scrutiny, otherwise I'd be overwhelmed by it.

I knew, too, that while the majority of people supported my appointment (a number of former team-mates called from the UK, and I received a nice note from John Eales, full of good and positive thoughts), there were a few individuals in the game who didn't want me to get the job. I conceded that at the time. A small coterie of people – a couple of journalists and a few officials –

didn't like me, while there were some men who would have preferred that I came from anywhere but Canberra. The last two Wallabies coaches had stepped into that role via the Brumbies, and for the captain to also be an 'outsider' was a bit much for these individuals.

My confrontation with Andre Watson in Dunedin a few months earlier, in a Super 12 game against the Highlanders was also cited as evidence I wasn't captaincy material, as was the manner in which that game ended. With time up on a wet and miserable evening, I decided that, rather than try to run one last play, we'd kick the ball out and accept a 16–9 loss, because we had a bonus point and didn't want to lose that. The way we were playing it was more likely we'd turn the ball over, concede a try or a penalty goal, and come away from the game with nothing, and we had an attitude that if you lose a game at least salvage something out of the wreck. It was, for me as captain, one of those situations where my gut feeling said, *It's not your night*. The romantics would argue that I should always be positive and go for the try that would have drawn the game, but I'll take my instincts over romance any day.

I knew I had massive shoes to fill. Just about all the cups and prizes it was possible for the Wallabies to win were in the ARU's trophy cabinet. At the media conference, the regular journalists seemed most interested in my relationship with referees, but also there was Dave Brockhoff, the proud former Wallabies coach and a huge supporter of the team. Brock is a regular at such events, and is always at the airport to see the Wallabies set off on tour, and here he asked a question about what I had learned from John Eales and another on how the team went about winning close games.

Of all the things Ealesy taught me about leadership, the one I valued most was about seeking input from individuals you respect. The final call is always the captain's, but listening to the right people can help enormously. From 1998 to 2001, Ealesy's on-field management was brilliant – he managed referees well, was decisive when he needed to be and had an impressive knack of getting the crucial calls right.

This last point is an interesting one because it enables a team to win through in tight matches. It comes down to self-belief and an ability to stay assured and composed in the key moments. It would be a significant difference between the Wallabies of 1998 to Ealesy's final Test as captain (twenty Tests decided by less than ten points, for fourteen wins, five losses and a draw), compared to the team I led from my first game in charge through to the end of 2004 (nineteen Tests decided by less than ten points, for eight wins and eleven losses). As you can see, there were a lot of close Tests but we lost the knack of winning them. The great teams have this skill and it comes through suffering from negative experiences and then learning from them. Maybe we lost that ability, because we often made the same critical errors . . . or maybe the earlier group was just an incredible Wallabies team.

One of the first things I had to do as captain was convince a couple of senior players to go on the end-of-season tour, as the full impact of the September 11 terrorist attacks set in. The first game of our European tour was scheduled for 1 November, a Test against Spain, and at our pre-tour camp I went from room to room, seeing how each player was thinking about the trip. In a group, players might have been naturally less inclined to speak about their reservations. It was a sensitive issue. Some of the guys had young families, a couple of guys' wives were pregnant. Matt Burke was about to get married. My own son was three months old. My opinion was that if anyone wanted to stay at home, it should never be held against them, and if the overwhelming majority view was that we shouldn't go, then the tour be cancelled. At the same time, I appreciated the efforts of the ARU, the Department of Foreign Affairs and Trade, and team management (and, I assume, the overseas rugby administrations, too), who were patient and understanding, and went to great lengths to ensure that the security in place for the tour was top-class. I was able to detail to the rest of the guys what would be happening to ensure we were as safe as possible. Eventually, everyone agreed to tour, though I sensed a couple of guys continued to waver until the very last minute.

My Test captaincy career began with a 92–10 win in Madrid, and then it was on to London, where we worked at the same training facility used by the Chelsea Premier League club. I remember being struck by how old school and amateur their preparation and pre-game analysis appeared to be, but our relatively state-of-the-art methods didn't count for too much when we were beaten 21–15 by England at Twickenham and then 14–13 by France in Marseille. The scoreboard might have showed that we only lost by a point, but the French were clearly the better team on the day. Still, I wasn't too downbeat as the team we put on the park was vastly less experienced than the teams which had been winning so famously for Australia in recent seasons. 'Our rookies were fantastic,' I said straight after the game.

I remember Chris Latham, the fullback, coming up to me after the game and saying how gutted he was for me. You don't go looking for such gestures when you're captain, but they do matter – in a way, the things that show how much your team-mates care are the things that mean the most when you're thinking back over your career. Eddie Jones and I were starting to take a little heat from the media, and I think Chris's reaction reflected the fact that within the playing group there was a strong desire to keep the good times rolling, even if we were down slightly on experienced personnel. I was touched by his support, but I stressed that we were a long way from the end of the road. 'Let's finish this tour well,' I said to the group when we got back to Britain for the Test in Cardiff. 'Let's not get down on ourselves.'

Coming at the end of such an intense home season, this was always going to be a difficult tour. Being my first trip as captain, I was probably more inspired than most, and the young players on tour were clearly enjoying the opportunities opening up for them. Every year is a long season, with just December off to recover from the rigours of an arduous campaign. The first week of January is 'pre-season' and you hit the ground running; soon you are playing trials, Super 12, Test matches, Tri Nations, European tour, and it's December again. It was only when I didn't go to the Northern Hemisphere because of injury – in 2000 and 2006 – that I had four months, rather than four weeks, to rehabilitate my mind and body and then prepare it for the battles to come. I don't think all players need four months off every year, but once in a while it helps. We don't play golf or bocce. We collide with people.

A constant during my football career was my ever-increasing recognition of the virtue of recovering properly and fully – this was a process that began for me at the AIS and was still happening in my final season. If today's elite players don't get the chance to recharge at appropriate moments, the lengths of their careers will be diminished and the quality of the football they provide will be downgraded. Of course, the other side of this argument is that we are professionals and these games are necessary to pay the rent; the answer, as with many things in life, lies in balance.

As football administrations come to grips with this, you'll see more situations such as what occurred in 2007 when Wales kept most of their best players at home rather than send them to

Australia, and South Africa didn't send their best squad to Australia for the Tri Nations Test. Both countries had a firm eye on the World Cup when they crafted their selection policies, but in doing so they were also acknowledging that they can only send their players to the well so many times. Rather than bad-mouth teams that do this, the officials need to accept the situation, or at least recognise the problem at the heart of it.

We looked at changing our game a little in 2002. Mostly, it was about subtle alterations – aimed at us playing with a bit more width – but if we hadn't done so Eddie was convinced the world would start to rush past us. We continued to be aggressive, typified by two decisions I made – one against South Africa, the other versus England – to go for tries rather than take kicks at goal. Both of these decisions were widely praised. New Zealand won the Tri Nations, but we ran them close, losing narrowly in Christchurch and winning by two points in Sydney. In South Africa, we lost by two damn points at Ellis Park, having won comfortably against the Springboks in Brisbane. Before that, we won two from two against the Frenchmen.

Sometimes the margin between greatness and the gutter can be very small. In Christchurch, we would have won if Jonathan Kaplan had awarded us a penalty try in the seventy-second minute, after Daniel Herbert was tackled without the ball. It was a 50–50 call, and it went against us. In Sydney, we snuck home on the back of a sensational late penalty from Matt Burke, but then, at Ellis Park in Johannesburg, we were beaten by a *very* late try . . .

This was quite a game, my seventy-eighth Test match. We didn't played well for a lot of it, but we showed a lot of character in the second half to chip away, chip away, and eventually get back into the game. In the seventy-fifth minute, George Smith ran 50 metres to set up a wonderful try for Brendan Cannon that got our noses in front – a calamity for the home crowd that led to half-full bottles being thrown at us as we celebrated. (This occurred just a week after a drunk fan had run onto the field in Durban to attack the referee in a New Zealand–South Africa Test. Fortunately, nobody was struck by one of those bottles; when I said afterwards that if any more had been thrown at us when we got back to halfway, I would have taken the team off the field, I was serious.)

The game was all but over when I tackled Bobby Skinstad out wide. I was slowing down this particular ruck by pulling Bobby close to my chest, so he had to work really hard to get the ball back. This was a skill we always practised. Here, I wanted the referee, Paddy O'Brien from New Zealand, to stop the play and give them a scrum. That would allow us to reorganise or, better still, if time was up it would be the end of the game. Instead, O'Brien let play go on. I can remember thinking, as I lay on the bottom of that ruck, *I'd back our defence nine times out of ten to come up with the tackle.* Sadly, not this time. Their fullback, Werner Greeff, ran a really good line, starting outside but cutting back closer to the ruck. Their half, Bolla Conradie, found him and he sliced through to score the try, then kick the goal, to win the game. I was still on the bottom of the ruck, hoping for silence, when I heard the roar as he raced through. Gosh, it was a big roar.

If ever the result of a football match tested my 'the sun will shine tomorrow' philosophy it was this one. Back at the team hotel, I was gutted, and I felt especially for defenders who had been in the vicinity when that last try was scored. They took the loss personally. But it wasn't through lack of effort that we were beaten, nor was it all about that last play. We weren't quite good enough, a point I conceded in a press interview: 'They just held

That's me as a little fella, at Mount Taylor in Canberra, 1976.

The whole family – Mum, me, Tendai, Dad and Susannah, 1976.

Playing halfback for the Tuggeranong Buffaloes under-6 rugby league team, 1979.

After my team won the under-12 NSW rugby union championships in Sydney in 1984, former Wallaby Steve Cutler offered his congratulations to the players.

As a kid, cricket was as much a passion as football. Here I am, head just above the stumps, playing for St Edmund's First XI in 1990.

I played for St Edmund's First XV in 1990, and we made it to the Waratah Shield final, where we were beaten by Scots College.

Playing for the Australian under-19 team in Christchurch against the Canterbury under-21s in 1992. The result was a 9–all draw.

My lucky break came when I played for a young Barbarians squad in the Fiji International Sevens tournament in 1994, and we then beat Cook Islands in the Plate Final. Also with me is a young Ben Tune (far right).

The Canberra Times

Matt O'Connor and me in 1994, when we were selected to be part of the Wallabies squad for a two-game series against Ireland. I didn't leave the bench in either match, but Matt was the first Canberra player in four years to get a starting role.

Tim Clayton/Sydney Morning Herald

The tackle. My hit on New Zealand's Jeff Wilson late in the Bledisloe Cup Test at the Sydney Football Stadium in 1994 was just a fortunate save, but it threw me into the limelight.

Before the start of the 1995 World Cup in South Africa, we visited the township of Zwilde. The smiles on the kids' faces were amazing. You can also make out Glen Ella, Scott Bowen, Troy Coker and Dan Crowley in the crowd.

Hooker Michael Foley about to score a try against Romania in a pool match of the 1995 World Cup, while I look on. We won comfortably, 42–13.

My one and only season playing for Randwick in the Sydney club competition in 1996.

In 1996 Greg Smith took over as Wallabies coach. Here he talks to the team at half-time during a Tri Nations match against the Springboks in August 1996.

Sport the Library

At a press conference with Brumbies coach Rod Macqueen after the Super 12 final against the Auckland Blues at Eden Park in 1997. We lost, but when we arrived home we were greeted by a big crowd who almost made us feel as though we'd won.

Getty Images

Congratulating Stirling Mortlock after he scored a try against the Hurricanes in Wellington in 1999, while Rod Kafer (far left) and Iliesa Tanivula (left) look on. We won the game 21–13.

Tim Clayton/Sydney Morning Herald

On a tour of the Guinness factory before the 1999 World Cup. Phil Kearns (second from left) is cracking up after a joke, alongside assistant Wallabies coach Jeff Miller (left) and Jason Little (centre).

Tim Clayton/Sydney Morning Herald

Right at the end of our quarter-final against Wales in the 1999 World Cup, I beat Daniel Herbert to the ball and scored my second try of the game, putting us 24–9 in the clear.

Springbok prop Os du Randt steamrolls over me in the 1999 World Cup semifinal at Twickenham. It doesn't look like it here, but I actually got him.

As the full-time whistle blows in our 1999 World Cup semifinal, Springbok Henry Honnibal is dejected while Richard Harry (left) and Owen Finegan (centre) and I celebrate. I am in rather a happy place!

AFP/Getty Images

The moment I knew we were world champions, after we beat France in the final of the 1999 World Cup.

Tim Clayton/Sydney Morning Herald

Sharing the moment with my mate Tim Horan, after the 1999 World Cup final.

The whole team celebrates following our victory in the 1999 World Cup.

After the '99 World Cup final, I found Erica in the crowd. Like all the other players' wives and girlfriends, she was wearing our semifinal jersey.

John Eales and me in the change rooms after the '99 World Cup final, ecstatic to get our hands on the Webb Ellis Cup.

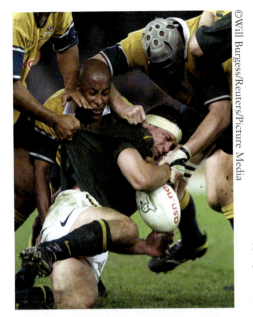

South Africa's Corné Krige goes down with the help of Mark Conner (right) during the Nelson Mandela Challenge in Melbourne in 2000.

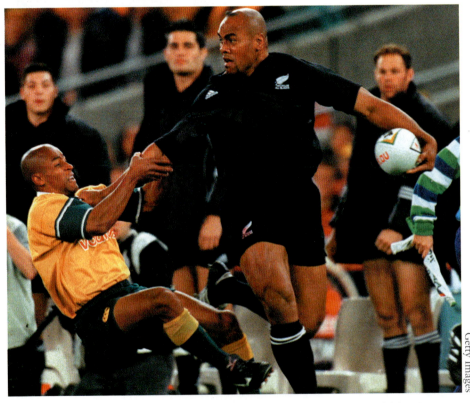

Playing the All Blacks in Sydney in July 2000. Jonah Lomu is a formidable player, but I used his body weight to pull him to the ground. We lost this match 39–35, but many consider it to be one of the best rugby matches every played.

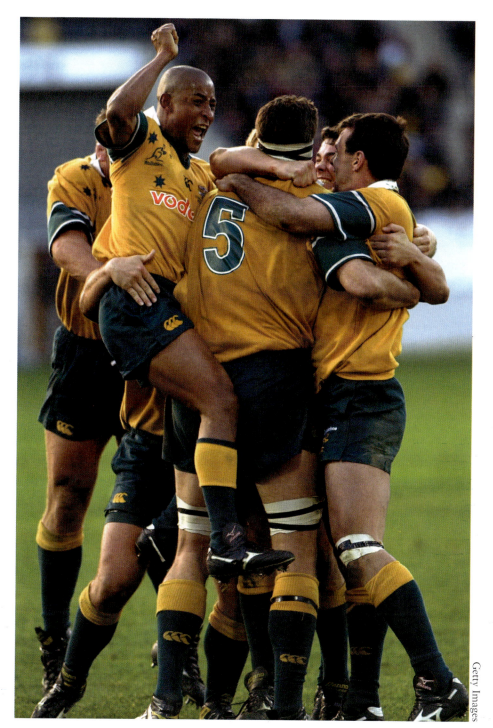

After Ealesy kicked the penalty goal in Wellington that won us the game against the All Blacks and clinched the 2000 Bledisloe Cup, there was a mad scramble to see who could hug him first.

Getty Images

The way Canberra celebrated the Brumbies 2001 Super 12 grand-final victory over the Sharks is a memory that will stay with me forever.

The tall and the short of it. Singing the national anthem alongside John Eales before the 2001 Test against the All Blacks in Dunedin.

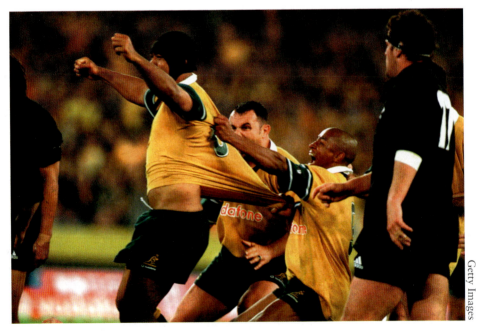

Just moments after Toutai Kefu scored the magnificent match-winning try against the All Blacks in Sydney in 2001. We retained the Bledisloe Cup and sent Eales off in style.

their nerve better than us, and they deserved the win.' We had a happy hour back at the hotel, and then a few of the guys headed out; I stayed in. Again, life went on. You'd beat yourself up big time if it didn't.

In any close game, you can always find a moment or three where you could think, *If only we'd done that . . .*

It might be a missed goal or tackle, a dropped pass, a refereeing decision, maybe just a bad bounce. I was usually inclined to think a different way: *Why didn't we win the game earlier? Why did we put ourselves in a position where one error cost us?* The other reality of a rugby match is that there is always going to be a winner and a loser. While one dressing room is celebrating, the post-mortems might have already started in the other. Peter Blanch, an AIS physiotherapist who worked with the Brumbies, used to say he liked the way I carried myself after a game. In his eyes, I enjoyed a good win, was able to cope with a bad loss, and was always thinking about what was ahead.

We knew it would take all season for us to adapt fully to our new style of attacking play, so I was more than happy with our efforts during the Southern Hemisphere winter of 2000, but things did go skewiff in October–November. We headed north with a big squad, and resolved to give everyone an opportunity early on, with the focus being on winning the Cook Cup Test against England.

One of the big stories of the team's European tour in 2002 was the fact that the Australian captain was permitted to travel home between the Irish and English Tests to witness the birth of his second child. I copped a bit of criticism, but for me we had a strong squad and watching the birth of my child was too important to miss.

Charlie, my eldest daughter, was induced on 11 November so I could be there. It was a Monday, so as to disrupt the team as little as possible. For me, whether or not I returned to Sydney for the birth was a pretty simple decision to make once I clarified in my mind that it was doable. That happened before we went away. The trip was an important part of our preparation for the World Cup, but it was a case of putting things in their right order. In my view, if I knew I could handle the travel (which, having seen plenty of planes and airports over the previous eight years, I knew I could), and if I knew the team's preparation for the England Test wouldn't be damaged by me being away for part of the week, then it was a no-brainer. I was bemused that some people thought they knew my body better than I did, and that they'd publicly question my motives, as if I didn't care about the team, only myself. In a way it was a throwback to the 'good old days' when men were men, wives didn't tour and so on.

Within the team set-up, there was no pressure placed on me to stay in the UK, even though we lost to Ireland. Eddie Jones and Phil Thomson were totally supportive, as was John O'Neill. All the critics were in the press box.

The fact I was a on a first-class flight on the Sunday meant I had plenty of time to review the Ireland Test. I slept at the right times (fortunately, sleeping on a plane has never been a problem for me), lost nothing in terms of my recovery, was able to witness one of the most precious experiences of my life – the birth of my second child – and hold little Charlie in my arms, all up spending thirty-six hours on Sydney soil and even seeing my son's first steps before I was back on a plane and arriving in London by the Wednesday morning. (I used the hospital fax machine to send some notes concerning the upcoming Test to Eddie at the team's hotel.) After I landed at Heathrow, I had a coffee with Eddie, took part in a sponsor's promotion, trained that afternoon and then slept comfortably that night. The team had Thursday off, a light training run on Friday, Test on Saturday. And I felt I played all right. We were leading until well into the game, the boys showed a ton of character, but then England's Ben Cohen scored a try in the sixty-sixth minute, a late goal attempt by Burkey swung just centimetres wide and we missed out, going down 32–31.

Eddie Jones is a tough little rooster, a man who rarely displays his emotions, but he had been hyped up before the Test. Tellingly, he wanted us to think about how good it would be to sing the national anthem in the dressing room after the game (we always sang 'Advance Australia Fair' that little bit louder when we were away from home, but we would have chanted it louder than ever if we'd won that day). Those cynics who in later years questioned Eddie's loyalty to his country and his country's rugby team would never have done so if they'd been in the Wallabies dressing room that day. There was a real sense of exhaustion, physical and especially emotional, in the rooms after that game, because we had put everything into it and come up just short – but later we had one of the best times I've had with the Wallabies when everyone toasted the birth of Charlie Gregan. There was a special spirit within that group, which carried on through 2003 to the World Cup.

One of the most popular members of that touring squad was Wendell Sailor, our high-profile rugby league convert. Wendell and two other league stars, Mat Rogers and Lote Tuqiri, would all make the switch before the 2003 World Cup. I didn't mind the ARU's policy of 'poaching' players from another code, what mattered was that he wanted to be a Wallaby, and that he realised there was a genuine challenge in becoming successful at the elite level in rugby. Wendell, Mat and Lote had not come over purely for the cash . . . all three worked hard and contributed when they joined the Wallabies squad.

There have been some rather snide comments in recent times about a 'league culture' being brought into rugby union, which I thought was a case of people talking in slogans without really being aware of their subject matter. I know league stars such as Ricky Stuart and Brad Fittler reasonably well, and we certainly respected each other's games and the fact we all worked hard, enjoyed the good times and had to cope with high levels of scrutiny. The landscape has changed for all professional sports in recent times, to the point that if you put a foot out of line your name is going to be in the papers for the wrong reasons. There have been unfortunate incidents in rugby union in recent times that involved ex-league players, and there have been others that have not. The life of a professional footballer in Australia in the twenty-first century is far removed from that of days gone by – the temptations are different and potentially more hazardous – and it crosses over all codes. You see it in union, league, and the AFL.

What is not recognised sufficiently, in my view, is that most players do their games enormous service that goes far beyond just staying out of trouble. We're also hit with a double standard from time to time – the lack of characters and larrikins in modern sport is bemoaned one day; a fellow is slaughtered for letting down the sport and acting unprofessionally if he is seen out having a drink or two the next. That's how it feels some-times.

Usually, Wendell is the life of the party. He has a big public image, yet he's one of those guys you don't get a fair idea about from what you read in the papers. He would do anything for his team-mates and I always like that in a footballer. He was a successful Test footballer and not too many people have managed that. I was surprised and disappointed when Wendell was suspended for failing a drugs test (for recreational drugs) in 2006.

The end of the 2002 European tour meant I could finally get some rest for a 'stress reaction' in my foot that had been bugging me since March. It was one of those injuries that never prevented me from playing at my best, but it still niggled. By late in any year, a lot of guys are carrying injuries that require some sort of surgery, or at least some extended rest. As I sat in the doctor's waiting room back in Canberra, I couldn't help thinking that we weren't travelling too badly coming into a World Cup year. The way the Test at Twickenham had panned out had us believing we could defeat England, whom we saw as the strongest of the Northern Hemisphere teams. A couple of lucky breaks and we could have beaten France twice, New Zealand twice, South Africa twice and England in 2002, which wouldn't have been a bad result.

14

UNDER FIRE

2003

'We've got incredible support from the public, but you just don't read about it. Don't get caught up in their agendas. Just let them go.'

GEORGE GREGAN TO HIS WALLABIES TEAM, AFTER THEY HAD
BEATEN SOUTH AFRICA 29–9 IN BRISBANE, 2003

The concept of a rugby union players' association was born out of the WRC battle of 1995. As part of the 'peace agreement' negotiated with Ian Ferrier from the NSW Rugby Union, the ARU agreed to support the concept of a players' association and make a loan of $10,000 towards its establishment. In late August 1995, the Rugby Union Players' Association (RUPA) was formed, and in the following month I became a member – with Tony Dempsey, Ewen McKenzie, Damian Smith, Mark Harthill, Tim Kava, Rod

McCall and Rod Kafer – of the association's initial interim committee. My role at that level was short-lived, however, as when the first committee elections were held in December, a number of us stood aside. Tony, a former Waratah and Wallaby (on the tour to Canada and France in 1993), was elected president, with the rest of the committee being made up of Dan Crowley, Rod Kafer, Tim Kava, Andrew Blades, Troy Coker and Mark Connors. In 1997, the RUPA negotiated the first collective bargaining agreement (CBA) with the ARU, NSWRU, QRU and ACTRU, which gave us players an employment framework, something which I believed had been necessary from the day the game went professional.

A second CBA was successfully negotiated in 2001. In the four years between these two agreements being reached, Tony and the RUPA had fought a number of battles on behalf of players over matters such as player welfare, the use of players' images and likenesses in sponsors' promotions, and the payment of World Cup bonuses. In September 2001, the RUPA was a founding member of the International Rugby Players' Association (IRPA), which included among its members the players' associations from England, France, New Zealand and South Africa. A year later, the IRB proposed that a match be played between the 'best of the Northern Hemisphere' and the 'best of the Southern Hemisphere' – a type of 'All Star' game, if you like. I thought the concept was terrific, but the timing was terrible. The plan was to stage the game at the end of 2002. That would be cutting into our down time, at the start of what would be a long and important World Cup year.

For the Australian players, there was a bit of history to this proposal. A not too dissimilar proposition had been put to the Wallabies for the end of the 1998 season, when a rich South African syndicate wanted to bankroll a match between the Springboks and a Rest of the World XV in Florida. The discussions within

Team Wallaby went as far as Rod Macqueen and the leadership group meeting with members of our medical staff to try to ascertain just how much a game of that type, played at that time of the four-year World Cup cycle, might take out of the players involved. We decided it wasn't going to be in our best interests to play, because it was going to encroach on our rest time, and also, perhaps, on our physical preparation leading into one of the most important years of our lives. The reasoning behind that decision, in my mind, set a strong precedent for any future enterprises.

John O'Neill was CEO of the ARU in 1998 and as far as I know he supported our choice. However, he strongly recommended that Australia provide some top-level players for the proposed IRB event in 2002. We considered his request, but in the end responded the same way we had in 1998. The only difference we could see was that this was an IRB game, whereas four years earlier it was a private venture.

An irony was that Eddie Jones had been appointed the coach of the Southern Hemisphere team, so we had both Australia's coach and CEO backing the game, while the players were not. Various compromises were suggested, such as only fringe Wallabies being available for selection, but that missed the point, as all of these players would soon be involved in preparation for a full Super 12 competition. We didn't say no to the concept, just the timing. Crucially, the RUPA's reading of the Standard Playing Contract was that the ARU could not compel us to make ourselves available for the game, and eventually – and sadly – we had to go to an independent arbitrator to get the ARU to back off. I think that some of the animosity that came out in 2003 stemmed from this standoff.

I didn't have to be involved with the RUPA, but I chose to be, and I never saw a conflict of interest, even when I became the Wallabies captain. I know others see the captain as more a member of senior management than an employee, but I always believed that first and foremost I needed to be a players' advocate. This difference of perception was what led to most of John O'Neill's specific problems with me. O'Neill is, by his nature, a political player who enjoys outsmarting opponents in business negotiations – such as, for example, the time in the 1990s when he bypassed the IRB to arrange annual Cook Cup Tests in Australia and England.

I was on the periphery of the negotiations that led to the second CBA in 2001. John Eales had been a member of the RUPA Executive Committee at one point when he was captain, but had relinquished that role by 2000. I welcomed the chance to put forward a few ideas. The spirit of those negotiations was excellent, the players' mood essentially being *We don't want to bleed you dry, that's not good for anyone, but there are certain aspects of the proposal that are not good for us, and we'd like them to be changed.* It was a negotiation, a good one, and the eventual agreement reflected that.

We were operating in a world where the media landscape was changing rapidly and the issue of players' intellectual property rights was a hot one. The new CBA had to reflect those changes. Two years later, however, the Rugby World Cup officials presented to the players, through their respective unions, a Participation Agreement (PA) that had not been adapted to suit this new world. If we were going to sign an agreement which would mean, in effect, that for the eight weeks of the 2003 World Cup our CBA would be superseded, then we needed to be adequately compensated. When the RUPA advised its members not to sign the PA as it was originally drafted, and sought changes through the ARU, John O'Neill reacted angrily, as if we were trying to sabotage the entire tournament. What followed was months of meetings and debate as we sought to get the PA modified to comply with our

CBA (and the agreements of players from other teams, too). O'Neill essentially said, 'Trust me.' But nothing was happening; instead the same document with the same flaws was presented to us, and eventually we were told we had to sign the PA as it stood by a certain date – and if we didn't, they'd start the World Cup without us. In response, the RUPA launched Supreme Court legal action against the ARU seeking orders preventing the ARU from approaching its players to sign the PA. At that point, finally, the IRB made some significant changes to the PA, and the players were able to sign up in the days after the Tri Nations Test at Cape Town in mid July. We could only wonder why it had taken so long.

Meanwhile, players from other countries had been able to sit back and watch the dispute unfold in Australia. When England were in Australia in June 2003, their captain, Martin Johnson, told me that was exactly what his men were doing. They had no intention of signing the PA as it was then written. New Zealand's Justin Marshall said the same thing of the All Blacks. A public relations war developed as the ARU tried to link the battle over the PA with separate negotiations over a player bonus for the World Cup. To me, the two issues were unrelated, but in merging them the ARU was able to paint the players as greedy mercenaries trying to hijack the game.

I felt no real angst towards the ARU, and had sympathy for O'Neill and his team having to deal with the IRB, which is a very conservative – and in many ways still amateur – body. However, I did object to a speech O'Neill gave at our base in Coffs Harbour in the first week of June, when he used some colourful language and others in the squad got to see a side of him which they hadn't seen before. He didn't want the RUPA to negotiate on our behalf, and accused us of 'ratting' on Australian rugby. His mood and the tone of his language meant that it was impossible not to interpret it as anything other than a threat. When I put my signature to an affidavit that was part of the RUPA's court submission, in which I stated that O'Neill had placed undue pressure on the team to sign the PA, our relationship was weakened.

In the previous weeks, O'Neill had rung me a few times, sometimes late at night, wanting to discuss the matter. But the players had agreed that the RUPA would be handling the negotiations, so he should have been negotiating with Tony Dempsey. He knew that, but didn't like it. O'Neill had nothing but disdain for Dempsey and it seemed to me that O'Neill was sometimes just as concerned with getting one over 'Demo'.

I'm not a guy who likes to go around picking fights and causing problems. If something needs fixing, fix it. The last thing the Wallabies leadership group wanted, midway through the Tri Nations and with the World Cup fast approaching, had been for team meetings to be scheduled so we could be updated on the latest information on the participation agreements and player bonuses negotiations. As the battle continued, I'd say publicly that it wasn't a distraction, but of course it was. One man might not want to get involved, while the guy next to him might be almost obsessed by the saga, and was eager to know what was happening next. It's hard to balance such contrasting stances in a team environment. Some players just wanted to sign whatever the ARU put in front of them so they could focus on their rugby; others were wanting a confrontation. It should have been resolved quickly and smartly in the 2002–03 off-season, but it wasn't to be.

Near the end of the process, Brett Robinson (now the head of the ARU's High Performance Unit) and Peter Friend (ARU counsel) journeyed to Cape Town. Robbo and Peter were handling the deal because of O'Neill's antipathy towards Demo. They had spoken to Eddie Jones on the Friday night before the Test and explained they wanted to talk to the players after the game, and hand out new, amended PAs for signature. The deadline the ARU had set for signature was the following Thursday (the IRB deadline was two weeks after that). They also had a bonus payments offer on the table. 'Okay, you can do that,' Eddie replied, 'but I'm not going to tell the players what to do.' Throughout the process, the coach had not been involved; it was a player matter and his only concern was that it didn't impinge on the team's preparation or performance. On the Sunday, the game having been lost 26–22 the previous day the two ARU guys spoke to the team and handed out the documents, which in most cases were autographed before the players boarded the plane to fly back to Sydney. There wasn't a problem, as I had received a phone call from Demo before the Test saying everything was sweet. 'Yep, it's all good,' I told the boys before Robbo came into the room. 'We can sign everything.'

The resolution of the PA meant that players from around the world could now all come to Australia. However, the matter of bonuses was still a matter for the individual unions, and two and three weeks later I was still reading stories about the All Blacks and the Springboks threatening to pull out of the Cup if an agreement wasn't reached. I'd moved on.

The affair became a part of two major media stories. One was a back-page report by Danny Weidler in the *Sun-Herald* of 29 June (a little more than two weeks after the RUPA filed its Supreme Court claim), under the bold headline 'BY GEORGE: ARU CAMPAIGN TO DRIVE GREGAN OUT OF THE GAME, which talked of 'the split between Gregan and the ARU' and suggested that 'the ARU is desperate to move Gregan along'. Weidler was just repeating gossip he'd heard, but suddenly over the next few weeks headlines appeared such as REPLACE GREGAN OR NIGHTMARE WILL GO ON in the *Sydney Morning Herald* of 28 July and GREGAN HAS TO GO in the *Daily Telegraph* of 29 July. Meanwhile players were being asked what they thought and, I'm proud to say, they supported me. But it really disappointed me that the guys were being asked to respond in this way. In truth, the mud that was thrown at me affected my team-mates and the players around me more than it affected me. Yet in the long run it didn't work.

O'Neill does have some very good qualities. He became the ARU's CEO in 1996, the right time for himself, the Wallabies and the game. The team had just been knocked out in the World Cup quarter-finals; it still included some wonderful players but it was clear some big decisions needed to be made. When Greg Smith lost the coaching job, O'Neill was smart enough to replace him with the best man for the job, Rod Macqueen, and he gave Rod everything he needed to put in place a program that gave us the best chance of success. The same process occurred in 2001, when he once again employed the best man for the job: Eddie Jones. Previously, rugby politics and interstate rivalries might have been involved in the head coaching appointment, but O'Neill was strong enough to prevent that from happening.

In 2002, we lost the knack of winning close games, and in 2003 we were inconsistent, but from 1998 to 2001 we were usually excellent and much of that came back to the programs O'Neill ensured were in place. It was his vision that led to the establishment of the High Performance Unit, an elite rugby program set up to help the ARU maintain a competitive advantage. He surrounds himself with good people, and can build a good administrative team. Overall, I would argue he did a very good job. But I could never understand why he seemed so happy to promote confrontation.

In the middle of the Participation Agreement controversy, we lost the Test against England at Melbourne's Telstra Dome in June. On the morning of the game, the *Sydney Morning Herald* quoted me as saying that I hoped the matter would be resolved quickly and that I couldn't imagine any players missing the World Cup because of it. That night, their centre, Will Greenwood, scored early, and after that England controlled the game, yet even with fifteen minutes to go, if we scored – and there were opportunities for us to do that – we were right back in it. But we did not take those opportunities. The result wasn't the catastrophe some believed, because we were experimenting a little (for example, with Stephen Larkham out injured, we tried Nathan Grey at No. 10, a position he had rarely played before). And this was the best England team I ever played against.

Then, two days after the Test, the *Daily Telegraph* in Sydney ran a headline: WHERE'S GEORGE? The thrust of the story was that I had been caught sneaking out of the team hotel to spend the night before the Test at a different location – with my wife in her hotel room.

There is some history that needs to be spelled out. In 1996, when Greg Smith took over, he introduced a policy where if your wife and family were staying in the same city as you were playing, they couldn't stay at the team hotel but you could go and stay the night with them so long as you were back in the team hotel an hour before any team commitment. If there was a team meeting at 10.30 am, for example, you had to be back at the hotel at 9.30 am. With Rod Macqueen, it was similar, though Rod and team management insisted that we stay at the team hotel on the eve of the Test. In 2001, before the start of the Tri Nations, the leadership group discussed this policy again, and we recognised that the team dynamic had changed, that more guys had young families and that we should try to provide as many opportunities as possible for players to be with their families, as long as it didn't damage the team's preparation. If a guy was playing a Test match in his home state, he was allowed to sleep in his own bed, so it seemed a bit incongruous that the guys who were from interstate were in effect being treated differently. Some senior players argued that it was good to keep the team together; others disagreed. I was in the latter camp.

It was decided that if you wanted to stay with your wife or partner, you just needed to let the team manager know. And it stayed that way until the World Cup, when we decided that everyone had to be back at the hotel by midnight before a match. That rule applied to everyone, even those who were playing in their home state. I can remember before the final, how we had the 'captain's run' (the traditional get-together the day before the Test) at Telstra Stadium (formerly known as Stadium Australia), then I had a little treatment with the physio before going home. That night, I had a bite to eat with my family, tucked Maxie in bed, gave Charlie a kiss, and was back at the hotel with time to spare.

So when that media storm broke after the England Test I was more bemused than anything. It was such an amazing scoop, revealing to an aghast public something that had been occurring for the previous two years. In the *Australian* – like the *Daily Telegraph* a News Limited publication – their chief rugby writer Wayne Smith wrote:

If Gregan's game against England was any indicator of how players would perform after getting away from the stifling all-male environment of a rugby team, then perhaps the Australian Rugby Union should seriously consider making such conjugal 'sleepouts' mandatory. The Australian captain turned in an outstanding performance behind a pack back-pedalling on top of him.

The Wallabies might have slumped to a historic defeat but there was no sign of capitulation from them and indeed

in the dying minutes Gregan marshalled his forwards to
put on a 30m drive straight up the middle of the English
defence.

Smith argued that the matter should have been discreetly dealt
with in-house. Instead, he believed it was 'burst into the public
arena' by people outside the team for the apparent purpose of
forcing the Wallabies captain onto the back foot.

It wasn't as if Erica and I had tiptoed off to some secret
rendezvous; in fact, Erica was staying at the same hotel as the
ARU officials who were in Melbourne for the Test. We had room
service and an early night – hardly the stuff of scandal.

For me, the 2003 season was chiefly about three big games: the
quarter-final, the semifinal and the final of the World Cup. The
matches before that were important, but those three were the big
ones. Win the first and we played the second; win the second and
we made the final; win the final and we were world champions.
This is not downplaying the importance of any of the Tests we
played before the World Cup – against Ireland, Wales, England
and then the Tri Nations – but it does show what I was thinking as
we approached the start of the international season.

When I am totally focused on something, I am able to com-
partmentalise my life so that everything else fades into the
background. The secondary things get dealt with, but they never
impose on what really matters. However, in 2003 there were a lot
of distractions put in front of me and the leadership group. But
it wasn't until just before the World Cup that the team leadership
group sat down with John O'Neill to discuss why there were so
many unnamed 'high-ranking ARU officials' saying disparaging
things about the team, or leaking little tidbits about senior players

or the coaching staff. We requested that the front office tighten things up. We were sick of some people at the ARU trying to railroad the team's World Cup campaign.

Throughout the year, we would hold meetings that involved captain, coach, team manager Phil Thomson and someone from the ARU. There were things discussed at those meetings that should have stayed confidential, but after the ARU representative reported back to his senior management, those matters were suddenly appearing in the papers. It was ridiculous that we had to ask for private Team Wallaby stuff to be kept confidential, but we did – and to O'Neill's credit the damaging leaks stopped occurring. The worst thing that can happen to the Wallabies is for the fans to stop backing the team, and that never happened in my experience. I don't think it has ever happened. The next worst thing that can happen is for the front office to stop supporting the team. That happened to a degree in 2003.

There was a feeling in some parts of the rugby community – the odd ex-player, many journalists and commentators, and some officials – that we weren't committed to the cause. This came to a head in the days before and after the Test against the All Blacks in Sydney, a game in which we were badly beaten, 50–21. We had also lost our previous two Tests: to England in Melbourne and then to South Africa, despite scoring three tries to two, in Cape Town. The critics were circling, and their chief sticking point was that the team wasn't showing enough 'passion'. I found it disappointing that some of this stuff was coming from former Wallabies. The general theme was that in our day we played with passion, but you professional guys don't exhibit any. At the pre-Test media conference, I was asked if this was fair criticism.

My response: 'I don't buy into that whole passion thing. I think it's a load of rubbish personally.'

In *One Step Ahead*, Rod Macqueen wrote, 'I believe passion is often used as an excuse for those who haven't done their preparation. These teams often know they are lacking in some way but believe by trying harder and being aggressive they will somehow win the game. . .'

I was making the same point, but I did it in a much terser way because I was really disappointed by the question. Having been in plenty of Australian dressing rooms between 1994 and 2007, and spoken to so many Wallabies greats who truly love the jumper and the tradition and history it represents, to question the passion of *any* Wallaby from any era is disgraceful. Nothing upset me more when it came to the reporting of the game than when a journalist or commentator said or wrote that we weren't putting in. When we were losing, it became popular for some reporters to try to outdo each other with their condemnation of the team. It was as if these guys were trying to bring the game and the Wallabies down – that's how I felt, and that's why I responded to that question with the answer I gave.

I've seen guys crying in the change room from that potent mix of pride, joy and trepidation that comes with wearing the Wallaby gold, and the bond in the dressing room is tight, maybe even more so than in days gone by because we spend so much time together, year after year. When the Wallabies run out on the field, they are bursting with pride. That is passion. Beating your chest, throwing a punch, pushing and shoving, swearing and cursing is not – its just foolish, a flash of false bravado. A player of that ilk will run out of energy very quickly, whereas a team with its emotions under control will absorb the brief onslaught and then keep coming, keep coming. That style of team rugby is more intimidating than some lightweight huffing and puffing.

It was frustrating when my comment about passion was pounced on so eagerly before and especially after that All Blacks Test, and it continued off and on over the next four years, whenever someone in the press box decided we weren't playing with sufficient energy for their liking.

That Test in Sydney was Tana Umaga's fiftieth Test and he put fifty on us, the most points ever conceded by a Wallabies team in Australia. However, we learned plenty from what was an ugly experience, to the point that we were unlucky not to beat them in Auckland three weeks later. Losing the Bledisloe Cup, which we'd held since 1998, was gut-wrenching, but the way we'd rallied in Auckland still said a lot about the character of the 2003 Wallabies.

15

UNDER THE SOUTHERN CROSS

2003

'If we win, it will be wonderful for those who have supported us. I'm not talking about the ones who jumped on the bandwagon, but those who supported us from start to finish.'

ZINÉDINE ZIDANE, AFTER FRANCE REACHED THE FINAL OF
FOOTBALL'S WORLD CUP IN 2006

The criticism had brought us closer together. The spirit in the squad was magnificent. And then Eddie Jones produced a masterstroke, taking us to the Northern Territory for what amounted to the greatest bonding session you could ever imagine. I've never been one for the big drink as a way of bringing the boys together (maybe the first night in Portmarnock before the 1999 World Cup excepted), have never been on a 'mad Monday', but

I do enjoy the good times when the whole group gets together and parties as only sporting teams can. I can remember a lot of great nights, around the world at both provincial and international level, but the trip to the Territory with the 2003 Wallabies was unique.

The absolute highlight was when, thanks to Glen Ella's contacts, the traditional owners gave permission to allow us to stay overnight in the wilderness near Mount Borradaile in north-west Arnhem Land, adjacent to Kakadu National Park. Having been there – and especially having been there with a group of good men and good friends who were about to represent their nation in one of the world's biggest sporting events – I now see it clearly as the spiritual epicentre of Australia. I feel so lucky to have seen rock paintings that are 30,000 or 40,000 years old, to have witnessed a special ceremony performed by the local Indigenous community, during which they presented the team with a painting of a wallaby reaching for the stars – which we carried with us. We had our faces painted, and sat in a circle under the Southern Cross and spoke about what it meant to be part of the Wallabies, and about what we each hoped to achieve during the World Cup. There was no media, no cameras – just us, in the middle of Australia, learning about our continent and rediscovering all that was good about being a team.

There was time for some relaxation – fishing for barramundi, a dusk drive along the river – and some clowning around, most notably when we did a cruise through the crocodile-infested waters, and were specifically told not to make an '*arrgh . . . arrgh . . .*' noise like that which a baby croc makes as it might stir up a mother. Sure enough, soon there was a boat full of Wallabies making this stupid cry. Suddenly one of the big crocs moved very quickly and all the lads dived for the other side of the vessel. The boat lurched dangerously and just for a moment I had visions of half our Cup squad being torn in two.

In Darwin, we worked hard, some of our most strenuous sessions ever, just as Eddie had planned it from the start of the year. By the end of it, we couldn't wait for the World Cup to start. Back home, the squad disbanded for a brief period, and then it was game on.

As I write this, a flood of terrific memories come back to me. A lot of shit had gone on during the lead-up, but from the day we landed in Darwin to the beers at Bill Young's pub the day after the final, it was all good.

We reassembled initially in Coffs Harbour, and then we came to Sydney for the official launch of the World Cup at the Opera House. We then based ourselves in Sydney for the couple of days before our opening match against Argentina. In that time, I wrote each player in the squad a letter, just me connecting a little with my team. I always try to discover the small but important traits about the people I'm working with, the things that make them tick, that they see as important. John Roe, who was studying to be a doctor, was new to the squad (he had taken the injured Toutai Kefu's spot) and when I asked him how he felt to be playing in the biggest rugby show on earth, he replied, 'I'm pinching myself.' In my letter, I asked him to 'stop pinching yourself because you are here and you could be called upon any minute'. I knew Matty Rogers' big goal was to be part of a winning World Cup team in rugby league and rugby union and to do it for his mum, who had passed away in 2001. We'd do everything we could, I wrote, to make his ambition come true.

I believed Benny Darwin was on the verge of becoming one of the game's best props, but the one thing holding him back was his lack of self-belief. So in my note to him I recalled the story of how the young Miles Davis doubted he was a good enough musician to play with the great Charlie Parker, and how Parker backed him, said he belonged and to 'go out there and play'. 'Now's the Time' is a song recognised as a Charlie Parker and Miles Davis classic; it was the song that first brought Davis's name to prominence. 'Benny,' I wrote in my letter to him, 'you've achieved your goal of being in a World Cup – now's the time to show you're a world-class prop.'

Eddie had decided that for this World Cup we were going to play with a bit more variety in terms of where we attacked. We had a two-pass focus as well as the ability to work off the No. 9, which appealed to me. A key to this was having everyone on the same page in regard to their roles at turnovers, in set pieces, general play and so on, and this was happening more and more. John Muggleton, our defence coach, like a lot of coaches, is always hard to please, and if we ever broke down his defensive system when we were doing attacking drills he could become a little agitated. We were seeing more of this as the Cup approached, not because his defensive patterns weren't working or his tacklers were slack, but because our offence was becoming so well drilled. We'd been written off in the media, so in a way we were flying under the radar, which was especially nice given that we were growing in confidence by the day.

While the papers might have been preparing our obituary, the vibe in the rugby community was wonderfully positive. It was the Olympics on a smaller scale, a celebration of rugby. John O'Neill and his colleagues at the ARU and IRB deserve a huge rap for the manner in which they staged the World Cup and how they managed to get the country to embrace it.

Nothing could spoil this party. At a media conference early in the tournament, I was asked – who'd have thought it? – if this Wallabies line-up had the same hunger and passion as the 1999 winning side. I responded this way: 'I will use an analogy. I own a Staffordshire bull terrier. Every time I feed it osso buco, he eats it like that's his last meal. My team is like my Staffordshire bull terrier, when it comes to meal times. That's how hungry, that's how passionate we are.'

We played pretty well against Argentina, and scored a lot of points against Romania and Namibia. Our last pool game proved more difficult. We got off to a good start, but in the second half it got very tight and we could have lost if an Irish drop goal attempt late in the game had gone over. In the end we only scraped past Ireland by a point.

Though we'd found a way to win, I wasn't happy with the way some of our players reacted when Ronan O'Gara kicked a penalty to get Ireland within a point near the end. 'I don't want to see anyone's head go down again like I saw when things got tight,' I said. 'Chin up, strong body language. If a game is there to be won, let's win it. That's the attitude we've got to show.'

We needed to be positive, and to take comfort in the fact we'd survived. That is, after all, part of what World Cups are about. The Irish had been a good test for us, and taught us something about the pressure we'd be facing in the coming games. Most teams that make a Cup final get involved in an arm wrestle at some point, often when they don't expect it, in the same way many Grand Slam tennis champions play a five-set match or two before they reach the final, and many major-winning golfers have a tough round or at least an awkward sequence of holes before they sink the decisive putt at the last. It was true of the Wallabies teams in 1991 and 1999, as well as 2003. Getting through the tough times can give you a stack of confidence.

Throughout this World Cup, we received any number of faxes from fans across the country. My phone was full of messages of support from other prominent Aussie sportspeople with whom I'd exchanged texts in recent years, including Steve Waugh, Ricky Ponting, Michael Voss and Ricky Stuart.

These were guys who at different times had spoken to the Wallabies. Steve had come along before the South Africa Test in Sydney in 2000 with his baggy green cap, and talked about what this iconic symbol meant to the cricketers. We'd allocated him fifteen to twenty minutes, and he was there for forty-five, answering questions, some about sledging (or, as he called it, 'mental disintegration'), most about his precious piece of green cloth. In the end, Rod Macqueen had to call a halt or there wouldn't have been any time for training.

Ricky Stuart spoke to us about the importance of not letting your mates down. 'They're trying for you,' he reminded us, 'so you must do the same for them.' Ricky was the Classic Wallaby who spoke to the team before the semifinal against New Zealand; he exhorted us to have faith in each other, and to trust the coach and the game plan. If this level of trust existed among the group, then we could focus on our own roles and not get distracted by fears about what others might or might not be doing.

Michael Voss came down to Coffs mid-week to address the boys in the lead-up to that same game. The Brisbane Lions, the AFL team he led, had just won their third straight premiership. They were a club with an uncanny knack of performing at their best at the right time: during the finals. He told the story of the Lions' effort in 2001, when in the grand final they faced the defending premiers, Essendon, who were rated by many as unbeatable. The Essendon side, he told us, always charged out really hard, as if they were trying to blow teams away, All Blacks-like, to establish the mood of the match and set up an early unassailable advantage. Brisbane's response was to make sure they were as fit and well-prepared as they could be, and to work really hard early, on the basis that if they could match them then they could forge clear at the end.

The key was for everyone to do their job from the opening bounce. The idea was not to win the game then, but not to lose it. When they followed through with this they suddenly discovered that this great Essendon team was human after all. The Lions trailed at three-quarter time but overwhelmed their much-vaunted opponents in the final term to win by twenty-six points. Michael underlined the fact that, in the end, they didn't have to do anything extraordinary to win the premiership. No one had to do anything more than fulfil their role within the team; the key was doing your job as well as you possibly could all of the time. To hear what is essentially a simple message put so eloquently by someone who had been successful is empowering. There's a lot to be said for surrounding yourself with winners.

A 33–16 defeat of Scotland in the quarter-final set up the semi against the All Blacks in Sydney. Despite that narrow defeat in Auckland three months earlier, few outside the Wallabies set-up gave us a chance heading into the semi, but it evolved into one of the best Wallabies wins of my life. After the game, I was talking to Justin Marshall, who had to come off with a rib injury in the second half, and he said, 'The way you boys started, we knew we were in for a tough night.'

We held the ball for the first two minutes and moved it accurately around the field, taking away their chance to start with a typical rush. That set the mood for the night, on the field and in the stands. I'm not sure if I've ever been as inspired by home-town support as the way that crowd backed us from start to finish.

Early in the game, Justin Harrison was into the All Blacks lineout, pointing out that they were, as he put it, 'Struggling, struggling!' It reached the stage where it seemed their hooker, Keven Mealamu, had nowhere to throw the ball. We had an outstanding lineout for that game, with Nathan Sharpe and Goog in the starting XV and David Giffin and Matt Cockbain coming off the bench, and on the night they were too good for their opponents. It's a good feeling for a halfback to see and hear his locks dominating the game.

We led 13–nil just before half-time, following two penalties and an intercept try to Stirling Mortlock. After each score, I kept stressing that we needed every point. 'Let's go back and do it again,' I shouted. They fought back to 13–7, and I imagine many expected the All Blacks to come out firing after the interval, but the way our forwards controlled the game in the second half was magnificent. We scored first in the championship minutes after half-time, and then we played excellently at the back end of the match.

Towards the end of the game, when Marshy's replacement, Byron Kelleher, spilt the ball soon after he came on the field I taunted him, saying 'Four more years.' It certainly wasn't re-hearsed, and I guess this could have been seen as a bit boorish and unnecessary, given that the game was won by this late stage, but I don't regret saying it. I do regret that everyone saw it, both at the ground on the big screen and on TV sets around the rugby world, but it's gamesmanship, it happens (though the next time I was in New Zealand the reception was a little frosty).

Right on full-time, with our place in the final assured, I tried to tackle their lock, Chris Jack, and went over on my ankle. Chris picked me up and we had a brief embrace. He said, 'Good luck in the final,' and I replied, 'I'll see you in the rooms.' With that, I dashed off the ground as quick as I could to get some treatment.

It had been organised by the two teams' management that after the game the losing team would go into the winning team's change room. This said something about the respect the teams had for each other. Not long after the final whistle, as I sat with my foot in a big ice bin I asked Phil Thomson, 'What's happening? Where is everybody?' It was taking forever for my team-mates to join me. What the rest of the boys were doing was enjoying an extended lap of honour, which I guess was fair enough, as it reflected the buoyant mood of the fans, who had been so good to us. Yet I wondered later whether it might have been better if we'd just given them a quick thank you, and then come inside. We hadn't won the tournament, we'd just given ourselves a chance to win the tournament. I know that if I hadn't been injured we wouldn't have been out there that long.

So it was that we had just a week to wait. The seven days between the semifinal and final was, in many ways, fairly routine. By this time, the team was back in Coffs, where we did our re-covery in the surf and on the beach, and after that it was supposed to be a light week. After such a very physical contest against the All Blacks, after all the work we'd put in over the previous few weeks, all we needed was a tune-up.

We had a last high-profile visitor to Coffs, during the week before the final: Cathy Freeman. I was fascinated by her explana-tion of how she dealt with the pressure of being a hot favourite in the 400 metres at the Sydney Olympics. Some champion athletes like talking about what made them victorious, but Cathy was succinct. 'I just shunted as much as I could out of my mind,' she recalled, 'and said to myself, over and over, "Cathy, just run."' The only reason this worked was because her preparation had been so complete, and that's where she gained her confidence. I was at Stadium Australia the night she won, and all I can say is if there is ever a sporting moment to beat that one, I hope I'm in the crowd to witness it.

I still get emotional thinking about what happened to prop Ben Darwin, how his World Cup dream ended in the semifinal against

New Zealand – in every other way a great day for us – when he went down with a frightening neck injury that cruelled his career. I was there when he came down to Canberra, to play with the Brumbies, in 1997. That year, he went on a development tour; the following year he was part of the senior squad. He was a 'new age' footballer, committed to training right and often, whose diet was 80 per cent carbohydrate, who was so organised he had a beeper that used to go off to remind him he had a meeting scheduled for an hour and a half's time. That would drive Eddie Jones mad – 'Would you mind turning that bloody thing off, mate,' Eddie would grumble – but in every other way Benny was a coach's dream. He was a guy who had a Wallabies jumper stuck on his bedroom wall when he was fifteen, as a reminder that he wanted to earn one of his own, and he never stopped setting himself goals and then achieving them.

Before the final, we had a meeting at our hotel, and I started to talk about Benny . . . and suddenly, this wave of emotion came over me. The main theme of my speech was supposed to be that we had to focus on the task at hand, to try to treat it like just another game, but here I was, starting to sob.

I had to stop for a moment. Regain my composure.

And then I said softly, 'If anyone is going to cry, it may as well be me, because it is the team that starts playing first that will win this game tonight.'

I remember after that meeting, Nathan Grey came up to me and chuckled, 'I thought you were a hard bastard.'

I'm not the crying type, but this was an emotional time. I love those guys with whom I shared this World Cup experience. The memory of us working together, refusing to yield and fighting to the very last second of extra time in the final is one I will always treasure. This World Cup reinforced for me the fact that the pure part of rugby is the training and playing and getting involved in a game, and it's a shared experience with your best mates.

Earlier in that talk, before I started talking about Benny, I recalled the story of the Chicago Bulls' 1998 NBA finals series, how Michael Jordan, one of my favourite athletes, claimed the championship for his team by landing the winning shot in game six with 5.2 seconds to play. The Bulls were breaking up after that season, and we were in a similar position, with a number of guys playing in their final World Cup. I thought this would be the last World Cup for me. I spoke about Jordan's composure under pressure, and how he wanted to take that shot, how he said later, 'It was my opportunity to win or lose the game.'

Five point two seconds. 'If it takes to the very end for us to win this game, then we will do it,' I said. 'We'll take that opportunity.'

As it turned out, the game went to one hundred minutes. But we didn't quite make the match-winning shot.

I've never watched a replay of the 2003 final, but some things remain vivid in my memory. When it comes to the actual football, the first thing I recall is the kicking of the little bull terrier, Elton Flatley. A couple of long-distance kicks early in the game fell short, and during the second half the message kept coming out from the coaching staff to 'go to the corners'. But I have always felt that if your kicker is keen to have a shot, then you need to back him, as confidence is a kicker's greatest ally. When we were awarded the penalty that took the game into extra time, I looked straight at Flats, thinking, *Jeez, he might not want to take this because it ain't easy* – 10 metres in from touch, 22 out. We could have attacked the line, and gone for the win. However, he had the headgear off and was walking over.

'Do you want it?' I asked as a matter of course.

'I'm going to knock it over,' he replied.

It was an easy decision for any captain to make.

Extra time. The first score after half-time in a tight match is always important, but it's nothing on the first score in extra time in a World Cup final. It doesn't mean you are going to win it – South Africa scored first in extra time in the 1999 Cup semi – but in this game, given that we'd come back from 14–5 down and that England hadn't scored a point since just before half-time, I was sure that if we got our noses in front the Poms would start doubting their ability to recover. But it didn't happen that way . . .

We'd scored with just about the first play of the game, off a scrum, when Stevie Larkham kicked high to create a one-on-one marking contest: Lote Tuqiri against Jason Robinson. But it wasn't the hot steamy Darwin-like night we'd been hoping for, as we'd prepared so precisely for those conditions. Rather, it was wet, more like Twickenham than Sydney in November, and gradually the Englishmen gained the advantage, first through three penalties to Wilkinson, then a try to Robinson. The second half was tight and thrilling, as the balance of power swung our way. But in extra time it was Wilkinson who kicked the first penalty, then Flats levelled the scores again, only for the England No. 10 to make himself the ultimate hero of the night by kicking the Cup-winning three-pointer with something like twenty seconds left on the clock. We knew they were setting up for that drop goal, but there wasn't anything we could do. Often in the latter stages of that final I kept reminding the boys that 'execution down the stretch' was the key. On that final play, the Englishmen executed perfectly.

Post-game, I made a point of shaking the hand of everyone associated with the England squad, players and coaching staff, and there were a lot of them! 'Well done, enjoy it,' I said, and I meant it – the four years to the next one goes real quick.

The next day, we were at Bill Young's pub at Concord West,

about twenty-five minutes walk from Telstra Stadium, and then some of the boys ventured into the city. I organised for my dad to pick me up and we headed home. It was over.

In the fortnight after the Cup there were almost as many functions as there had been in 1999. There were no ticker-tape parades, but once again we were invited by the Prime Minister to the Lodge, and often it was hard to decide whether people were even slightly downcast that we had lost. I felt like we'd failed, but everyone outside the team seemed happy with the way we'd failed.

At the same time, I was so proud of the team. I said that to the boys in the rooms straight afterwards. I think I even said, 'I couldn't be happier.' But that wasn't right – it was just that I was fearful that if I said anything too negative it might take something away from the Englishmen and it might also be interpreted wrongly as a knock on our team. I couldn't have asked for anything more from them. I know that everyone gave everything of themselves in the final and throughout the tournament – not just the men on the field but everyone in the squad. Guys who weren't in the final XXII, such as Matt Burke and Chris Latham, must have been gutted at missing out, yet they were in the gym 48 hours before the final, achieving personal bests. It was optional to go to the gym that day but everyone turned up, and there was so much positive excitement about those PBs, and not just from Burkey and Latho. I've never experienced anything like it, and I've been in some tremendous groups. You can't fake that sort of spirit. It really was a special, special team.

16

GETTING OVER IT

2002–2004

'You can't be standing still, and that is one thing – a good
lesson in life – that the Super 14 competition teaches you.'

GEORGE GREGAN, 2007

There was every chance I was going to finish up after the 2003
World Cup. How close did I get to retiring? Probably within
one miserable field goal by Jonny Wilkinson. There wouldn't have
been much more for me to achieve. We'd come so close. Part of me
said, *You've got to try again*, while another part of my brain kept
thinking, *Playing four more years of rugby is not going to be easy*.
If we'd won, if we'd successfully defended (something that had
never been achieved before), had we won in front of our home
fans and I'd had the chance to lift the cup at Telstra Stadium, I'm
fairly sure I would have been happy with that.

But it hadn't happened that way. I had received a massive dose of perspective within minutes of the World Cup final ending, when my son Max came out onto the field to be with me. As I tried to come to grips with my disappointment, I looked in his eyes and realised that he didn't really care whether we'd won or lost. He was just happy to see me, to be with his dad. *Good on you, mate*, I thought as I smiled back at him, and gave him a kiss.

The second good lesson came in December, after I was invited to go to the Australian PGA golf tournament at Coolum, on Queensland's Sunshine Coast. I played in the Pro-Am and stayed on afterwards with my family to watch some golf and just relax. All up, it was one of the most enjoyable seven days of my life. It was also, in terms of my rugby career after 2003, one of the most important . . .

The day after the World Cup final, we'd had that great day at Bill Young's pub. The team was ripping into prawns and KFC and having the odd beer, playing two-up and having a good time. After that, we 'disassembled', and we all had time to reflect. If ever there was a time when my philosophy of looking forward to a new day, or not getting caught up in regrets, was tested, it was now. Every day, everywhere I went, well-meaning people came up to tell me how proud they were of the team. The overriding message was *Don't think of yourself as losers; you're winners in our eyes*. It was a lovely sentiment, and I knew it was said from the heart and with all good intentions.

But we hadn't won. We'd lost.

As well as we'd played, as fantastic an effort as the boys had put in, nothing could change the fact that England had won the Webb Ellis Cup and Australia had finished second. That's not what I'd aimed for, what I'd worked for, and every time another person came up to commiserate I cringed inside. This went on for nearly three weeks, until we landed at Coolum and I found myself having a few beers with some of the golfers, and a few past and present members of the Australian Davis Cup team, including Lleyton Hewitt and Pat Rafter.

I have known Patty for a number of years. 'Mate,' he said as soon as he saw me, 'come and have a drink. But I should warn you, the boys will give you a bit of lip.'

Gee, that'll be great, I thought to myself.

Erica was pregnant with our second daughter, Jazz, at the time, so she, Max and Charlie stayed in our room while I headed down to the Village Square at Coolum, a terrific outdoor area that is a favourite haunt for families who enjoy a pizza or burgers as the sun sets over Mount Coolum. When I arrived, around 7 pm, these people were just finishing up, while the tennis lads were starting to make a little noise outside one of the bars on the edge of the square. Then they spotted me, and started singing, to the tune of 'Camptown Races' . . .

Georgie lost the World Cup,
Doo-dah! . . . Doo-dah! . . .

So now everyone was looking around, and I was starting to think, *Maybe this is going to be a good night . . .*

Georgie lost the World Cup!
Oh, doo-dah day!

This went on for quite a while, all good Aussie fun. After a while, I was giving as good as I got, and laughing and cracking jokes for the first time since that day at Youngy's pub.

Later, I had a good chat with Patty about the distress I was experiencing. 'I know how you feel,' he said. 'I lost the Wimble-don final two years in a row, and everyone kept telling me how well I'd done . . . But I'd lost.'

For a moment, there was silence, and I thought Patty was going to go all sombre on me. Then he looked at me and, with a smidgin of a grin, quipped, 'Don't worry, mate, you never get over it.'

I think that was the moment when I started to get over it. Speaking to someone who genuinely knew what I was feeling, what I was going through, was so comforting. Pat had been through what I was going through. He'd come up short on the biggest stage, and as a result had felt ordinary while everyone was telling him he was brilliant. 'Are you going to keep playing?' Pat asked, and I admitted I didn't know.

'Are you still enjoying it?'

'Oh yeah, the football, the team, they're still great.'

'Mate, I reckon that's all you need,' Pat said. 'When you're not enjoying it, that's when it's hard.'

We talked a bit more, and then Pat declared, 'Let's have another drink.' Back we went, to sing 'Georgie Lost the World Cup!' a couple more times, and then for me to ponder, on the walk home, that life really does go on. The next day, I enjoyed a round of golf with Greg Norman, no less, and Lleyton (who was carrying Greg's bag in the tournament) – a wonderful experience. I remember a tip Greg gave me about bunker play, which I'm keeping to myself, and a moment when I tried to negotiate Lleyton's caddying fee. 'From what I understand,' I said to the golfing superstar, 'the normal cut is 10 per cent. But Lleyton's a big name, he's boosting your profile, I'll try to get him to do it for 30 per cent of whatever you make on the weekend.' If there is one Australian sportsperson who doesn't need his profile boosted it's Greg Norman, the man who has done so much for Australian golf, whose 'Great White Shark' trademark is known across the world. But Max Gregan remembers him not as the Shark, but as the 'Kangaroo Man', because around dusk the two of them went off in a golf buggy looking for the roos that roam the fairways in the twilight. Greg is such a good man, a great Australian.

The piss-taking continued in the first week of January, when I was invited to a private function to celebrate Steve Waugh's farewell to Test cricket. I received a special 'leave pass' from Brumbies coach David Nucifora – 'Yeah, mate,' David said, 'you've got to do that. Those sort of nights are one-offs' – and flew up to Sydney that day, to enjoy a special evening with, among others, all the champion Aussie cricketers of the previous decade. They are an amazing group, who had at that time established themselves as the best team on the planet, winners of the previous nine Ashes series and the last two cricket World Cups (under Steve's captaincy in 1999 and Ricky Ponting's leadership in 2003).

At one point, I was joined by Mark Taylor, captain from September 1994 to January 1999; he had been at the helm for the 1996 World Cup when Australia was beaten in the final by Sri Lanka. He came over to me with a beer and said, 'Here, mate, grab this.' Then he added, 'How about a private toast?' *Okay*, I thought, *maybe he wants to raise a glass to the Waugh years, or the strength of Aussie cricket?*

'Here's to you and me,' he said, as a few people gathered around, anxious to hear Taylor's wise words. 'The two people here who are losing World Cup captains.'

For the Brumbies, the seasons from 2002 to 2004 had been transition years. They had sometimes been turbulent, too, especially in 2004, when the place was overtaken by a coaching drama.

David Nucifora, the former Queensland and Wallabies hooker, had arrived in Canberra at the start of this period to replace Eddie Jones. I was on the committee that assessed the coaching applications, alongside Eddie, Owen Finegan and Brumbies general manager Mark Sinderberry. David Giffin also contributed to the selection process, as did Andrew Blades, who had been working as Eddie's forwards coach but was unavailable for the top job. David Nucifora was the standout candidate. Even though he didn't have much coaching experience, he was clearly very well organised and had a track record in business, just as Rod Macqueen had. On his appointment, he said he recognised the unique culture of the place, noting that our success was 'due to the input from a whole lot of senior players and the younger players, too'.

The departure after 2001 of Rod Kafer, Joe Roff (for a season only) and Jim Williams meant that some guys – such as Mark Bartholomeusz and Peter Ryan – moved up to take on important roles within the squad. Peter's contribution was particularly significant. Three of the best hits I've seen in union were made by him: fierce collisions that sounded as if a gun had gone off. Rhino is not a big man, maybe 90 kilos, the kind of forward who at weigh-in would sneak a dumbbell or two into his pockets if he could, so he'd officially be a little heavier than he actually was. He was massive for the team; you lose a little bit of the heart and soul of the team when a player like him departs. He'd do a lot of work at training and after training with the younger players. During the pre-season, he was one of the guys who'd convince the younger players to do the extra work that they needed to do . . . by doing it with them.

Why is that so special? When you are in your thirties and you're carrying niggles in your knees or ankles from a decade or more of top-level senior football, and it's thirty-plus degrees in mid January, I reckon in one sense you've earned the right to not do that extra work. In truth, if you dodge the work in January and get away with it, bad instincts are instilled that will return later in the year. Rhino would say, 'C'mon boys, let's do it,' and he'd lead the way. Consequently, there was nothing hypocritical about him when he was really hard on standards and discipline when the games were on. Just one example: one of my pet hates is when you're doing sprints, and you are meant to leave on the *go* in *three, two, one . . . go!* and some guys think it's clever to get a jump, to leave on the *one*. If you're haphazard in a simple drill like that, the ill-discipline can spread like a fever. Rhino was ruthless on guys who cheated in this way; they didn't do it for long. When you are team captain and you've got a player like that supporting you, helping the team, it makes your life so much easier. The fans don't see that contribution, the media doesn't see it, but I love it.

The grit Rhino and others provided proved critical when we recovered from four straight losses to make the semifinals in 2002, where we played a Waratahs side reeling from a late-season collapse. Bob Dwyer had made the headlines after our round-eight game in Sydney, when he labelled me 'arrogant' in the way I spoke to referees, but while I thought his remarks were unnecessary and didn't reflect well on him, they didn't really worry me. It was, I guess, an example of a coach trying to play mind games, in this case either with me or with the officials, but it backfired on him spectacularly when we earned a rematch against them in the semi.

A man of Dwyer's stature and his experience should have known better. I know his senior players weren't thrilled about it – it was almost a reflex for them to think, straight after he said it, *That's coming back to bite us if we play the Brumbies again.* It was part of our psyche for us to look after our own, but it's also true of every team I've played for that if the captain is attacked, the rest of the side will seek retribution. If you can bring a captain down, you have won a significant victory, but a team will always respond when their opponents try to do that, and if the captain survives it invariably makes the team he still leads stronger. We'd never beaten the Waratahs in Sydney before this semifinal, but they had no playoff experience and we had plenty. We won 51–10.

The final was a classic. There is no doubt that the Crusaders deserved to win – they were an outstanding team who won every Super 12 game they played that year.

On pretty much the first play of the final they ran the ball from just outside their 22, we charged up too hard on Andrew Mehrtens, and he took the hole. After that, we were just on the back foot the whole time, defending, defending, hanging on, hanging on, and by the fifty-fourth minute we were down 14–3. But then we got three points from a penalty and Andrew Walker nabbed an intercept try after Justin Marshall went down the short side. That really should have been a major momentum shift, and I really thought we might be able to get down their end of the field and somehow manufacture a penalty on them. Instead, they reasserted themselves: Mehrts kicked a drop goal within two minutes of Walker's try, and then they scored two tries in the last five minutes.

Walks, who played for Australia in 2000 and 2001, was the most natural rugby player I ever saw. Not the greatest player, but the most natural. I remember a try he scored for the Brumbies in 2001, in a game in which he initially wasn't going to play because he had a bad hamstring – we kicked the ball down into their 22, and he ran 50 or 60 metres to make a tackle and find himself at the bottom of a ruck. They counterattacked, and then booted the ball to Joe Roff, deep in our half. Roffy decided to link up with his left winger, Walks, who had disentangled himself from the ruck and run back those same 50 or 60 metres so he could take Roffy's pass. He should have been exhausted, but instead he just stepped,

stepped, stepped, stepped off his left foot, cut through and scored near the right-hand goalpost. You can't teach that. There were so many natural instincts and skills involved in that try it was freakish.

The first time he played for the Brumbies, in a trial match, I asked him to kick off with a long drop kick. So he kicked it way over the dead-ball line, and I said, 'Walks, not that long!'

'Oh, sorry, Greegs,' he said. From then on, it became something of a trademark – if I wanted a high kick to a certain part of the field, he would ask, 'How high?', and then land the kick exactly where and when we wanted it. He was a master at kicking the ball for territory, and we really missed him when he injured his knee in 2003, and then left at the end of that season. When Walks had his family with him, and he felt comfortable in his surroundings, you couldn't find a harder working guy, but sometimes on tour, or even in camp at Coffs Harbour, when he was away from his family, he made some bad choices.

We all tried really hard to help him, but the concept of travelling for days to play a game of footy never really won him over. One week you are playing in Canberra and the next in Johannesburg, feeling absolutely rubbish because you're jetlagged. It's hard work. The grind got to him more than most. But I'll never give up on Walks. He has so many great qualities. In 2008, he was selected in the Australian squad for the Hong Kong Sevens, and indications are he's got his life together away from footy, too.

In 2003, there were plenty of changes in the Brumbies' front office. At the beginning of the year we lost Mark Sinderberry, the CEO, who did a great job with the Brumbies from day one, and then there were some changes in the coaching staff as a couple of guys departed and it took longer than it should have to get their replacements sorted out. Further, we changed the way we prepared for the off-season, as David put some of his ideas in place, which he was perfectly entitled to do. The mistake he made was to impose these on the team without any consultation with the leadership group. All of this added up to something of an upheaval.

The irony was that we had always embraced change at the Brumbies. We saw ourselves as innovators, and we realised the importance of staying ahead of the game. But in the 2003 pre-season we neglected some fundamental things that had helped us be successful. For example, we didn't do our homework on opponents as we had in the past, and we went into the first block of games as if we were cramming for an exam. We had a bad run with injuries, most notably in Stirling Mortlock, who missed most of the Super 12 season. Andrew Walker was suspended for breaking curfew in South Africa. Jeremy Paul was dropped. The appointment of the new CEO, Rob Clarke, wasn't announced until there were only two weeks of the regular season remaining, after we'd been thrashed, seven tries to three, by the Highlanders in Dunedin. In a World Cup year, we didn't have a major sponsor, which had the players thinking – shades of 1996 – *Are the Brumbies on the skids?* A number of things we'd taken for granted weren't in play and many of those were out of the players' control. A number of contract negotiations were left till the end of the season and were then handled badly, with some players being asked to commit long term, others left in limbo, and some, including Justin Harrison, in a year in which he would play in a World Cup final, being told they weren't wanted anymore.

In past years, what had made the place unique was the way the players worked with the coaches, discussing how we were going to play, how we were going to move forward. We thought David had recognised that himself when he was appointed, but gradually the lines of communication were blurred, and a sense of mistrust grew. We had always aimed not to have any distractions at the pointy end of the season, but we had plenty in 2003.

It was a fluke that we made the '03 semifinals. We lost to the Crusaders in the last round, giving us a six win/five loss record, but then every result went our way and we snuck in. I was actually packing up my unit in Kingston, expecting to go back to Sydney, when I received a text from David that read, *We're still alive*. But the Blues finally put us out of our misery the following week.

When David Nucifora took over in 2002, one of the first things we talked about was my workload as Wallabies and Brumbies captain. I can remember saying, 'Mate, there is going to be a point when I would like to have a break from being captain. I'm not going to be here forever and I think it's important that the player who succeeds me doesn't take over without having had any experience.' Taking over 'cold turkey' can be hard. I had led the team in a number of games when Brett Robinson was injured in 2000, so I felt very comfortable in the role when I took over full time in 2001. By the end of 2003, after the World Cup and all the battles with John O'Neill, I was exhausted. Giving Stirling the Brumbies captaincy for 2004 was the logical thing to do.

There were a number of examples of Test captains not leading their provincial sides: Sean Fitzpatrick at Auckland, John Eales with Queensland. My ambition in 2002 was that the person who became the Brumbies leader after me would be taking over a successful team and understood how we operated and what was involved in leading the squad. When, following the World Cup, I began seriously thinking about the 2004 season, I knew immediately that if I was going to play on there was no way I was going to continue as Brumbies captain. That would have been too much.

During a January meeting with David, he asked me if I was still happy to relinquish the captaincy, and I said, 'No problem, mate. Things haven't changed.' It was a good decision. I don't think I would have played for as long as I did if I had stayed on as Brumbies skipper.

Stirling was an excellent candidate to take over, but he wasn't the only one. Stephen Larkham could have done the job well, or George Smith (who did eventually get the job after Stirling, in 2008, and will become a great captain for the Brumbies and maybe the Wallabies, too). But at that time I'm not sure if either Stephen or Georgie would have wanted the job, and one thing I've learned about captaincy is that you do have to want to take it on. Stirlo is a man who plays 'big', the type of player who demands, almost by his physical presence alone, that his team-mates follow him.

David's contract expired after the 2004 Super 12 season, and it wasn't renewed. He had been hired to coach the Brumbies from 2002 to 2004, he did that job to the best of his ability, we made the finals every year he was there and won the competition in 2004, and then the Brumbies decided to employ a different coach. On the surface, it looks a strange decision to jettison a coach with that record, given that he wanted to continue, but part of the problem was that David wanted a decision on his coaching future made halfway through the 2004 season, at a time when morale in the camp wasn't good. Under pressure to make a decision, Rob Clarke gathered information from board members and players, and then came to the view that we'd have a new coach for the following season.

I was one of the senior players who was asked my view on the coaching situation. There is no doubt that his relationship with many senior players, from a football point of view, was strained. On a personal level, I think we were okay, but that communication between coach and players that had been a hallmark of the Brumbies had broken down. The team dynamic in 2003 wasn't great and things hadn't improved through the 2004 pre-season or the early games. We wanted to help with the way we planned for matches, as we'd always done, but David was adamant that the way he operated was the way to go, and it made some senior players feel unwanted. He argued that the place needed to get younger. A buzz word with bringing young players up is 'mentoring', but more experienced players need managing, too. The culture that had set us apart – of all parts of the Brumbies family working together was being hammered – and no one with any inside knowledge of the brief history of the franchise was happy about that.

We had pre-arranged a meeting of players, management and coaching staff in Johannesburg to take place after the game against the Lions. We just lost the game to a last-minute field goal, a straight swap for what happened in 2001, when Rod Kafer kicked a late three-pointer to get us home. This time, we kept fighting and Roffy snuck us in front near the death, but it wasn't quite enough. On the Sunday, before we flew home, the players expressed concerns about our early season preparation, and we identified a number of areas where we felt we were deficient. We wanted to correct the problems, but David was defensive, saying he didn't need the players doing this extra work. 'It's not extra work for us,' I responded. 'It's the work we always do and we want to do it.'

I didn't enjoy the 2004 pre-season, and having cleared my head after the World Cup, I really thought I would. Before we played Auckland in the opening round, we had another meeting where the issues discussed were almost identical to those we'd put on the table in Jo'burg the previous year. After game seven, a 47–28 loss to the Crusaders in Christchurch, the decision was made; many people point to the fact that we won the final six weeks later as proof that David got a raw deal, but I disagree. Had the decision gone the other way, the mood in the camp might have darkened, and our season could have fallen away. One of the main reasons we won was because we had a very good squad featuring many current or future internationals, including Mark Bartholomeusz, Mark Chisholm, Scott Fava, Owen Finegan, Mark Gerrard, David Giffin, Matt Giteau, Nic Henderson, Matt Henjak, Stephen Larkham, Stirling Mortlock, Jeremy Paul, Clyde Rathbone, Joe Roff, Radike Samo, Guy Shepherdson and George Smith. It was some team.

I was impressed by the way David handled the controversy. After the decision was made, he said to the squad, 'You know what's happened ... we've always talked about winning the competition, nothing has changed. Let's knuckle down to that.' First game after the news broke, we beat the Highlanders 50–18, with me on the bench – a joint decision that came about mainly because I had spent a large chunk of the week in Sydney, to be with Erica, Max and Charlie for the arrival of our third child, Jazz. It also enabled us to give Matt Henjak, already on the edge of the Wallabies squad, a Super 12 start.

Stirling had to miss the final because of an injured knee, and Owen Finegan was captain when we dashed out to a 33–0 lead after nineteen minutes. Yet even then, I wasn't sure we were over the line, only because we were playing a championship team in the Crusaders. Our opponents are a proud team, and sensible, too, and I knew that, even though the scoreboard said they were no chance, they'd regroup and see if they could have a good half of rugby. Andrew Mehrtens settled them down, and they actually snuck up to within fourteen of us with less than twenty minutes to go.

For Roffy, this really was the end of his Brumbies career, and for the second time in three years he was chaired from the field. Of course, I chipped him for being so much the centre of attention, but inside I knew he deserved all the accolades, for he really was one of the great players of my time. I never saw a winger who ran better than Joe Roff. He added to that by having a rare ability to turn up in the right place, throw the critical pass, run the crucial line. He's one of those players opponents talked about – I know, from listening to Tana Umaga, that the All Blacks really rated him. But a lot of people took for granted all the things that made Roffy great, because he'd been doing them since day one.

I have two memories of Roffy as a young man. One, he was a prodigious football talent from Marist College, Canberra, who was good enough to make the 1995 Australian World Cup team as a nineteen-year-old. Two, he was a grot, a guy with no concept of the importance of soap. For young Joe Roff, the water pressure in the shower was reputedly enough to get him clean.

Always with Roffy, the bigger the game, the bigger he played. Still, even as we celebrated his great career in Canberra and the Brumbies' second Super 12 victory, we couldn't escape the fact that there had been too much tension and politics in it for us veterans to recall it quite as fondly as our triumph in 2001. The saddest part of this entire episode is that David Nucifora is a terrific person. Especially, in 2002, when he had the balance right, I used to enjoy the one-on-one meetings we had, coach and captain.

17

CENTENARY

2004

'The thing that keeps me going and motivates me is the feeling that I can improve as a player and that there is always room for more improvement.

GEORGE GREGAN, 2006

South Africa's rugby footballers are hard men, born to play the game . . . and good guys, too. You know what you are going to get when you play the Springboks – they are going to try to physically dominate you, try to belt you. The challenge is always to match them in that capacity and then outskill them. But it's hard to outskill a big guy when he's trying to beat you up.

One day, I was speaking to their great lock Victor Matfield. 'You guys are just a different animal when you play at home,' I said. 'You go crazy.'

'I don't know why that is,' he replied.

I know why it is. There is an almost overwhelming pressure on them to perform. A Test in South Africa against the All Blacks or the Wallabies is a massive event; some fans appear to regard such matches as the most important things in their lives. The passion around Newlands when I first played against South Africa, in the opening game of 1995 World Cup, was compelling, something I had never experienced before. I did see it again, quite a few times in the seasons that followed, but never quite with that same intensity. The Springboks, of course, beat us that day and went on to win the tournament, but they were not a truly great side – physically they were tremendous, strong and committed, but there were not an abundantly skilful side. The hometown support was crucial to their victory. However, gradually over the next twelve years, they added a little subtlety and skill without diminishing their physicality.

So many South Africans love rugby. Before the game, they'll sidle up to you and say, 'Good luck on Saturday, you are going to need it,' and then chuckle as if they've just cracked a really good gag. They are, in their unique way, good sports and hugely proud and parochial all at the same time.

I always thought that the atmosphere in Durban captured something of the South Africans' commitment to the code. Around ABSA Stadium (formerly Kings Park Stadium), the city's premier rugby venue, there are a number of rugby fields, and families drive in there on game day, park their cars, set up their barbecues and build a real carnival atmosphere. They are there to celebrate their sport. Post-game, they return for their post-mortems, fine food and laughter. We would always mingle after Super 12 and Super 14 games; maybe share some food and conversation with the Sharks fans.

They were always gracious in both victory and defeat.

The Sharks might not have won with the same efficiency and regularity as the Canterbury Crusaders have over the years, but I still enjoyed the way they played, the manner in which they attempted to operate with high skill, ball in hand. Men such as Gary Teichmann, Henry Honiball and Andre Joubert were always tough to play against.

Away from Durban, another Springbok I always rated highly was Johan 'Rassie' Erasmus, who played Test football as a flanker between 1997 and 2001. I always thought he was ahead of his time. Tough, versatile, invaluable players such as Rassie are often underrated when lists of the game's most important players are compiled, while more flamboyant showmen are given precedence. South African players today, such as Victor Matfield, are always studying their laptops, doing their research, breaking down past games. Rassie was doing that before it was fashionable, which was how, I think, he came to know some of our calls. That was always disconcerting. An under-21 provincial flyhalf, like the great All Black, Zinzan Brooke, Rassie brought a range of skills to his role as a back-rower. He could pass, kick, tackle hard and had a real awareness of all that was happening around him. He was one of those players who always seemed to pop up in the right places.

He also hated losing, but this hardly made him unique among South African players, for none of them copped a loss too well. Back in 1995, I was often told that they'd never lost a Cup match – as if the first two tournaments didn't count because they weren't involved in them on account of the apartheid boycott. It wasn't until Stevie Larkham kicked that field goal at Twickenham in 1999 that that record was broken. Their great players back themselves and have a sense of purpose which really shines through in World Cup competitions.

Just as Rassie was on the way out from the South Africa XV,

another great character was emerging in John Smit, who would go on to become the most capped Springbok hooker and captain. 'Smitty' is a big guy, and an impressive leader. When we played together in the tsunami game in 2005, we had a call, 'Slice', that involved a big forward getting the ball and then cutting back into the players left at the previous breakdown.

Three weeks later, before the Brumbies played the Sharks in the Super 12, I texted Smitty: 'Mate, if I'm in the line, no slices on the weekend. Call slice off.' They had just the right players in their team to make that play effective and, for me, potentially painful.

Back came the reply: 'There will be plenty of slices.'

And, of course, there were. For all the professionalism, the scrutiny, the passion and the patriotism, this sense of fun and camaraderie across teams and nations remains a *pure* part of rugby.

In 2004, the Wallabies played the Springboks in Perth – my 100th Test. It was inevitable, given that I was reaching such a major milestone, that I would receive a lot of attention in the lead-up to the game. It was all nice, and much appreciated, but I just wanted to play. I was coming back from a shoulder injury that had kept me out of the previous Test, in Wellington, and we had a very good South African team to beat. Having lost to the All Blacks, we needed to get our Tri Nations campaign back on track. As soon as I dared, after a couple of questions from reporters about the milestone, I said, 'Let's talk about how important the *game* is.'

My team-mates knew how I liked to prepare for matches, and they made sure that – despite the fact it was my centenary – as little fuss as possible impinged on that. At the same time, a friend such as Matt Burke, who knows exactly which cigars I like, made sure he had those (and a '94 Grange) ready to be consumed in the change room after the game.

On the field, Burkey and I had combined late in the game to make a tackle on De Wet Barry that helped seal the win. It was an important moment late in the game, but my first reaction was that it was a good test for the left shoulder. The things you think about. It was a cracking game, in which the lead changed hands eight times in the second half. Barry kicked through for Gaffie du Toit to dive over, Percy Montgomery's conversion made it 26–23 to the Boks, but near the death Lote Tuqiri and Stephen Larkham combined to send Clyde Rathbone over in the corner, Burkey calmly landed the conversion and we were home.

During the game, Smitty found himself arguing with the referee, Chris White of England. This went on for a little while, and then I stopped the Springbok skipper in his tracks by asking plaintively, 'Are you the ref, mate?' He spun around and just looked at me, shocked that I'd have the hide to say this to anyone. By the time he'd regained his composure I think he'd forgotten what he was arguing about. I was just trying to help the guy in the middle. It's a hard job!

After that game, the South African boys presented me with a commemorative jersey, as they did with Stevie Larkham in Sydney in 2007, and Smitty called me a 'warrior'. That meant a lot to me, that tribute, coming as it did from a battle-hardened rugby man such as him.

Soon, the whole celebration process was repeated when I played my 102nd Test, in Durban, to beat David Campese's Australian record. Again, there were heaps of media questions and text messages and the like (my father flew over especially for the match), and this time we were playing for the Tri Nations title. But there was no happy ending. We didn't play well, losing by more than the four points we were behind on the scoreboard, and afterwards I was left with a hollow feeling. I was now Australia's most capped player, but as we flew back over the

Indian Ocean it felt more bitter than sweet, like we'd lost two grand finals in nine months.

Another disappointing defeat came in Paris in November. I wasn't on the wrong side of a scoreline in a Test against France until November 2001, when we were defeated in Marseille, but I'd lose against them twice more, in Paris in 2004 and Marseille in 2005. At the Stade de France, the Test turned on a big moment when Frédéric Michalak scored a try just before half-time, which meant that instead of us going into half-time with our noses in front, the home team led by a point, and we were the ones that didn't cope well with the pressure in the second half. The championship minutes were crucial once more.

The French team always have good skills from 1 to 15, and they are inevitably excellent scrimmagers and tough at the lineout. Part of this, I think, comes from the influence of the forwards from the south, where many promising rugby types also get involved in wrestling and judo at an early age. But they are incredibly inconsistent in their performances, which is probably best summed up by the great French scrum-half Fabien Galthié, who once said matter-of-factly of the French team: 'Some days we fly with the birds and other days we play like shit.' That's French rugby. A week after they beat us in 2004, they lost to Argentina in Marseille and then, another seven days later, they were thrashed 45–6 by the All Blacks! It seemed the game that really mattered to them was the one against us.

After that loss, at the post-game media conference, Eddie Jones was critical of some on-field decisions made by me and Stephen Larkham, and claimed we ignored instructions. However, I didn't learn of this until later, next time I met the press, when the journos sought my reaction to his comments. It was the first time Eddie had publicly questioned us through the media and naturally I was disappointed – not with the criticism, but because he went public. The leadership group had always been solid on these things – win or lose, we'd back each other up. Eddie told me later that he wanted to see more leadership throughout the group, and that had motivated him to speak up in the way he had. Too many guys, he felt, were sitting back and waiting for the senior players to take command, and he felt he needed to do something radical – such as use the press – to achieve his objective. I could see his point, but I didn't agree with his actions.

It was a move born out of a sense of frustration I'm not sure Eddie ever lost for the rest of his time as Wallabies coach. He is a rugby man who strives for perfection, which I can relate to, but as coach of the 2004 Australian team I think that virtue became something of a vice. We were poor in the two big games of that year – against South Africa and France – and he was at a loss to explain those performances. We beat Scotland twice on the tour, Matt Giteau kicked two really important late penalties at Twickenham to get us home in a brilliant Test against England, and we had lost both Stevie and Stirlo to injury, so our backline was very inexperienced, but still the general feeling was that it had been a disappointing tour. Looking back, the results weren't too bad, but at the time the mood was a little glum.

18

KEEPING
PERSPECTIVE

2004

*'I didn't cope too well when Max was fitting badly. It is
natural for a parent to panic and I couldn't eat or sleep.
George, however, was amazing. He was the one sleeping
beside our son's bed and coping with his seizures. I think
that is why he is such a great leader – he simply copes with
enormous pressure naturally. It's not that he feels it less,
but rather that he gets on with what needs to be done.'*

ERICA GREGAN

Before I departed for the Wallabies overseas tour in late 2004,
I was enjoying breakfast with Max one morning, pulling faces
and giggling and then, suddenly . . . he wasn't giggling anymore.

'Stop mucking around, mate,' I said with a laugh.

But Max wasn't mucking around. He was having a seizure
and I was scared. At the same time, I felt prepared . . .

My son is having a seizure, I've got to put him in recovery position, check his pulse, ring the ambulance . . .

Max's central nervous system had short-circuited. The little guy – only three and a half years old – was locked up. And when he came out of it after a couple of minutes – which seemed an eternity – he was shattered. The amount of energy he had expended was awesome. It was a very abrupt, in-your-face experience, and I have no idea what is the 'natural' way to react in such a situation. I doubt anyone does, until you find yourself facing such a crisis. Max had had one episode about a year before, but we had been told it was almost certainly a one-off, so this had come out of the blue. Maybe my instinct as a parent kicked in. More likely, the first aid training I'd received at university gave me just enough knowledge and confidence to react appropriately. We got him to Royal North Shore Hospital, twenty minutes from home. And then we waited . . .

For the next week, Max was at North Shore and then the Children's Hospital at Westmead while they tried to ascertain what was wrong and get the seizures under control. This was probably the most difficult time of my life, as I felt very out of control watching Max having constant seizures and being drugged out on meds. Eventually we found out: it was epilepsy and it was treatable. For a while it looked like I wouldn't be making the tour, but we were reassured that Max was doing well, so I left with the boys. That was bloody hard, but in a way me staying in Australia would have been going against the doctors' advice that life should go back to normal. The epilepsy was treatable. We also had to give our son confidence and show him he can enjoy life to the fullest and not to be embarrassed by his condition.

The experience was an eye-opener for Erica and me in so many ways. Our time at North Shore, one of the many hospitals in Sydney that has benefited from the fantastic work of the

Humpty Dumpty Foundation, a non-profit organisation that Phil Kearns does a lot of work for, gave us a chance to see first-hand and appreciate how a charity can make a difference.

Eventually, we were told Max needed to see a neurology specialist based at the Children's Hospital at Westmead, in western Sydney. We'd been assured he was going to be okay; now we were going to find out how to manage the illness. We stayed at Westmead for the best part of two days and, as is always the way at hospitals, there was plenty of free time while further tests were being analysed.

The weather was good and Max wanted to get out and play. Out the window he could see the playground at Ronald McDonald House, an accommodation facility for families so they can stay near the hospital wards while their sick child is being treated. It is, however, only for kids with cancer, and there are a lot of other sick kids at Westmead.

I had to tell Max no, we weren't allowed in that playground. In the distance, beyond the hospital boundaries, he could see some terrific parkland. It was hard to explain, 'Mate, you can't go in there, either.' There just wasn't a playground or anything similar where kids could get out of the hospital atmosphere and go muck around.

Some of the other patients needed to get out even more. Many had been in hospital for months, and giving them the opportunity to go out and enjoy the outdoors with their families or therapists seemed like an obvious thing to do.

Why can't they just build the kids a playground?

So I asked senior figures at the hospital about it. They quickly replied that there was a committee that had been seeking funds for over ten years.

'How much are you looking at?'

About half a million dollars, they replied, which seemed a large amount at first, but then they explained that a specialised children's outdoor playground at a hospital had to meet a wide variety of safety requirements. Top-class architects and occupational therapists needed to be consulted. The playing surface needed to be cushioned, access for wheelchairs and portable drips was imperative. Erica and I had been strongly considering setting up a foundation of some kind, and from the moment I had this conversation we knew what our objective was going to be. Further, we wanted to support research into epilepsy, by backing the work of specialists studying the condition.

This was certainly not going to be something we went into half-heartedly. We set out to find the best people in the business, and then asked for their support. Without exception, everyone we hoped would be involved immediately jumped on board (including David Clarke – Chairman of Macquarie Bank – who agreed to be our chairman), which meant that not only has this endeavour been extremely successful and rewarding, it has also allowed us to really get to know some wonderful people. A great momentum has built up. We have had some fantastic fundraisers and are supported by a massive list of ambassadors including: many past and present Wallabies; other sporting greats, such as Pat Rafter, Michael Campbell, Peter O'Malley and Ricky Ponting; and actors and musicians, such as Sam Neill, Bryan Brown, Rachel Ward, Rob Sitch, Jimmy Barnes, Mark Lizotte and Jon Stevens. To these and many more we are so grateful.

From the moment we committed to the playground idea to that first one being built was about a year of hard work. Mirvac and *Backyard Blitz* came on board to help make it a reality, and the reward was seeing the playground packed full of kids, including some who were really sick. Parents tell us that visiting the playground is the part of the day they all look forward to and that it is a much nicer place to receive visitors than the ward.

To date we have raised in excess of $3 million on the smell of an oily rag, but we have lots still to achieve. We have now started building a wonderful, interactive playground at the Royal Children's Hospital in Brisbane and are waiting for the contracts to be signed so we can get to work building a playground at Canberra Hospital.

There is no feeling to compare to seeing one of these playgrounds open and the kids playing in them, smiling, and hearing the positive comments of parents, doctors and nurses. I've really enjoyed my rugby career and take enormous pride in my sporting achievements, but what we are doing off the field means so much more to me.

Erica once asked me, 'Who are your heroes?' I can honestly say my heroes are kids overcoming adversity. I see them in hospitals all the time, and I'm lucky enough to meet some of their families and see the way they make the most of very difficult situations. We feel honored to know these people.

My family has put my rugby life into perspective. They make everything sweeter and everything more real. They are there through the good times and the bad. Watching my kids learn to speak French has blown my mind; they just never stop amazing me.

When we lost the 2007 World Cup quarter-final in Marseilles, Max came into the change room and told me not to worry as we had done our best and he was proud of us. (I guess I should mention, however, that he did cry when his beloved All Blacks lost.)

My family and friends have been very good to me throughout my playing career. They have travelled all over the world to support me and the team. Erica's father, Joe, and other family members who know nothing about rugby have flown all the way to the other side of the world on several occasions just to be there to see me play. Almost the entire family on both sides went to the World Cup in France. Erica rented a house in a beautiful medieval town in Provence, about an hour from our base camp in

Montpellier. Our family and friends used it as a base and came and went throughout the World Cup, and it also was a great escape on my odd days off.

My brother now lives close by in Sydney, and although my sister lives in Melbourne her son Shaye often joins us for holidays – he is like a big brother to our kids. We live next door to Erica's sister Melanie, and we always seem to have a house full of kids and somebody to share a coffee or beer. We also live in the same suburb as many of my former team-mates' families, who for years have adopted Erica and the kids when I was away (which was often). Erica is a little concerned that my retirement will mean that she has to give up her routine, including Sunday 'poker and Thai night' at the Barnes house. But I think my parents will be the ones who'll miss rugby the most as they have always been involved and they too have their network of friends, who are proud players' parents.

19

BLOODY HARD WORK

2005

'We could have easily sidestepped the issue, but George was
being truthful – and isn't that what we want our role
models to be?'

EDDIE JONES, AFTER A STORM BROKE OUT OVER THE USE
OF CAFFEINE TABLETS IN PROFESSIONAL SPORT, MAY 2005

In the space of two months in the first half of the 2005 season,
I found myself involved in two major rugby stories that caused
a degree of moral outrage not always associated with rugby. One
was an important issue but I was not directly involved; the other
caused a big storm but I thought it was something of a beat-up.
I also managed to miss ten weeks' playing time after I broke my
leg in a game against NSW.

The first controversy concerned my old mate Justin Harrison, who, while playing for the Waratahs in a Super 12 match in Johannesburg, racially abused the Cats' winger Chumani Booi. I was in South Africa when the story broke, having arrived there to prepare for the Brumbies' upcoming game in Jo'burg, so I was immediately aware that it was a big incident that would damage the reputation of the player who made the remark. For a few days, there was some conjecture as to the identity of the offending NSW player, with a finger being pointed at Nathan Grey, but Goog took responsibility for his actions.

I felt genuinely sorry for Goog, because I knew it was totally out of character. I knew he'd be seriously regretting what he'd done. He had always enjoyed being involved in the verbal side of the game, but he'd crossed a line in this instance.

When I next saw him, the subject came up and I knew immediately he was very remorseful. 'I know it's totally out of character for you, Goog,' I said. 'I know what was said, and you showed a lot of character for owning up. You're just going to have to deal with it and live with it.'

We knew that people would tag him as a racist. The challenge for Goog was to prove these people wrong, to demonstrate there is more to him than that, and that the moment of madness in Jo'burg was an aberration.

As Australian captain, it was perfectly logical that I would be asked about the incident, but I didn't want to add too much to what was already a major controversy. I emphasised the fact that there is no place for racial abuse in sport, or in life. When I was asked if this was a true representation of Justin Harrison's character, I said quickly and sincerely, 'No.'

A month after Goog found himself in trouble, I broke my leg on the body of Chris Whitaker, my NSW rival and Wallabies team-mate, on a day when the Waratahs beat us at home (which hurt more than the fracture). Whits and I went for the same loose ball, collided in mid-air, and I came off second best.

Initially, I thought it was a cork. I was down on the ground when I copped a serve from Mat Rogers, who strode up close to let me know he thought I was weak because I couldn't stand up. I wouldn't cop that, so I stumbled to my feet, only to almost immediately find myself having to mark up on Matty, of all people, a player who is fast and elusive on his feet, a natural attacker with the ability to break tackles. *This isn't good*, I thought, but rather than take me on he kicked for the line. It's possible he took it easy on me, but I still shot back, 'Shit, Rogo, you gave me a gobful when I was on the ground, but you didn't even have a go at me on one leg!' And then I hobbled off the ground. I couldn't run.

After the match, they sent me to the AIS medical area to get some precautionary X-rays. By this stage, I was walking okay, if a little slowly, so I was stunned to learn I'd fractured my fibula, a silly bone in your leg that doesn't really do much. You could probably pull it out and be all right. But when it breaks, well . . . it breaks.

The injury was good for me as it gave me a rest, even if I missed the rest of the Super 12 campaign. I thought I'd be right if we made the semis, but as it turned out I wasn't fit again until the second Test match of the year.

The second major controversy concerned one of professional sport's biggest bugbears: drugs. During the 1999 World Cup, there had been whispers that the Southern Hemisphere players were on performance-enhancing drugs; that was why we were stronger, fitter, bigger. To refute the suggestion, Michael Lynagh used me as the example in his newspaper column to demonstrate that the allegations weren't true:

He trains as hard as anyone I have seen and turned himself into such a ball of muscle that he can compete with, and most of the time embarrass, much large opponents ... coaches and players in the southern hemisphere also think more laterally about the game. They don't necessarily accept what has gone before.

I was happy for Noddy to use my name as he did, but I never felt I was doing anything special on the training track. Yes, I was always dedicated, especially since those days back at the AIS when I was shown the sort of benefits that could be won by hard work and the latest individual training programs. From that time, I was always looking at doing things better.

As professionalism really took hold in rugby, attitudes to training changed markedly, and whereas in the late 1990s I was one of the more dedicated trainers in the Wallabies squad, by the tail-end of my career I was just one of a large number of serious players seeking an edge. I never lost my dedication to training or recovery, never wavered in my belief that I could find a point of difference between me and my rivals through the nature of my preparation, and I always wanted to discover new methods. I have no doubt I was fitter and physically better prepared in my final season than in any preceding year. But as Wallabies fitness coach Steve Nance said when asked what our secret was, it was all down to 'BHW.' Bloody Hard Work.

I have never seen instances of deliberate illegal drug-taking in rugby. However, it is true that athletes take advantage of legal vitamin and mineral supplements to gain and maintain muscle mass, and to aid recovery after heavy training sessions. The important thing to add here is that in modern professional rugby in Australia, any decisions as to what product is used and when it is used can be made with expert advice close at hand. It is not as if a player might read about any old supplement in a health-and-fitness magazine and then sneak out the back to consume as much as he wants. In both the Wallabies and Brumbies set-ups, we had access to doctors, dieticians and nutritionists who are among the best in the world. I was fortunate to be introduced to some of these people before I played senior representative football, while I was at the AIS. I learned that what is good for one person may not be good for another; the key was always to work *with* the medical experts to ensure that I wasn't damaging my body, or sacrificing my long-term wellbeing for a short-term benefit.

Another important thing to stress is that any advantage an athlete might gain from using a supplement is miniscule compared to what can be obtained from sheer hard work. I can think of team-mates who trained religiously to get in the best physical shape of their careers; they might have used supplements that assisted their recovery or allowed them to maximise what they got from their work in the gym and on the training paddock, but it was the effort they put in that made the key difference, not the supplements. We work so hard, if there is a way within the rules that can get us an edge, however small, we should have a look at it. I took a range of supplements, such as protein shakes and minerals, during my career; some of them helped me, others didn't, all were 100 per cent legal. I know that because I never tried anything unless it had been approved by experts I knew and trusted.

Senior players in Australian rugby are left in no doubt as to what they need to do in relation to drugs. If anyone makes a mistake, he has no one to blame but himself. Even a simple matter, such as taking a cough mixture, needs to be cleared with the doctor. It isn't for us to decide what we can and can't take; the world anti-doping authorities make those decisions and we abide by them. I appreciate these rules, and have no wish to see them relaxed, as I never want to see the day when competitors in any sport are sacrificing their health in pursuit of 'greatness'. But if there is something out there that is legal, won't hurt you and will give you edge, I think an athlete would be mad to ignore it. Yet that was what some commentators and doctors' groups wanted me to do in mid May 2005, after it was revealed that I was taking caffeine tablets to assist my performance.

This episode began when the Australian men's hockey team, gold-medal winners at the Athens Olympics in 2004, used caffeine and found that you could measure a distinct average increase in the work output of a player over the course of a game. The World Anti-Doping Agency (WADA) had removed caffeine from its list of banned substances on 1 January 2004 because the substance failed to satisfy two of the three criteria a drug has to meet for it to be ruled illegal: performance-enhancing; harmful to a person's health; and against the spirit of sport. Doctors and strength-and-conditioning coaches with links to both the hockey team and Australian football then introduced caffeine tablets at a number of AFL clubs and quickly players in most teams were using them. The AIS released a fact sheet outlining the benefits, and offered advice on how to take the pills. One pill was said to contain the equivalent of twelve cups of coffee. The great boxer, Kostya Tszyu, revealed he had used caffeine tablets, and then a UK survey claimed 36 per cent of British sportsmen and women and as many as half of all top-grade rugby league players had used supplements containing caffeine. Maybe it was because of my links to coffee – by 2005, Erica and I had established a number of *GG espresso* cafes in Sydney – but I saw no harm in trying the tablets, once I'd got the all-clear from our doctors, who controlled the dosage for the players using them. If it was legal, and I found that it did help my performance, then I would have no problem with using caffeine. Not everyone agreed with me, as I discovered after I confirmed, in response to a question at a press conference held in Melbourne to promote the upcoming Test against Italy, that I was taking caffeine tablets.

Eddie Jones and the ARU's CEO Gary Flowers came out in support of me, as did Dick Pound, chairman of the World Anti-Doping Agency, and Dr Louise Bourke, the head of the Department of Sports Nutrition at the AIS. However, the *Daily Telegraph* in Sydney headlined its story on the matter 'MADNESS' and quoted David Campese as saying I was 'stupid' for admitting I used the tablets. The Australian Schools Rugby Union was also critical, with a spokesman commenting, 'Maybe some things are better not talked about, because of the message it gives.'

In the end, the debate turned a bit silly. We rely on the drugs agencies to monitor what is right and wrong yet, even though they had made the decision that caffeine tablets were legal, we were being censured for acting within the letter of their law. The main thrust of the critics' argument was that if the Australian rugby captain was seen to be taking these pills, then youngsters without access to the best medical advice might blithely follow my example and do themselves harm. I was told I was being irresponsible, neglecting my duty as a role model. However, I felt this was a naive and in one sense hysterical argument. It was made without appreciating the fact I have just outlined – that elite athletes across many professional sports use a range of nutritional supplements, under the guidance of experts, to aid performance and recovery. If any of these products are used to excess, they can cause grief, but we weren't using them to excess; on the contrary, we were using them *under strict medical supervision*. It was just that the word 'caffeine' made for a loud headline.

What clouds this issue to some degree is that there are conflicting views on which 'performance-enhancing' products should be permitted. Are painkillers okay, when they undoubtedly aid the performance of an injured athlete? What about the sports drinks which make a virtue of the fact they replace the electrolytes athletes sweat out of their systems? The question of where to draw the line needs to be addressed by sensible debate, led by experts. That didn't happen on this occasion. As the controversy petered out, there were whispers that WADA was going to have another look at the situation, but if they did, nothing ever came of it.

I would seek any competitive edge I could find, provided it was legal and recommended by health experts I trusted. They are professionals, who were always intent on getting me on the field in the best possible condition, physically and mentally. I always trusted them to do their job, just like a coach must trust his players to do their job. Everyone at the Wallabies is there for one primary purpose: to win, within the rules.

I was randomly tested countless times while I was with the Wallabies. We all were. Sometimes, it could be a real imposition – I can remember after the World Cup semifinal in 2003, when the Wallabies and All Blacks got together for a post-game drink in the winners' dressing room, Aaron Mauger had to speak on behalf of the Kiwis because their captain, Reuben Thorne, was being tested. But it never bugged me, because I knew why the tests had to be done.

Rugby footballers at the top level have a fantastic life, but I guess there will always be some guys in the sport who have a reckless streak, or who wonder if the grass is greener elsewhere. Maybe I'm old school, but I'm happy to settle for a couple of beers or a few wines.

20

HARD TIMES

2005

At the start of 2005, looking towards the World Cup in 2007, Eddie Jones told us he wanted to introduce a pattern of play that would allow us to play across the width of the field. The options it would give us, if we got it right, would be phenomenal. It might take us three or four phases to get players into the parts of the field where we wanted them, but once we did so we could attack wide or we could attack close, predominantly off the No. 10 or either of the centres, who were 'split' on either side of the halfback. For it to work, we needed a great No. 10 – which, of course, we had in Stephen Larkham – and we needed players with very good vision and the ability to communicate well. Initially, the scheme worked well, and it was great for Stevie because he was getting the ball with lots of people in and around him.

Our first four Tests of 2005 were against Samoa, Italy, France and South Africa, and we won the lot and won them well. The media coverage was positive, and Stevie was in magical form. The only problem I could see, and I remember speaking to Eddie and Rod Kafer about it, was that the method hadn't really been tested. As we got into the Tri Nations, it was inevitable that there would be a few steps back as we moved forward. But so be it . . .

After the first Test against the Springboks, which was played at Telstra Stadium, we travelled to Johannesburg, where first we had to live through the off-field drama that led to Matt Henjak eventually being sent home for disciplinary reasons, and then we lost 33–20, even though we managed to match them, scoring three tries apiece. An intercept try we conceded made a huge difference, but even if we didn't play particularly well, the effort we put in was first-class. A week later, Stevie did his shoulder during the second Test of the tour, at Pretoria, where we went down 22–16. Stirling Mortlock was also out through injury, so a young Drew Mitchell came into the side to make his Test debut against the All Blacks and by the end of the Southern Hemisphere season, as we prepared to return to Europe, he was almost a senior player. As we tried to introduce a new attacking system, the last thing we needed was one of the most diabolical injury runs of my experience. That's what happened, though.

We went into the Test against the All Blacks in Sydney without Stevie, Chris Latham, Wendell Sailor or Mat Rogers, got off to a 13–nil start in the first thirteen minutes and then lost Matt Giteau and Morgan Turinui either side of half-time. Jeremy Paul badly hurt his shoulder as well and we ended up losing 30–13. I was being criticised for not running at defenders, but the new attacking plan didn't really allow for the half to do so, as our attack revolved around our first receivers. For me, the focus remained on moving the ball one or two passes away from the breakdown.

The injury toll was brutal, the media criticism was getting ridiculous, the team had lost three straight, and the pressure was on: *Do we stay true to our new system?*

Our next Test was against South Africa in Perth. Elton Flatley was to start at No. 10, but during the final warm-ups, twenty minutes before we're due to run out, he began to suffer from dizziness and double vision. That was linked back to previous concussions and was essentially the end of his career. Gits went to 10, we changed the game plan slightly so more of the play could work off me – afterwards a few people complimented me on my running game returning (funny how it works!) – and we fought back from eight points down in the second half to hit the front 19–17, only for Bryan Habana to score the match-winning try fifteen minutes from time. It was one of the gutsiest performances I was ever involved in, but still we came up short.

Afterwards, I asked Eddie whether we should be working a little bit more off the No. 9. I knew that we had committed to this new form of attack, but with the incredible change in personnel due to injury I felt we needed to adapt a little. In my view, we were not getting to our attacking set-up consistently in games. The earlier discussion – that we would have to 'take a few steps' back with this new attacking system – was at the forefront of both our minds, but we needed a win. Eddie listened, as he always did, but we persevered with the new system. I could quote pages of the most savage criticism received in this period, from reporters whose ambition seemed to be to claim a scalp, whether it be captain or coach. It was impossible to totally ignore this coverage, because it had consumed so much of the debate going on in the Australian rugby community, and I think one of the ramifications was that Eddie lost a degree of patience with players who weren't able to adapt to the new system. At the same time, I was becoming frustrated by our inability to operate efficiently on the field. When we played New Zealand in Auckland, we fielded a very young side and the All Blacks were too good for us, but we kept fighting. During the game, though, there was an incident that showed just how much the criticism and the run of losses had damaged the team's mindset.

The Kiwis shot out to lead 20–0, but maybe the mood of the contest was starting to change. I called for a five-man lineout, ran at their tight-head Carl Hayman, passed to Mark Gerrard, who made the break, on to Mark Chisholm, try. However, when I'd asked for that lineout, our forward leader, Nathan Sharpe, responded, 'Mate, I can't give it to you in case we lose it.'

And I'm thinking, *Sharpey, we're twenty points down!*

'No,' I said, 'let's at least have a crack. It's our best scoring option.'

Nathan was preoccupied with not losing the lineout, and he was right – our five-man was not our best performing lineout – but calling it did give us a chance to get on the scoreboard. Whatever the circumstances, we needed to back ourselves. We actually fought back to 20–19 before going down by ten points, but it was another loss and Eddie was right when he said afterwards, 'We got ourselves into a position to win the game and we let ourselves down again. It's not good enough.' But I just wondered if it would have been better if he'd looked for positives – such as the fact that one of the youngest Wallabies teams I had ever played in had put themselves in a good position to win a Test against the All Blacks, and that with this experience we'd be better equipped to handle the next opportunity we got to close out a big game. I said that to him, but we had to agree to disagree. An unhealthy sense of fear was pervading the team.

Eddie always liked to challenge players, wanted to make them think. He liked to be challenged, too, and if you didn't do that, he could get frustrated. If, after a game, someone said, 'I thought we should have done this,' he'd reply curtly, 'Why didn't you say so at the beginning of the week?' That, to me, was an error on both sides – the player should have said something earlier if that's what he thought, but the manner of Eddie's response could stifle debate. Raising a concern is important, because if something is wrong we've got to fix it. The 2003 World Cup final is an example – some of the forwards said quietly, months later, almost as an afterthought, that they were 'overdone' because of the work they did at Coffs Harbour in the week beforehand. I didn't see that at the time, but with hindsight, given all they did against the All Blacks in the semifinal, maybe they were. The coaching staff should have picked up on it, so should I, but the forwards who felt that way should have raised it immediately with Eddie or with me.

What I loved and respected so much about Eddie was that we agreed to disagree on some things but agreed on plenty of others in the years we worked together, from 1998 to 2005, and he would always hear me out. Sometimes he'd stick, sometimes he'd bend my way; always, he'd say words to the effect, 'Yeah, I heard what you said, and I respect you for bringing it up.'

A good example occurred during the 2003 World Cup. I always rated Joe Roff as a big-match player. However, after we played Ireland, our last pool match, Eddie and his fellow selectors swapped Roffy, who been playing on the wing, and Lote Tuqiri, who'd been on the bench, because he was dissatisfied with Roffy's kicking game. Lote played so well in the quarter-final and the semifinal that there was no way he could be dropped, but there were some concerns over fullback Mat Rogers, who did not have the same experience as the others. The competition for the No. 15 jumper, between the two of them and Chris Latham, was terrific.

Eddie is not the sort of coach who would usually discuss a tough selection. However, every once in a while, with really tight ones, he might come up and ask my opinion. This is what he did before the final.

'What do you think about the back three, mate?' he asked. 'We're thinking of sticking with what we had in the semi.'

'Don't change a winning team,' was my first response. But then I thought about big-match experience. 'You've got guys like Burkey, Roffy, Latho who have played these big matches,' I said, musing aloud. 'Particularly Burkey and Roffy ... but Burkey hasn't played much, and when he has it's been predominantly at 13. So it's really between Roffy, Latho and Matty ... Latho hasn't played since Namibia, but he's played big matches in the past. He's ready to go ... I know you're concerned about Roffy's kicking ... but the bigger the game, the bigger Roffy plays ... If you want my opinion, I'm probably leaning towards Roffy ...'

Eddie went away and he and his fellow selectors decided to stick with the same team, which was a good decision. In 2004, when we put fifty on the Poms in Brisbane, Roffy played superbly at fullback, but that was then. Matty handled things really well in the final. I just liked the fact that Eddie and I could have that conversation, I could offer my view, and then we would move on.

Through the second half of 2005 there almost seemed to be a competition running among the reporters for the first person to successfully predict my retirement date. I just let them go, and focused on the things I could control. It actually gave me some more perspective – made me appreciate who was important: my family and my team-mates. It also, in a strange sort of way, made me appreciate what a great game rugby is; as the media campaign to get rid of me was at its height, it was natural for me to think,

Is it all worth it? And the answer, absolutely, was yes. I knew I could never get ahead of myself, that my next game could be my last, but I'd achieved a lot in my career, and I was going to treasure the rest of it.

The end-of-season trip away to France, England, Ireland and Wales was like a development tour, we had so many senior guys out. Against England, we were smashed in the scrum and that's what all the post-game talk was about, but it was 16–all well into the second half after Drew Mitchell scored. In prominent parts of the Australian media, though, the focus was all on me and how I 'had to go' if the team was to improve. I remember the press conference in Cardiff before the Test there, when one Sydney journo sat in the front row, which he rarely did, and asked, 'Do you take responsibility for how poorly the team is playing?'

'I know about leadership.' I replied slowly. 'I hear about it every time I watch *A Bug's Life* with my son. Hopper's first rule of leadership is: "Everything is your fault." '

It was such a ridiculous, provocative question – asking a captain of Australia if he took responsibility for the way his team was performing. If I said yes, then I set myself up as the scapegoat; if I said no, I'd be accused of deserting the ship. This is what the team was dealing with.

There was a race to have the exclusive on my impending retirement. I played a lot of 'last Tests' in this period. Media conferences weren't about upcoming Test matches anymore. People talk about my difficult relationship with the media, but I think during this time a level of suspicion was built between the entire team and the media that will take a while to break down. During this period, we never shirked away from the fact that we were losing and that there were things about the way we were playing that needed to be addressed. However, our commitment was strong and the effort was total, so it was hard to read – but not expected – that we were 'flops', 'shameful', an 'embarrass-ment' and that we all 'had to go'. It became quite a wacky world.

If the journos didn't agree with a decision, they went over-board. I had to be sacked because Australian rugby needed to look towards its future. Instead, for the England Test, Eddie left out Matt Giteau – because he was frustrated with the little guy, wanted him to get more serious about his footy. He saw Gits as a key figure moving forward and felt he needed to rev him up. In one way, you could argue Eddie was looking to the future by making this tough call, but instead it just provided more evidence in the cynics' eyes that I was a 'protected species'. In many Tests in 2005 I was being substituted late in games, which gave the press box another opportunity. *What is a captain doing being replaced with the game on the line?* It didn't look good, and I didn't like it, but if Eddie thought the change was for the betterment of the side then I was out of there. And the player who was coming on, Chris Whitaker, was outstanding. Eddie was looking for something different as players tired late in the games, and in that sense the substitution could be deemed to be shrewd. But when the game is close, important decisions have to be made, and experience counts. Sometimes I wondered who was making those decisions on the field after I went off.

On November 21, the *Daily Telegraph* ran an 'exclusive' story that the Test against Wales on the following Saturday would be my farewell. This story encapsulates what I disliked most about the way these reporters operated. The story was totally false, yet the guy who wrote it got away with it, moved on to his next piece, despite the effect it had on my family, friends and the team. The manner in which this story was written suggested the infor-mation had been deliberately leaked so that everyone would notice I was departing. My manager issued a denial, but it didn't undo the original damage. When I did play my last Test, almost two years after that story was written, I was able to go out on my terms.

The media's negativity dominated the tour, but there were some good times. Earlier in the year, in Auckland, after I played my 114th Test, to equal England prop Jason Leonard's world record for most Test appearances, the All Blacks players gave me a beautiful green tiki as a memento of the occasion. I was genuinely honoured, and my sense of pride was accentuated even further when Steve Hansen, their assistant coach, grabbed me straight after the presentation and said, 'Son, do you know what that's all about? It's respect. It might not look like they like you out there –' he pointed to the field, 'but they love you, son.'

Then, in London, Jason Leonard – who is a great guy – presented me with a bottle of 1973 vintage champagne at our team hotel after I'd broken his record by playing my 115th Test, in Marseille. Jason had also played five Tests for the Lions, so it would be a little longer before I could claim the 'most caps' record unequivocally.

The two of us, big prop and little halfback, sitting there enjoying a chat was really nice. Jason and I had enjoyed many a battle on the field, going back to the World Cup quarter-final in 1995. I didn't say much in that game, but later, once I got to know him, I was always happy to introduce myself. 'Haven't seen you in a while, you big bastard,' I might say at the first scrum or after the match.

'What are you doing still playing?' he'd reply.

'I'll give it up when you give it up,' I'd laugh. He's a good man.

I was in Coolum on summer holidays in early December 2005 when I got the call from an ARU representative telling me that

Eddie was gone. I was told there would be a media conference in the very near future. I rang Eddie straight away. There was no doubt that we had to break the losing cycle (eight losses from our past nine Tests), but I didn't think we needed to sack the coach. The ARU asked me for my view on how the squad was operating, and I answered honestly, outlining areas where we'd been struggling, highlighting things that weren't too bad. Everything I said, I'd already said to Eddie. I've outlined them here. I expected them to stick with him, but they didn't.

'I don't know what to say, mate,' was how I started our phone conversation. We had been a leadership team since 1998, first with the Brumbies and then with the Wallabies from 2001, which represented a lot of history together and a whole lot of respect. Later, we exchanged letters. We have a bit of a book thing going between the two of us, where if I read a book I think he'll like, I send it to him and vice versa. We've been doing this for so long he's started posting me books I sent to him a few years ago. With the first book I sent after he was dismissed, I included a letter that referred to the experiences and challenges we'd shared, and how he had improved me as a footballer and a person. The thing I learned most from him was the value of planning. The guy is a machine in this area. He sent a nice letter back.

One thing that nagged at me was that Eddie's loyalty to me had cost him in the end. The media campaign had been so vehement that one of us had to go. The results had been bad enough that a big decision had to be made. But Eddie refused to drop me, even temporarily, because he didn't think that was in the team's best interests. Had he done so, he might have bought himself some more time.

On the day of the dismissal, the ARU asked me if I wanted to make myself available to the media, but I declined. I had said privately to Eddie what I needed to say, and with so much already written and said in the press I didn't want to add to it. I was mindful, too, of the fact that he would most likely have things to say and I didn't want anything I said to crowd in on that. I was also still angry with the way our recent tour had been covered. With hindsight, maybe I should have issued a brief statement, because some reporters leapt on the fact I hadn't paid tribute to the coach as evidence that I had no compassion, that I was glad to see him go, which was total rubbish. At a Players' Association lunch a couple of weeks later, I was asked questions about Eddie's departure and my answers were then written up as my first comments on the saga.

As Peter Lonard, the knockabout Aussie golfer, said to me at Coolum when the criticism started coming, 'You can't win, mate. You ring him personally and out of respect you don't say anything in public and you get slaughtered. But if you'd said something, you'd have been slaughtered, too.'

It had been that sort of year.

THE SKY AIN'T
THE LIMIT

'I've always told the musicians in my band to play what
they know and then play above that. Because then anything
can happen, and that's where great art and music happens.'

MILES DAVIS

*I've loved jazz since my final years of school. Specifically I was
into acid jazz; I loved the way it was a bit funky, that it
was always changing. Not far from where I grew up in Canberra,
the father of a good friend of mine was heavily into jazz. When I
went around to visit, he would always be playing a record from
his massive jazz collection, and from the first time I heard the
music I thought it was a nice sound – mellow, very different to
the Police albums I was listening to on my turntable at home. The
thing that stands out in my memory is that the jazz seemed to
command silence inside the house, which was a good trick given
that there were usually four or more boys playing in the backyard
at the time. As I grew older, I felt compelled to learn more about*

jazz, the different varieties, how it evolved. The sound and story of Miles Davis enchanted me, and Kind of Blue, his masterpiece first released in 1959, was a favourite. I love the fact that throughout his career, from the 1940s to the 1990s, he refused to be bound by tradition or the expectation of others. 'When you're creating your own shit, man, even the sky ain't the limit,' is one Davis quote that strikes a chord with me.

Miles Davis was a leader. He was also a complex character, flawed for sure, but judged purely as a musician and on the impact he had on the people he played with, he was definitely one of the greats. Early in his career, he played with Charlie Parker, the jazz saxophonist and composer regarded by most jazz historians as one of the most influential of all musicians. As the story goes, Davis was really nervous. He couldn't believe he was playing in front of Charlie Parker, and he missed a few notes, which annoyed him. He thought he'd let himself down. But later Parker kindly explained to him, 'If you are not missing notes, you are not trying.' Parker's attitude was that he would rather play with someone who makes a few mistakes and learned from them, than with someone who doesn't really test themselves and is happy to stay at the same level. Later, Davis would advise, 'Do not fear mistakes. There are none.'

Davis was always improvising. He might play twelve live shows on consecutive nights and each would be different, depending on where his mood and creative spirit took him. He wanted others in his group to share his bravado and to respond to criticism and praise as he did: by working and testing the boundaries even harder. Davis had a way of just empowering the people playing with him. At the same time, he was often criticised, especially by those who feared innovation. But it never worried him what others thought, he just kept challenging himself and the people he worked with. I like that.

Herbie Hancock, the great jazz pianist and composer, played in Davis' band for five years, and later described Davis as his 'mentor'. He said, 'Miles told us that he paid us to search for new things, to explore territory, to explore new territory, not to rest on your laurels, not to just stay in the comfort zone.' This philosophy fits with my approach to life and to rugby. Hancock was on a tour of Australia a few years ago, when he described Davis' philosophy to rehearsing: Every time I practice, I aim to become better. *He believed that if he didn't do so then he was wasting his time and he was wasting his band members' time.*

21

OLD MAN RIVER

2005–2007

'I can't see myself playing past age thirty. I don't think my body will hold up. I have been lucky considering we are playing high-intensity football from the end of February through to late November. That's longer than the past and it will affect my longevity.'

GEORGE GREGAN, SEPTEMBER 1997

When I first made the Wallabies team, there were some crusty old forwards who used to sit in the corner and make a mockery of my lotion packs. At one stage, Toutai Kefu called me 'Nivea'. But in my last season, thirteen years after my Test debut, I'd look at all the toiletry bags in the Wallabies dressing room and I'd think, *I'm like a mud-caked cowboy out of the Wild West compared to these guys.* They had cosmetics for their hair and eyes, cooling gel moisturisers, hair-restoring shampoos . . .

Things change. When I announced I was going to play on after the 2003 World Cup, I only committed to one more year, because I wanted to see how I'd feel once the grind of the season kicked in. My attitude never changed, I took it one winter at a time, but deep down I hoped to make it to the 2007 World Cup in France. Getting there involved two main considerations: I needed to continue to enjoy the game, and I needed to keep believing I could improve as a player. If those things happened, then I was sure I would still be worthy of my place in the side. As it turned out, my level of enjoyment never dropped, and I do think I kept improving, in a number of ways.

One related to my defence. We changed the way I defended at the Brumbies, which flowed through to the Wallabies. I became more aggressive – not in a 'punchy' sense, but in terms of leading the defensive line forward, almost like a rugby league 'up and in' style, to meet the attacker on his side of the ruck. I had the job of deciding when we attacked in this way, and then led the assault, which I found stimulating. New Wallabies assistant coaches, such as skills coach Scotty Wisemantel and backs coach Scott Johnson, were outstanding at working on the individual skills of players, and I benefited as much as anyone. My son, Max, had started to pay attention to my play from about 2004 on, and he was into me for not scoring enough tries, but my support play improved and I did get over the line. I also worked on my kicking game with my skills coaches at all levels. Finally, I was also improving in all aspects of my fitness, such as aerobic capacity, speed, strength and flexibility. At the start of 2007, after I missed the Wallabies' European tour, I was probably in the best shape of my life. But I needed to be, as the game keeps getting faster and harder every year.

I enjoyed working with the young players. Until he signed with the Western Force Super 14 team for the 2007 season, Matt Giteau was my training partner at the Brumbies, and he was always pushing me, especially during the pre-season. We had our targets and we would be on each other's backs to make sure we didn't miss them. He might have called me 'Old Man River', but we kept each other honest during those sessions. He would beat me in the one-off sprints, but when we went to repeat sprints, things balanced out. To me, the fittest players are the ones who can complete an intense effort, and then recover quickly and do it again . . . and again.

In my fourteen seasons of Test rugby, I only played under five coaches: Bob Dwyer (1994–95), Greg Smith (1996–97), Rod Macqueen (1997–2001), Eddie Jones (2001–2005) and John Connolly (2006–07). In the Super 12/Super 14, I had four coaches: Macqueen (1996–97), Jones (1998–2001), David Nucifora (2002–2004) and Laurie Fisher (2005–2007). All up, over 139 Tests for Australia and 136 matches for the Brumbies, I only worked with seven coaches.

Laurie came through the Canberra rugby system, as a hooker and then coach, before joining the Brumbies as a part-time consultant in 2003 after Andrew Blades departed. A Canberra man from head to toe, his trademark is his beard and long grey hair, which flops well past his shoulders and sets him well apart from just about every other senior rugby coach in the world. As had been the case in 2002, I was on the panel that selected the new coach in 2005 – this time with Stephen Larkham, Stirling Mortlock, Bill Young and Rob Clarke – and when Laurie came in saying he would bring the new ideas and intellectual leadership that we felt had been lacking, I thought he was the right man to move us forward. And I think, to a large degree, he managed that, even if it wasn't quite reflected on the competition ladder.

In 2005, he was beaten by injuries, with not just me but also Larkham, Stirlo and Gits missing large chunks of the season, and we ended up fifth. Nine players made their Super 12 debut that year. It was the same result in the following two years, as both times we finished one win out of the semis. Given that there had been a major turnover of players, with a number of founding members departing, you could argue that we did okay, though in the back of my mind was a nagging thought that the old Brumbies would have found a way to do it, to get over the line, to find that extra victory that would have earned a finals appearance. If that's true, the only people who can get that culture back are the players – that had always been the Brumbies way.

Of the three years from 2005 to 2007, 2006's result was the most disappointing. For me, the season ended early when I was suspended for a week after I messed up a tackle against Otago and was charged with making a spear tackle. I didn't mean to tip their winger, Richard Kahui, the way I did, and he made it worse for himself because he panicked while he was in the air. I accepted the punishment as the tackle was dangerous, and it looked terrible. But I didn't drive him into the ground and my disciplinary record over thirteen years of rugby showed it was not in my nature.

The match I missed was our last one of the year, as it turned out, against the Crusaders in Christchurch. We only needed to earn a bonus point to qualify fourth, but we came up with nothing. The mistake we made was to go into the game thinking that all we needed was that bonus point. The focus was on getting that one point instead of getting ourselves right and doing the little things well, which would lead to a good performance and outcome. They finished us off in the championship minutes, which was typical of them. It was the only time all season we were out of the four.

My first conversation with John 'Knuckles' Connolly after he was appointed Wallabies coach in 2006 was a case of going from one end of the spectrum to the other. Compared to Eddie Jones, Knuckles was really relaxed. He didn't turn up to team meetings with an assortment of folders under his arm, preferring to rely on his very good rugby memory. His football philosophy was uncomplicated, always has been, but he was smart enough to surround himself with good coaches who added a lot of the detail.

One of the first things he did was show me some footage of Brett Sheehan, who had played some games at halfback for the Queensland Reds in 2005 before linking up with the Waratahs for the new season. On the screen, Brett was making some breaks around the edge of the ruck, and I quickly learned that the new Wallabies coach was very keen for me to do the same.

'That's fine,' I said. By the end of the 2005 tour, I felt that because we were running all our plays off the fly-half or the No. 12, I had no opportunity to run. 'But a halfback has to have some options. If a No. 9 is constantly going one out, he'll eventually get belted.'

'You'll get that support,' Knuckles promised. He was true to his word.

The footage of Brett was from early in the 2006 Super 14 season, when he was usually coming on late in games, to replace Waratahs captain Chris Whitaker. There was no doubt that Brett was backing himself around the edge of the ruck, but every move he made on that film was the same and he was a relatively unknown entity in the competition. 'Knuckles, all it will take is one or two games of his doing that,' I mentioned, 'and opposition coaches will be on to him.'

At the Brumbies, under Matt O'Connor's watchful eye, I had been attacking effectively, so the new Wallabies coach's plans for me, or whoever played halfback, were hardly a turn-off. Scott Johnson was also a strong supporter. 'What's all this rubbish about you not running the ball?' he argued when we gathered at the start of the 2006 international season. He produced some stats from the Super 14 competition (the old Super 12 having been expanded with the inclusion of two new teams – the Western Force from Western Australia and the Cheetahs from South Africa), which showed I'd made more line breaks than any other Australian No. 9, and then later in the year showed me some more, which proved that I was running more often for the Wallabies than I had in the previous couple of years. The new coaches had challenged me to adapt my game to their tactics, and I felt I had responded positively.

Not that I needed statistics to tell me that. Producing stats on any number of items that might or might not indicate why a team is winning or losing has become a bit of an industry across all football codes, a practice which, if it's not handled appropriately, could be dangerous. It irritates me whenever someone appears to put their personal figures ahead of the team's needs, and it was equally aggravating when stats were twisted to suit a particular agenda. As an example, a player can make a break and all he has to do is draw the fullback and pass to the man outside and it's a try. Or he can take the tackle and his team gets another phase, but nothing eventuates from the subsequent play. According to the stats, he's made a line break and been responsible for delivering quick ball at the breakdown, but to his team-mates it's a selfish play.

At one of the first meetings I had with the coaches in 2007 I was told I needed to be 'a little bit more selfish' when it came to my running game. I knew what they meant, but I couldn't help thinking, *I hope they are not telling too many people to be more selfish*. That's cancer in a rugby team. Selflessness beats selfishness just about every time.

I once heard Phil Gould, the rugby league coach and commentator, offer another example of a flaw in football stats. Player A has the ball, player B runs a good line which opens up a hole in the defence, and the pass goes to player C, who runs into the space created by player B. The stats only give credit to the man giving the pass and the man scoring the try, not the guy who ran a great, unselfish line. Another great one is the charge down. How many do you see in a game? But often it can be *your* job to run 15 or 20 metres, and maybe you don't quite get there, but the pressure you put on the kicker leads to a shank that gives your team excellent field position. Again, the stats won't measure your effort, but your team-mates will know and the coaches should. There are so many things in rugby that occur off the ball that can have a huge impact on the result. When I was asked, on my retirement from international football, how would you like to be remembered, I said, 'As someone who wanted to be the hardest-working player off the ball.'

Three days out from a Test, Knuckles was keen for us to train the way we were going to play. Unfortunately, the first time we tried this, before his first Test as Wallabies coach, against England in Sydney, we weren't too flash, and as we prepared to finish up Knuckles said he wanted us to come back the following day to try to get it right. It had been a long session, reflecting the fact that the players and coaches were still getting to know each other. 'Knuckles,' I said, 'I don't think that would be right. The guys need time to recover from that run. That rest two days before a Test match is really important.'

The coach was non-committal, but I pushed the point. 'Why

don't we go another fifteen or twenty minutes now?' I think he was glad we did it that way. Not surprisingly, he was actually very nervous, as it was his first Test match, and he needed time to settle in.

Knuckles developed the concept of the squad rotating from match to match. I knew, even though I was captain, that I was only going to start two of the first three Tests of the season, and as it turned out I missed the game against England in Melbourne. I had no problem with this concept; I could see positives and negatives, and the fact that I remember it as a good week – without the normal commitments as a captain or starting player – suggests that the break in a year that, like any other, included the Super 14, the Tests in Australia against European teams, the Tri Nations and a European tour, wasn't a bad thing. A different week in the middle of a long year was, in its own way, a refreshing change.

All up, Australia played thirteen Tests in 2006, all against high-class opposition. Afterwards, John Connolly said he made a mistake playing George Smith in six Tests straight, and it was obvious that rotation was going to play an even bigger role in the World Cup year.

For the coach, though, there was no such break. Big games take a lot out of everyone involved: emotionally, physically and mentally. We played really well against the All Blacks in Brisbane, but came up just short, 13–9. The following week we played South Africa in Sydney in a pretty diabolical game, which we ended up winning by two points three weeks after we'd thrashed them 49–0 in Brisbane. We went into half-time in the Sydney game leading 10–0, the coach seemed happy with the way things were going, but his strategy for the second half was stunningly simple: kick it, kick it, kick it. It was a really conservative approach at a time when I thought we needed to get more aggressive, and it went against the nature of an Australian team to constantly boot the ball away. But

With my son, Max, during Camp Wallaby at Coffs Harbour, 2002.

A sensational late penalty from Matt Burke helped us sneak home against the All Blacks, 16–14, in Sydney in 2002 and retain the Bledisloe Cup.

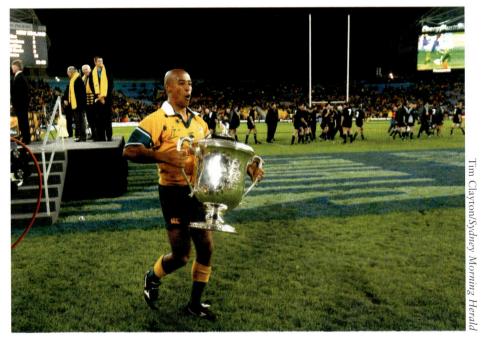

Holding the Bledisloe Cup following our victory in Sydney, 2002. Sadly Australia hasn't won the cup since.

Sharing a laugh with Wallabies coach Eddie Jones in 2003 at a team photo session.

Tim Clayton/Sydney Morning Herald

Ireland was a tough opponent in our 2003 World Cup pool match. Keith Wood won this collision, but at least Australia won the game.

Tim Clayton/Sydney Morning Herald

With seconds left on the clock, Stephen Larkham and I can do nothing to stop Jonny Wilkinson booting home a field goal to win the 2003 World Cup final for England.

Congratulating the English captain
Martin Johnson following the 2003
World Cup final.

Despite our loss in the 2003 World Cup
final, my son, Max, cheers me up.

Tackling Aaron Mauger on the way to a Brumbies victory in the Super 12 final
against the Crusaders, May 2004.

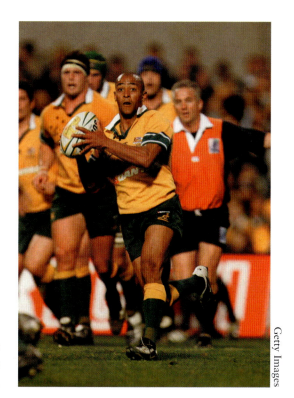

A milestone. My 100th Test came playing against the Springboks in Perth, 2004.

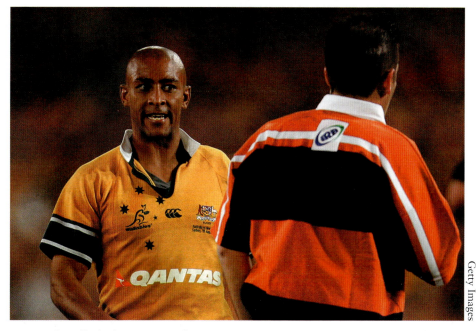

During the All Blacks Test in Sydney, 2004, just getting my point across to referee Jonathan Kaplan! Apparently this is the famous death stare, which I inherited from my mum.

Facing down the haka in Sydney, 2004. Seeing this extraordinary ritual close-up is an amazing experience.

Ali Williams stands nearby while I hug Matt Burke after our victory over the All Blacks in Sydney, 2004. It was a terrific way to farewell a great mate.

Clyde Rathbone (left), Matt Burke (right) and I celebrate after beating the All Blacks in Sydney, 2004.

With Erica and Max at the Australian PGA Championship Pro-Am in Coolum, 2004.

Tana Umaga and I try to keep warm while training for the IRB's North versus South Rugby Aid match in 2005. It snowed all week!

Coming off second best in a collision with my NSW rival and Wallabies team-mate Chris Whitaker. I broke my leg, but losing to the Waratahs for the first and only time at home hurt more.

In 2005 I was named in the Wallabies Team of the Decade, alongside such great players as (left to right) John Eales, Richard Harry, Andrew Blades, Jason Little, Phil Kearns and George Smith.

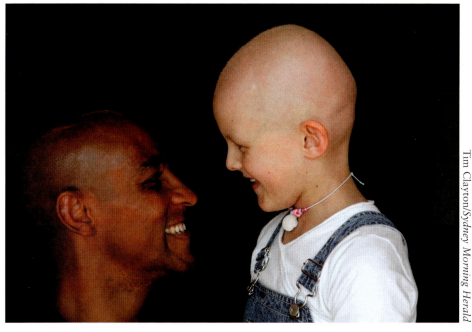

Katie Power, the youngest ambassador of the George Gregan Foundation, has the most amazing smile I've ever seen.

Celebrating New Year's Eve 2005 with our friends Rob Sitch (left), Jane Kennedy (centre), Pat Rafter (back) and Lara Rafter (right) and all our kids.

Getty Images

Scoring a try against Ireland at Subiaco in Perth – my happiest hunting ground in terms of getting over the paint, 2006.

Talking with Wallabies coach John Connolly during the captain's run at Eden Park in 2006, the day before an All Blacks Test.

Thanking the crowd after my last Test on home soil, in Sydney, 2007.

After winning our last Test match in Australia, against South Africa in Sydney, Stephen Larkham and I lead the singing of the national anthem in our change rooms after the match, 2007.

Matt Giteau makes a nuisance of himself as I try to keep a straight face while at a photo shoot for the World Cup, August 2007.

Getty Images

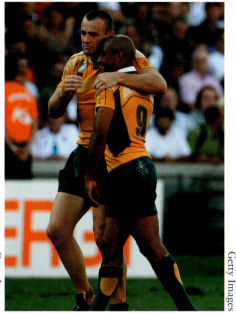

Getty Images

Tackling Andy Gomarsall of England during the quarter-final of the 2007 World Cup.

Heartbreak. Chris Latham and I console each other after our loss in the 2007 World Cup quarter-final.

The day after I retired following Australia's exit from the 2007 World Cup, my son, Max, runs with the game ball.

Sam Neill and I find the best way to see the countryside of Champagne, France, October 2007.

Training with my Toulon team-mates, including Anton Oliver, Tusi Pisi and Orene Ai'i, in December 2007.

Left to right: Andrew Mehrtens, Justin Marshall, Benoit Gouez (Moët & Chandon's chef de cave) me, Dan Luger and Anton Oliver enjoying a tour of Moët's cellar, 2008.

Celebrating Toulon's Pro D2 championship in 2008 with Victor Matfield (left) and Andrew Mehrtens (right).

Partying in St Tropez for Gunnar Sachs birthday with (left to right) Andrew Mehrtens, Tarik Al Said, Ed Sellar, Jean-Michel Hueni, Gunnar Sachs (kneeling), Pat Rafter, Michael Brosnan, Damien Hill, Damien Smith, Dan Luger and Frank Ingraham, 2008.

With my wonderful family (left to right): Charlie, Erica, Jazz, Max and me, St Tropez, 2008.

in the middle of a long season, at half-time in our seventh Test in nine weeks, the coach seemed drained.

I made sure we followed Knuckles' instructions in the second half, but later I sat down with him and put my view. I didn't think it was the right message – to me, it showed a lack of faith in the players. He countered by saying that the boys were weary after all the football they'd been playing, but I argued that if the tactics had been more positive we would have risen above that tiredness. A coach's faith in his men can be inspirational. Yet John had the ultimate counter – we won the game, and we both knew that at that stage of the four-year cycle between World Cups, the win/loss statistic was important, if only to keep the wolves in the media pack at bay. He had seen his predecessor sacked because he lost eight times in nine games. Yet the feeling in the dressing room after the game was downbeat. We hadn't played well, and South Africa, coming off such a thumping the previous time we'd met, had taken more out of the game than we had.

If I was slightly frustrated by Knuckles' conservative nature, I was being won over by his loyalty, his passion for the game, and the manner in which he let his assistants do their job. There wasn't that sense within the squad that we were groundbreakers, as there had been with Rod and Eddie, that we were on some great adventure, but the mood was good and progress was being made. New Zealand's Richie McCaw had played unbelievably well in Brisbane, when the All Blacks beat us in that tight Test match, but for me the lasting memory will be an example of how we developed as a unit. Scott Johnson was into us after the game over a key moment when Stirling Mortlock made a line break and passed outside to his winger, Mark Gerrard. A try looked certain, until McCaw – who seemed to be all over the field that night – not only made the tackle but also turned Mark over and regained possession in the maul. Scotty conceded it was a brilliant bit of football on McCaw's part, but felt there was a lesson for us in terms of backing up the man who made the break. Where was the support on the inside? A year later, at the MCG, Stirlo made another break against the All Blacks, and this time there were four guys queuing up to take the inside pass. Scott Staniforth scored under the posts and we won by five points. We'd lost by four in Brisbane.

When I had that first discussion with Knuckles after he got the Wallabies coaching job, I said that if I was going to be at my best in 2007 I'd need to miss the end-of-season tour, so I could enjoy a good block of pre-season training. He was okay with that, provided I made myself available to join the team if circumstances, such as a bad run with injuries, demanded it. Ironically, by late July I had damaged the area around my shoulder and neck to a point where I knew I wouldn't have been able to tour anyway. As had been the case in 2000, I needed to let the aggravated nerve regenerate.

Another thing we had discussed at that first meeting was the captaincy. I was given no guarantees; nor did I seek any. I knew as well as anybody that no player should be guaranteed his place in the side, let alone a leadership position. In June 2007, after Stirling Mortlock had captained the side to the UK and Italy, winning three Tests out of four, Knuckles opted to make Stirlo and Phil Waugh co-captains, a concept which at the time I wasn't sure about and now I think was probably the wrong call. Please don't interpret this as a complaint from me about losing the job or even the slightest knock on either man – they are both terrific leaders and good men. But the dual-captaincy method gave an impression of indecisiveness, that maybe neither man was quite capable of doing the job on his own, which was not true. I know the co-captains model has worked with some teams, such as the

Australian women's hockey team and the Sydney Swans in the AFL, but my view is that you need a rare team dynamic for it to be a superior model to having just one leader. In the Wallabies set-up, the captain plays a major role in planning, and in putting in place a number of enterprises relating to tactics and team development. I think we lost a bit of that with the co-captains idea – not because the guys weren't capable, but because it just wasn't feasible to do such things within this framework.

Probably the most frustrating aspect of losing the captaincy was that Knuckles refused to rule out the possibility of me being returned to the job for the 2007 World Cup. It was as if he was hedging his bets at a time when he needed to make the tough call. It wasn't fair on the new co-captains to have this conjecture hanging around, and it wouldn't have been fair on me if they had called me back because it would have been equivalent to saying, *We tried everything else, it didn't work, are you interested*?

Despite this, through the early weeks of the Tri Nations stories began to circulate that I was about to be offered the captaincy for the World Cup. I don't know where the stories came from, and I wouldn't have taken the job if they'd offered it to me. Thankfully, the good win over the All Blacks in Melbourne, with Stirlo leading the way, put an end to the speculation. He was the World Cup captain, and Waughy and I were named as his deputies.

Losing the captaincy was a funny thing. I think people pre-sumed I'd be bitter but for me it was more of a blessing, in that I was now free of a number of off-field commitments. I knew I wouldn't be captain forever, and to have led the Wallabies in more than fifty Tests was a privilege I had not expected or dreamed of when I was a boy, so it would have been very silly to feel hard done by. I think the only thing I didn't enjoy was the occasional feeling that some guys were happy to bow to my opinions as if

I was some kind of wise 'elder' within the group. At the first team meeting we had with the new leadership group, after Stirlo and Waughy had spoken, one of them looked my way and asked, 'George, what do you think?' It was as if he needed my approval. All I could do was say I backed what they had already said, and then later reiterate, 'Mate, the boys are following you now, so it's important that you lead with conviction. I'm behind you. If I think I can guide you, I'll talk to you privately.'

I had been told at the beginning of 2007 that I wouldn't be in the starting XV for the early Tests. I felt I'd demonstrated in the Super 14 that I was the best performing halfback in Australia, but I was okay with having to prove myself. Knuckles explained that I'd probably only start one of the three Tests before the Tri Nations, with Gits (who'd played halfback on the European tour) wearing the No. 9 in the other two, and then they'd be a lot closer to determining what was going to be their top side going into the World Cup. As it turned out, this probably worked to my advantage, because the team didn't play well against Wales and I was back in the team for the Test against Fiji in Perth and the opening match of our Tri Nations campaign, against South Africa in Cape Town.

What I loved being able to do during this process was complete the promise I'd made to myself back in 1994, when I'd first made the Wallabies starting XV and the player I'd replaced, Peter Slattery, had been so good to me. I was determined to do for Gits what Slats had done for me: kicking and passing drills, coffee breaks to talk about the role, anything I could do. I loved doing it and it was good for me. And when I got on the field, I just went out and played. In 2006, my former Brumbies team-mate Peter Ryan had said to me, 'You know, mate, when you get to our age, it's automatic. You know what to do. You are not stressed about it; you just go out and do it.' Provided a senior player's still got his motivation, Peter is absolutely right.

*

I played right through the Tri Nations, the last game of which was my final game in New Zealand.

To me, the All Blacks are New Zealand. They are fiercely proud men who love their jumper and will do anything they can to represent it well. They are fully aware of the great tradition, built up over more than one hundred years, which they are required to uphold. The standards set for them are high, yet often they reach them. Occasionally during my career, when gladiators such as Tana Umaga and Zinzan Brooke were at their peak, they exceeded them. I never played against a bad All Blacks team.

As I prepared for this last game, I stopped to think about the haka, how – unless we met at the World Cup – I'd never again get a close-up view of this extraordinary ritual. The most memorable one for me was the first one, back in 1994, because of the sense of expectation. I was so eager to see it, to feel the adrenalin it exudes, and all around the Sydney Football Stadium the mood was the same. It lived up to the hype I'd given it, and the place was buzzing.

Aussie players have different views on how they deal with the haka. Some guys like to engage the All Blacks, eyeball to eyeball; others are more relaxed, thinking, *Okay, stand back, just let 'em do it*. I was one of those players. Greg Smith was a bit obsessed by the haka when he was Wallabies coach, and told us to ignore it, but that rebounded spectacularly when the All Blacks, affronted by the insult, promptly belted us in Wellington in 1996, winning 43–6. Of course, you should respect the haka. Through it, All Blacks players are demonstrating the passion they have for their country and pride in their heritage, and the intensity on the faces of the champions such as Zinzan Brooke, Tana Umaga, Taine Randell and Carl Hayman, who led hakas in Tests I played, reflected this. They are laying down the gauntlet.

I learned a lot from the All Blacks. More than anything, they taught me the value of intensity, provided you are in control of it, and of having trust in your skills. Without these things, we couldn't compete with them. It was as if they were saying, 'Come, join us in battle,' and if we didn't, we'd be blown away.

I've always felt that one way to judge a truly great player is to see how they deal with the big moments, and these often came against New Zealand outfits. I'll never forget the way George Smith played open side for the Brumbies in 2000, especially in the last regular-season match in Christchurch against the Crusaders, when we were playing for home-ground advantage in the semi-finals. That's a tough environment, playing at Jade Stadium, and the New Zealanders belted him, but he just shook it all off, kept making his tackles, kept bouncing back to his feet. Near the end, when a try would change the outcome, he earned a big turnover, got the ball back to me, we cleared our line, and he was still in the game, totally unruffled, jogging to the lineout, as if he was saying, *You've thrown your best at me, what happens next?* That's when I knew for sure he was the next superstar of Australian rugby.

There is never any fanfare about Georgie Smith, a reason why the tough All Blacks forwards admire him so much. He just loves his team, loves his family and will do anything for either. The quintessential team man, we nicknamed him 'camp dog', largely on Justin Harrison's urging, because Goog said Georgie's dread-locks reminded him of the mangy dogs he'd seen when he was growing up in the Northern Territory, especially when a strange streak of red appeared in the dreads. He was also tagged 'Jorge' (Spanish for George, pronounced 'Haw-hey') by David Giffin, because when he first came into the side someone would shout out 'George' and he and I would both turn around.

After the Brumbies won the Super 12 in 2001 we did a lap of honour. I remember saying to him, 'Sorry, Georgie, I know at times I ride you hard, but I know how good you are and I want you to go all the way in this game.' Since then, he has been amazing, but my sights for him were so high I'm not sure if he has got there yet. But he will.

It would have been good to win my last Test in New Zealand, but it wasn't to be. We led after half an hour, but Dan Carter kicked seven penalties and we went down 26–12 on a wet, cold night. This result meant I never played in a winning Wallabies side at Eden Park.

A lot of friends had come over for the occasion, but of all the quiet drinks and reminiscences, the one that stood out most for me came after the Test, when I was in the bar at the hotel where Erica was staying, the two of us enjoying a nice Central Otago pinot. Who should I see walking towards the exit but my old mate Robin Brooke, Zinzan's younger brother and an outstanding forward in his own right. There had always been a bit of shit between Robin and me on the field, but off it we were good mates – the way it should be.

Nine seasons earlier, the Auckland Blues, winners of the first two Super 12 titles, had beaten New South Wales in a pre-season trial at the Hyatt Regency in Coolum, and after that game Robin had been into Andrew Blades: 'The reason why Australia never beats the All Blacks is because we've beaten you before you go out,' he began. 'We've got more skill than you because we've grown up playing rugby in the streets. I bet you a night out that you won't beat us this year.'

When the Wallabies first got together at Caloundra, Bladesy was still fuming. 'These blokes are good,' he muttered. 'But they're not *that* good.'

That year we beat the All Blacks in all three Tests, and the accuracy of Bladesy's telling of the story was confirmed when I caught up with Robin for a beer after the second Test, Christchurch. 'Obviously, you're buying,' I said, and he laughed because he knew exactly what I meant. It was the start of a tradition. Every year, if we ever caught up, the result of the Test determined who paid for the drinks.

In 2007, when we bumped into him, I convinced him not to go home, to stay a little longer. Then I said, 'Mate, it was my last Test. I reckon you should pay for this one!'

For a second he looked like a lock who had just been chipped by a halfback. But then, the good fella that he is, he went and got another bottle. I enjoyed that. He's a good man.

22

THE CHANCE
TO WIN

2007–2008

'*I remember my first Australian team. It was at the Hong Kong Sevens and there were guys like Tim Horan, Jason Little, David Campese and David Wilson. What they promoted was positive reinforcement and self-belief.*'

GEORGE GREGAN, MAY 2007

My long last season – which began with the Brumbies' opening Super 12 game in Hamilton in the first week of February 2007 and ended in France in June 2008 – was a beauty, almost all of it totally enjoyable. I relished the pressure of trying to go out on a high, and spent 2007 ticking off boxes: last game against Queensland (a 6–3 win on 17 February); last Super 14 game in South Africa (14–9 over the Lions in Johannesburg on 31 March); last game against NSW (a 36–10 victory in Canberra on 8 April); last game in Canberra (15–6 defeat of the Crusaders on 28 April); last Super 14 game (29–10 over the Highlanders in Dunedin on 5 May); last Test in Brisbane (31–0 over Wales on 2 June); last Test in Perth (49–0 over Fiji on 9 June); last Test in South Africa (a 22–19 loss at Cape Town on 16 June); last Test in Melbourne (a 20–15 defeat of the All Blacks on 30 June); last Test in Sydney (25–17 over South Africa on 7 July); last Test in New Zealand (a 26–12 defeat in Auckland on 21 July). Then it was off to France for the World Cup.

All the time, I looked forward. I've been doing that all my sporting life. As I caught sight of the finish line, I began to get genuinely excited about breaking the tape and moving on. I understand that the playing-rugby part of life has been fantastic, and that many of my experiences will help me during the next stage of life, but that never caused me to stop and pine for extra time, wishing that somehow I could go back and do all the good bits again.

I know now that retiring is a personal thing. From watching guys such as Brendan Cannon and Bill Young, who had to retire early because of injury, I knew that my playing career could end at any time, so in my mind I had prepared for it even when my body was telling me there were still more miles in the tank. I have been criticised for being too cool after a defeat and refusing to dwell on the past, but only by people who interpreted my demeanour after a game as meaning I wasn't worried about the misplays that I or the team might have made. I always try to learn from mistakes, in football and in life. With rugby, this process happened every week, usually starting on the Monday after the game, sometimes sooner. A long-haul flight back from South Africa, for example, might have been the time to study the DVD on the laptop. This was a task I never shirked, always found time for, and by doing it I discovered that even on my poorest days I was able to do something positive, and also that I never played a game that I was totally over the moon about – not from an individual perspective. I'd still say, 'Yeah, that's good, but . . .'

You need the buts!

My last game at home for the Brumbies was the second-last round game, against the Crusaders. It was also the final appearance in Canberra for Stephen Larkham and Jeremy Paul. There was a big build-up in the media before the game, but we just wanted to go out there with our kids, acknowledge the crowd briefly, and then play. Any major festivities could wait until after full-time, when, hopefully, we would have made a good night of it by getting the win. There was still a chance we could make the Super 14 top four, if other results went our way, but even if that hadn't been the case, the result was still paramount. Max was turning six and loving it, walking out there with me in front of the crowd, and Stephen's daughter and Jeremy's daughter were also having a great time. There was time to have a quick look at the newly renamed Gregan/Larkham Stand on the eastern side of Canberra Stadium, and then we played and the game evolved into another Brumbies–Crusaders classic.

For me, Canberra will always be a special place. I have had the joy of watching the affinity grow between the city and its Brumbies, and the Brumbies and the city. It's a special place to play rugby. After the game, there was an on-field presentation (for which every member of the Crusaders stayed on the field – what a class act!) and then the three of us did a lap of the ground, which was scheduled to take fifteen minutes, but went for closer to an hour and a half. So many people stayed to say goodbye, we missed the entire recovery session. No one seemed to mind, though, and I was, as ever, grateful for the support.

I really enjoyed the fact that I was able to share this celebration with two great players in Jeremy and Stevie.

For a hooker, Jeremy scored an amazing amount of tries, largely because he had a sixth sense that told him where an attacking move would eventually lead. We called it 'fat man's alley', the way he'd follow the play down a lane near the middle of the field and the ball would eventually come that way, usually in the manner of the last pass of a try-scoring movement. If that was easy, everyone would do it. Watch videos of Brumbies and Wallabies games and you'd see him in the background, trailing the play, often with his hand in the air. It was uncanny.

On a wide range of subjects, Jeremy would get his words mixed up while sounding like he was an expert. One year, a few players (Jeremy, Rod Kafer and Justin Harrison) invested in a bar in the Canberra suburb of Kingston. It needed some extensive renovations before it could open, and during this process, they met up at a nearby cafe for a coffee. Soon, Jeremy was holding court.

'You know, guys,' he said, 'isn't it amazing how a concept from a drawing can come together so quickly?'

'It sure is,' someone replied as the others nodded in agreement.

'They can take the shell of a place and turn it into something completely different,' he continued. 'And once they finish the chiprock it's going to take on a whole new dimension.'

'Did you say "chiprock"?' Kafe interrupted.

'Yeah, when they start chiprocking. From what I know, the chiprockers we're using are the best in the business.'

If it happened once, it would just be an unfortunate slip-up, but it happened all the time, and they were always delivered with such authority. We were always eagerly awaiting the next 'Jeremy Paulism'. Once, in Cape Town, we were at a Japanese restaurant and there was a variety of seafood dishes on offer. The next day,

Jeremy was raving about the Atlantic salmon, Mozambiquan tiger prawns and the 'elephant tuna'.

'What was that?'

'Greegs, it was the best elephant tuna I've ever had.'

I stopped for a second, and then asked slowly, 'Would that, by any chance, be some rare breed of fish related to "yellowfin tuna"?'

When they announced they were naming a grandstand after Stephen Larkham and me, it was an honour and, more significantly, it meant that a combination of two boys who grew up in different parts of Canberra, before joining forces at the Brumbies and then the Wallabies, would be recognised. Although we are very different people and we were very different footballers, our combination on the field worked beautifully, not least because of Stevie's innate feel for the game and his rare ability to adapt whatever a game threw at him. There were so many times when I was lucky he was out there.

At the same time, there were things about him as a footballer that used to drive me mad. He was one of those players who, during pre-season, would be looking for short cuts and ways to 'beat the system'. In games, he would go against a call if he saw a better opportunity, which could be annoying if no one else knew what he was doing. However, I quickly realised that when Stevie backed himself, he was invariably right, and that flair became one of the team's greatest assets.

Originally, in junior rugby, Stevie was a halfback and then when he came into the Brumbies squad in 1996 he played at fullback or outside centre. That's how he became a Wallaby, but Rod Macqueen saw a No. 10 in him, something few others recognised because Stevie was hardly a big communicator. Everyone knows that I'm a massive talker on the field, and my partner didn't like me yapping at him all the time. In fact, I'm sure he didn't like me at all, because I was always on his back, but as I said to him, 'I need you to open your mouth so I can find where you are. That's going to help you. It's going to help everyone.'

Over the next few years, he built a reputation as one of the great Wallaby No. 10s, with a style all his own. He had a remarkable gift for accelerating without anyone noticing, so he ghosted rather than cut past opponents. He was a great defender, which is unusual for most No. 10s, and, of course, he landed *that* field goal – the kick that gave us the lead in extra time of the World Cup semifinal against South Africa at Twickenham in 1999. But I reckon it wasn't until 2002, when Eddie Jones decided that the No. 10 would make a lot of our attacking calls, that he truly came out of his shell on the field. Previously, I had made a lot of those calls, but now that I was captain, Eddie decided Stevie could assist in this department.

His natural reflex was to say no to added responsibility, but we insisted and he became comfortable with the notion of steering the team around the field. By the end of his career he was brilliant at it.

One of his greatest skills was that when receiving any pass, short or long, he could catch and pass at pace. Many can do this with a short pass, but with a long one the majority of players have to catch, reload and then pass. I could also throw the ball further in front of Stevie than others, because of his 'ghostly' pace off the mark. Our understanding became uncanny, and I loved every minute I played with him.

I have the utmost respect for English rugby, and part of that relates to the twinge of arrogance they bring to their game. Through the late 1990s, in the early years of professional rugby, the Southern Hemisphere teams definitely raised the bar when it came to preparation and intensity of performance. The England camp needed an infusion of self-belief and coach Clive Woodward and captain Martin Johnson provided it. At the 2003 World Cup final there was me, the Australian captain and halfback, 173 centimetres short and 80 kilograms, standing next to Johnson, who is about 2 metres tall and around 125 kilos. But rather than feeling like David to Johnson's Goliath, I felt a strong affinity with the big man.

We went about our business in a similar way. Martin Johnson is a winner, revered at his club, the highly successful Leicester, and with Woodward and their kicking genius, Jonny Wilkinson, he became the face of England's World Cup victory. It is may be true that not everyone likes him, at least they don't like his rugby persona, but he never seemed to care what people thought of him, if gaining that affection meant compromising his beliefs and resolve. There is no bullshit about him.

The year before the 2003 World Cup, after we lost by a point to the Poms at Twickenham, Martin Johnson and I met in mid-pitch after the game, had a quick handshake and hug, and then stopped for a brief chat, which started with him saying, 'I'm getting too old for this,' in reference to the thrilling finish.

I laughed. 'Me too,' I said, continuing, 'I'll see you next year in Sydney, mate. It'll be good.'

And this time he didn't laugh. 'I don't know, mate,' he said seriously.

'What d'ya mean? They still need you out here. You're an important part of the team.'

'I'll have to wait and see,' he said, hinting that his team's management might not have valued him quite as highly as he would have liked.

'If they don't pick you,' I told him straight, 'we will be the happiest team in the world.'

There is an enormous value in experience that should never be underrated. Selectors who persevere with players who have come through the toughest battles, and showed character when it matters, are usually on the right track. Johnson was a spiritual leader of that England team. Losing Wilkinson wouldn't have been as big a setback. Johnson, of course, went on to demonstrate just how important he was during the 2003 World Cup. A great player, he was the best and most influential British forward of my experience.

Going into the 2007 World Cup tournament, I'd likened my mindset to how the great Denver Broncos quarterback John Elway approached his long pursuit of a Super Bowl victory. The Broncos had been beaten in 1987, 1988 and 1990, and then in 1992 found themselves in the AFC Championship game (one win away from the Super Bowl), and Elway was asked if the previous setbacks had discouraged him. 'If I have to go ten times, and get beat ten times, I will. I just want another chance to win it.' That's what I'd pursued, what I wanted to experience again: the *chance* to win. The way we had played in the recent Tests in Cape Town and Melbourne, when we had matched it with the Springboks and then the All Blacks, gave me confidence. I was wary of the French, but our record against them is good, and we had won three of our last four Tests against England, who on paper at least did not look as powerful as before. For me, it had been a long battle to get to the Cup, so I was determined to enjoy the experience, and give it my best shot.

Our campaign began in Portugal, where we trained extremely hard. We were staying in a resort town that was full of Poms trying to get extra sun before winter, so I certainly didn't get to experience any of the true Portugal. Instead, I played a bit of golf, mostly with Gits and Matt Dunning, and worked well with the coaches. Our first game was against Japan in Lyon, and we won 91–3. Then we went to Cardiff, where we produced what proved to be our best forty minutes of the tournament. We lost Stevie to injury the night before the game, to be replaced by young Berrick Barnes from Queensland; the transition was seamless, and we scored twenty-five points in the first half as the entire team showed a lot of maturity. In the second, we took the foot off the accelerator, but there was still time for Chris Latham to score an unbelievable try. Thirty metres from his own line, he put in a huge left-footed up-and-under that Wales's Stephen Jones dropped 30 metres out from the home team's line, and Latho grabbed the ball at full speed on the first bounce and careered away. My final Test in Britain was a 32–20 victory.

Chris had done an amazing job to even be at the World Cup, as he had ruptured an anterior cruciate ligament at the start of the year, missed the entire Super 14 season and then made it back for forty minutes of Tri Nations football. He had first played Test football in 1998, but I don't think he felt truly entrenched at the top-level until as late as 2004, when he was the Wallabies' best player on our European tour. In the next two years, however, he established himself as a match-winner in the Joe Roff mould, a guy with that rare ability to score tries that had team-mates, opponents and fans all thinking, *How on earth did he do that?* The most important skills he had developed, in my opinion, was to rise above criticism, and to avoid getting too down on himself if something went wrong. Suddenly, he was a footballer with a rare ability to get the ball to bounce for him. It's amazing what self-belief can do.

I was trying hard not to spend this World Cup in a reminiscing mood, but I couldn't help thinking how Latho took me right back to my early days in senior rugby. I knew how hard he'd worked on his game, because I played with him at Randwick in 1996, when he was a young guy coming through the Colts. He wasn't a natural kicker then, but he put in countless hours and now boasts one of the most powerful and effective kicking games in world rugby. One day at Coogee Oval, Randwick's home ground, Latho was making his first-grade debut and he made a break, but instead of passing to the unmarked man outside him he took the fullback on and the try was lost. His team-mates ripped into him, which I thought was a bit extreme. He had made an error in judgment, but sometimes you have to back yourself. I think I was the only guy to go up to him and say, 'Mate, it's not that bad. You'll get another chance. Learn from it.'

In the following twelve years, we had both learned a great deal. Eight days after the Wales game, we were in Montpellier, taking on Fiji. With Stirlo having damaged a shoulder against the Welsh I was named captain for one last time, and in the thirty-first minute we had a moment that captured part of why I liked being in a leadership role. We were camped in the Fijians' half, sustaining pressure, and they cleared the ball from near their own line. Modern rugby being the way it is, the conventional play was to use the seven-man, drive it forward, wait for the penalty, take three points. Not only is the attacking team thinking this way, so is the defensive team, but I wanted to think outside that square. We'd had three or four cracks with the seven-man earlier in the game and never come up with more than a penalty and now we were 20 metres out from the Fijian line. I looked at our backline, and asked if they wanted a five-man. They sure did. Drew Mitchell scored on the third phase.

We ended up winning 55–12, and then we went to Bordeaux, where we defeated Canada 37–6 in a game I watched from the bench until the seventy-fourth minute. (It's funny, I played in three Tests against the Canadians during my career – at Port Elizabeth during the 1995 World Cup, at Ballymore in Brisbane in 1996, and at Bordeaux – and each time it was as a replacement, for Peter

Slattery, Sam Payne and Sam Cordingley respectively.) We were into the quarter-finals, to play England in Marseille.

Unfortunately, that is where our World Cup ended. We led 10–6 at half-time, but we were down on confidence; we weren't absorbing the pressure the Poms were throwing at us, or exerting any consistent pressure of our own. The effort the boys put in was tremendous and we scored a try just before half-time, but we were scrambling, and in the second half Jonny Wilkinson kicked them to victory.

Afterwards, for me, there were no recriminations. Our preparation had been first-class, and it was hard to find something concrete about which I could say, *If we'd done that, we would have won.* The one thing that nags at me, and it comes back to one of the major lessons I learned during my football life, was that at the half-time break we should have been more positive and specific about what we had to do in the next half. So often during my career, I had seen instances where focus and self-belief won the day, where players kept faith with themselves, their team-mates and the quality of their preparation, and that confidence took them to victory. I felt that we could have been better at this interval in building the faith and confidence within the group.

The margin between the best teams in rugby is often tiny. How often did I see that during my rugby career? Four World Cup games – our losses to England in 1995, 2003 and 2007, our defeat of the Springboks in 1999 – are proof enough. In a sense, a half-time is a microcosm of a season, a career. If you can honestly assess how things are going, learn, be positive, and back yourself, you're a chance to win. How a team uses the half-time break can be enough to turn a loss into a victory, and vice versa. You often hear commentators say, after a team comes back in the second half, 'The coach must have given them a spray at half-time.' From my experience with some great Brumbies and Australian teams, this method never worked. That's because the team was always trying, so how could a gobful improve on that? It's not an easy job, but if someone in the leadership group can press the buttons that gets the team back to adhering to the game plan and believing in themselves again, it's amazing how quickly things can change.

Even in the last five minutes of the quarter-final, I thought we might sneak through, and Stirlo had a difficult penalty shot with time almost up, but in the end the better team won. The final score was 12–10.

Outside the dressing room, a reporter asked me the standard question: 'George, how do you feel?'

I answered in short, concise, often half-sentences . . .

Very disappointed . . . big effort from everyone in the squad . . . take a while . . . hard to describe how we feel at the moment.

Emotionally stripped of any sort of feeling. We'll stay together as a group as Australian teams always do, regroup together and enjoy each other's company, have a few beers. That's the way to get over it.

We started pretty well . . . field position . . . one of those games where we got some momentum, they got some momentum, but we never got our rhythm in the whole game. The try before half-time was the closest to how we wanted to play.

'After fourteen years, what's it like in the room?'

I feel very lucky to have been able to be in the room. I was just saying to the young fella [Max] that it'll be the last time I'll be in the change rooms in the company of such great men and great people. I've enjoyed every minute of it.

The aspect of sport you have to learn is that you have your good times and your bad times, but you share them all with great people.

My life as an ex-Test rugby footballer had begun.

Postscript

2007–2008

When my final super 14 season began, I had no idea that one of the last clubs I'd be playing for before I finished up would be Rugby Club Toulonnais (also known as 'RCT Toulon' or just 'Toulon'), playing in the Rugby Pro D2 competition, the French Second Division. The first direct approach I received came from Tim Lane, the former Australian backs coach, who was coaching there, and it came a week or two after the Brumbies had played the Hurricanes in Wellington on 23 February. As we'd been doing religiously since 2003, I caught up with Tana Umaga after that game and we started talking about his experiences playing in France. It sounded fantastic, and I said so.

Two years before that, during the week of the tsunami game, Tana and I had spoken about the fact that we'd never played in Europe at this time of year, when the weather in many rugby-playing parts of the Northern Hemisphere could be ugly. He claimed he would never come over to play club football north of the equator, but then, after the Super 14 season in 2006, it was announced out of the blue that he was joining Toulon for big money on a short-term deal. The club's wealthy and ambitious owner, Mourad Boudjellal, was keen for the once-great team to return to the French top division, but while Tana made an enormous impact in his seven games, they narrowly missed promotion. 'It was a great life experience,' he told me in Welling-ton. 'I loved it.'

Soon after, I received a text from Tim. 'What are you doing after the World Cup?'

'Retiring,' I replied.

'Would you contemplate playing over here?'

My initial response was a straight 'no', but then I texted back that if I was to consider an offer, it would have to be for immedi-ately after the Cup. I wasn't going to fly back to Australia and then return to France. That was good for them, as the season proper started on 28 October (the World Cup final was scheduled for 20 October). A month after my chat with Tana in Wellington, I signed a contract in Durban. It had happened quickly, but the more I thought about it the better the concept became, for I saw it as potentially a wonderful experience for my young family. In the end, I felt compelled to do it. And it proved to be superb.

In Durban, after the news was announced publicly, Matty O'Connor drew on his experiences playing and coaching overseas to say, 'Mate, you will be finishing your career almost the way you started. It's professional, I know, but all the things that drew you to the game you'll be doing again. It's competitive, but it won't be the same pressure environment as Super 14 and Test-match rugby.'

Three months later, we were in Cape Town, in the middle of a fantastic Test match that was decided by a pair of field goals landed in the final ten minutes by twenty-year-old Francois Steyn. One was a really well-planned drop goal, but the other was quite ridiculous, kicked from 45 metres out and near the sideline. It never looked like missing. Earlier in the game, when it seemed South Africa were getting on top, there was a stanza when our forwards were asked to defend and defend and, not surprisingly, at the end of this phase of play it took them a while to get to their feet. 'Aren't you fit enough?' the Springbok forwards sneered. 'Get up, get on with the game.'

Then the tide turned, we were in the ascendancy, and it was the South African forwards who were staying down. The boys ripped into them, and into the great Victor Matfield especially, but I tried a different tack, saying, 'Hey, don't pick on Victor.' He is a legendary player, one of those great forwards who carries an aura with him around the field, and I saw a chance to reduce the impact of that. 'I'll vouch for you, mate,' I then said to him. 'I know you're a good guy.'

He looked up and gave me a grin. 'And while you're down there having a drink, let's talk about Toulon,' I said. I knew the club was pursuing him. 'Remember how we talked about a tsunami game reunion? We've got an Aussie, we've got some Kiwis, you're the missing link. What do you say? Is it happening?'

Victor gave me this astonished look that said, *We're in the middle of a Test match!* Then he shrugged his shoulders, and clambered to his feet.

'Listen, Victor, we'll do it this way. I know if you don't call at a lineout the ball is going to you. You only call if it's going somewhere else. Before you call or don't call, give me a wink for "yes", shake of the head for "no".'

He gave me a wink. This might have been the first deal of this kind ever sealed during a Test match. Three days later, Victor put pen to paper to make the Toulon arrangement official.

Matty O'Connor was right. There was still pressure when we ran out on the field; everyone expected us to win – given that we had players in our ranks such as Victor, Andrew Mehrtens and Anton Oliver, and we were coached by Tana – and a lot of players were also trying to belt us. But the team was a cosmopolitan one, with players from Argentina, Australia, Georgia, Italy, New Zealand and South Africa, as well as France and Britain, which added to the sense of adventure, and we won many more games than we lost taking out the Pro D2 championship. Our home stadium was located at the business end of Toulon's big and busy port, so it almost felt as if the ground was there first and they built the city around it. And when the team is playing at home, at the compact Stade Mayol (aka 'Mad Mayol'), it *is* a rugby town, and just a little bit crazy. The home support is committed and passionate, and it can be a very intimidating place for an away team to visit. Thirteen or fourteen thousand people make the noise of ten times that number, especially when they roar the song 'Pilou-Pilou', which was created in the 1940s by a club player, Marcel Bodrero. The lyrics envisage the Toulon players as fierce warriors charging down from the Toulon mountains to the coast.

> *Ah! Nous les terribles guerriers du Pilou-Pilou*
> *(Pilou-Pilou!)*
> *Qui descendons de la montagne vers la mer*
> *(Pilou-Pilou!)*
> *Avec nos femmes échevelées allaitant nos enfants*
> *A l'ombre des grands cocotiers blancs*
> *(Pilou-Pilou!)*
> *Nous les terribles guerriers poussons notre terrible cri de*
> *guerre*
> *(AAAARRRGGGGHHHHH!)*
> *J'ai dit NOTRE TERRIBLE CRI DE GUERRE!*
> *(AAAARRRGGGGHHHHH!)*
> *Parce que TOULON*
> *(ROUGE!)*
> *Parce que TOULON*
> *(NOIR!)*

Parce que TOULON
(ROUGE ET NOIR!)

Do a search for 'Pilou-Pilou Toulon' on YouTube and you'll get a feel for how raucous it can be. When Victor ran on to make his debut, with about twenty minutes to go in our game against La Rochelle, I seriously thought the roof of the grandstand would explode, such was the noise. The big man was amazed. I just looked at him, grinned, and said, 'Welcome to Mad Mayol.' Fabian Pelous, the big lock who has won more Test caps for France than any other player, told me that for many years it was considered you hadn't proved your rugby manhood until you'd played well at the Stade Mayol.

We finished the season well on top of the ladder, and the town really went crazy. They blocked off all the streets for the celebration. Mourad Boudjellal's ambition became a reality, and next season Toulon will proudly run on in first division.

In terms of geography, Toulon is a long, long way from Canberra. But in a rugby sense the two cities are the same. The supporters genuinely love RC Toulon, and they get a strong sense of pride and even identity from their team. I treasured my twelve years with the Brumbies. And I'll never forget my one season with Toulon. There was an amazing group of players I was lucky enough to call my team-mates and friends. Victor Matfield said to me after his final game, 'In years to come we will look back on this year as one of the best life experiences.' We were quite a group, getting together for meals often with Victor, Andrew Mehrtens, Anton Oliver, Dan Luger and Tana Umaga and their families. It was special.

I have just signed a contact to play for Suntory Sungoliath in Tokyo, Japan, and I'm looking forward to the season with much excitement. I first went to Japan in 1996, with the Brumbies, and was there again in 2006 with the Prime Minister's XV. I love Japan – the people, the culture, the food. My family and I are looking forward to moving there and I hope to be able to contribute positively to my new team. I also look forward to playing against and spending time with my great old teammate, Toutai Kefu.

GEORGE GREGAN ON MATT BURKE

My first memory of Matthew Burke goes back to the winter of 1990, when St Joseph's College from Sydney came to the ACT to play Marist College Canberra. It was an annual affair between these two schools and one that was looked upon with much anticipation by the Canberra lads – it was a kind of yardstick match for them. I was watching with a few of my Eddies (St Edmund's College) team-mates and we were all in awe of the Joeys' No. 13: Matthew Burke. This was one of the best Joeys teams ever, also featuring Peter Jorgensen (who would represent the Wallabies in 1992), Dave Kelaher (who would be my captain in the Australian under-21s in 1993) and a number of other outstanding schoolboy footballers. But as good as any of the other players looked on the field, none of them stood out like Burkes.

On this day he was kicking goals from everywhere, beating players with his speed and agility, and defending strongly. But the most impressive things were his decision-making and timing. These are what separate the good and very good players from the class ones. Matty was all class.

Burkes had a big influence on me at this time because I saw him as being much like Ricky Stuart, a player with great qualities. In any walk of life you can learn and be inspired by others, but in terms of sport I think it is critical because it gives you a target to aim for.

The first time I actually met Burkes was during the spring of 1992, at an AIS rugby camp, when we hit it off straight away. He was reasonably quiet and unassuming compared to a lot of the guys who attended these camps, which consisted of a lot of physical testing, and lectures from sports-science and sports-medicine gurus, trainers and coaches. In the downtime, all the lads got together and, with drinking alcohol out of the question, videos, games and general chat were high on the agenda. Most of the talk, as it is with any guys of that age, was based around girls, nights out, games of footy and other funny yarns – and then it was back to girls!

It was a great environment in which to meet future team-mates and opponents, a chance to spend time with guys away from rugby and families. For me, this was just the first of a number of AIS camps, and I became very good mates with Burkes and a good friend of his, Scotty 'Mango' Bowen. We really enjoyed each other's company and, importantly for me, they provided plenty of motivation for me when they won their first Australian caps in 1993. On one level, they had me thinking, if they can do it, so can I. But further, once you made the Wallabies, you were no longer eligible for the AIS camps, as their purpose was to propel young players into the national squad. So if I wanted to catch up with Burkes and Mango (in more ways than one), I had to get in the Aussie team myself.

All three of us ended up going to the 1995 World Cup, and then Burkes and I went on to play in another two together, in 1999 and 2003.

Anyway, enough of Burkes the rugby player. As a person, he is loyal, trusting, a caring husband and father, hardworking, extremely competitive and a little obsessive compulsive! I should probably go into the last characteristic. He and his wonderful wife, Kate, would often come around to our house, especially after we had Max, because Matty just loved seeing the little fella while the girls caught up and had a few beverages. During this time, he became attached to the coffee machine we have at our house, which can punch out the same quality of coffee that you get at one of our cafes, but is half the size. The steamer used to froth the milk has a lot of pressure behind it, so it takes a bit of getting used to – if you turn it on too hard, or your technique and feel are poor, then you will either burn the milk or cover yourself in a milk bath! Burkes has experienced both the burn *and* the bath!

This is where his obsessive compulsive disorder kicked in, because on every subsequent trip to our place he brought about four litres of milk with him so he could hone his technique. If the milk was too hot, he would dump it; if there were too many bubbles (too much air), he would dump it; if there was not enough creamy froth minus the bubbles, he would dump it; if the sound and motion of the milk was not right, he would dump it. It was not until the temperature, texture, sound and motion were right that he would present the jug to Erica (I am not going to lie and say it was me) for inspection. It was very funny seeing him behind that coffee machine with an extremely focused look on his face. I can honestly say the only other times you will see that look is on the rugby field or when he is about to drain a putt to beat you in golf!

I could tell a book's worth of stories about his escapades on the golf course and about his uncanny ability to remain a ten handicapper while consistently shooting in the low seventies. I honestly do not know how he lives with himself! We would often play golf on our day off leading into a match during the 1999

World Cup. Matty had come back from his shoulder reconstruction and he was hitting a big draw that he was struggling to control. Well, this was probably the only time I was getting the better of him on the golf course, I knew it was bugging him a little, and contrary to what people may think I was not gloating. Anyway, to lift his spirits, I let him know about a personal stat that I had been keeping on him in regards to his golf and his goal kicking – they were inversely proportional.

In other words, the better he played on the golf course, the worse he kicked and vice versa. To be honest, I wasn't too sure about this long term, but he had been kicking beautifully throughout the tournament, while his golf had been ordinary. After our last round, before the final at Cardiff, I got the points at the beautiful Celtic Manor layout near Newport and immediately predicted a flawless kicking display from the big fella.

History shows that Burkes was kicking them long and straight at Millennium Stadium on the afternoon of 6 November, which for me confirmed the quality of my extensive golf research!

MATT BURKE ON
GEORGE GREGAN

The first time I heard the name 'George Gregan' it had nothing to do with the rugby ball. We were brash twenty-year-olds attending a rugby camp at the AIS, but we were in the indoor football arena playing cricket and it was my turn to bat.

I did fancy myself as being somewhat proficient with the willow in my hands. As I stood in front of the makeshift stumps, I glanced down the pitch to see who would be thundering in. It was a bloke about five-foot-six (I'm probably being generous at that) with an afro that took him to just under six foot. My first thoughts were to ask for the field to be pushed back because I was going to open up the shoulders, but then a call came from behind the stumps: 'This bloke can bowl; he actually chose rugby over cricket.'

Well, what came at me could only be described in cricketing terms as 'chin music'. The ball came so quickly out of a short arm-action that I had no chance of playing any type of shot. From that point, there was instant respect. If this bloke could do that with a tennis ball with some tape around it, how good could he be at rugby? As history tells us, pretty damn good.

One of my earliest memories of GG was when he started making a name for himself and was doing one of his first TV interviews. The television guys like to paint a picture for the viewers, and do this by trying to get as much background material on their subject as they can. At the same time, a young footballer will often say yes to too much, which means he can get himself in situations where he knows he will look silly, but he doesn't have the confidence to say no. When I look back at some of the stuff I said yes to, I can only cringe. George must have hoped this interview would never raise its head again . . .

It took place at his parents' home in Canberra, and included all the usual 'fluffy' stuff. 'How good are you?' . . . 'What's your potential as a rugby player?' . . . 'Are you going to take Nick Farr-Jones's spot in the future?' At all times, modesty reigned.

Then the closing shot: 'Hey, George, why don't we get a shot of you reversing out of the driveway in your car while you're waving at the camera?'

The car was a 1965 Kingswood with bench seats front and back, and a paint job that could only be described as baby-poo colour. (Sorry, but there really is no other way to describe it.) It made for riveting television. Little Georgie boy sat at the wheel, still sporting his afro, and waved goodbye.

By the look of it, it had taken a couple of takes because the end result was some of the most vigorous waving I have ever seen. Talk about hamming it up for the cameras! This overacting obviously had a lasting effect on him, because the best you are going to get out of him in an interview these days is a little raise of the eyebrows.

You will find George at anything that has a competitive element to it. He loves his golf, prides himself on his tennis, talks up his forehand in table tennis and even fancies himself as a goal-kicker. But when it comes to computer games you could say he is a little out of his depth.

A long, long time ago, on a trip to New Zealand with the Australian under-21 team, Daniel Herbert took his PlayStation with him in case of boredom. What he actually provided for the team was one of the most competitive environments ever staged on a tour, where hours were lost in playing one game: Tekken.

The object is to kick the shit out of your opponent. Good, old-fashioned, meaningless stuff. The rules: pick a player and become king of the ring. The better you are, the longer you stay on. GG had a few goes and was whipped every time. What would he do in that situation? Practise, practise and practise some more . . .

The battle commenced. George Gregan versus Rodney Hayes. The two No. 9s going for it. The problem for GG was that he had been set up from the start. While he sat close to the TV to get the best view, Haysie sat behind him and pretended he was playing, but he had actually handed the controls to the far more experienced Herbie, who beat GG every time. Round after round, Gregan hit the floor to the cries of 'One more! One more!' and time after time, Gregan lost, to the point of a nude run being called for, for losing in the worst possible manner.

For days, he believed that his chief adversary had got the better of him. Only later was he told that he had been beaten by the owner of the game.

And there it was. The first time I had seen The Stare. How good is it!

It is a look that says, 'Don't f**k with me.' Perhaps this was the moment that instigated one of the most famous and intimidating looks in rugby. Fortunately, I haven't been on the receiving end of any of these looks, but there are plenty who have. Referees copped the brunt of them!

Now the stare is not just reserved for the rugby field. In fact, my friends, the golf course takes pride of place. Combined with The Sniff, it makes for a potent combination. I can only describe the sniff as a call that says, 'That's right, you know it – how good am I?'

I can recall a game of golf at Terrey Hills in northern Sydney, where GG is a member. He and I were going head to head. George is off five or six. I am off six or seven. (This stuff about me being off ten is a figment of his imagination.) We were both travelling well until the thirteenth, a par four, not too tough, probably a driver and a six iron. GG leaked his second right and recorded a double bogey. Not happy, Jan!

There was absolutely no chat from Old Grumpy Bones as we walked to the next hole: a par five. I blasted one down the middle, and as he took to the tee there was a little smile and a call of 'nice shot'. So sincere. It was then I saw the eyes: the stare. His drive went past mine on the fly. Talk about getting angry! Then came the sniff; like, 'How does that feel?'

There was a little more chat as we approached my ball. A three wood for me, which landed short of the green. Three iron for GG and it's 20 feet from the pin. Stares and sniffs were going in every direction. I chip it dead for a birdie four and GG lines up for a three. He takes his putt and about one foot from the hole gets one of the luckiest 'headers' from a divot that directs it into the back of the cup. Eagle! Thank you, sniff, stare, sniff. He is back on song and ready to pounce.

One of the perks of becoming a Wallaby, aside from playing for your country, is the invitations you get to events outside of rugby. My favourite one involving GG was televised on Channel 10, consisting of a group of top sportsmen from a range of sports competing in a decathlon of sorts. From lifting to running, kayaking to swimming . . . this was where the almighty fell.

When you first glance at George you see a magnificent specimen of a human being. Sculpted body, a true competitor in every sense of the word. On this occasion, the final event, the swim required the athletes to complete a swim–run–swim course. Let's just say that the style was magnificent, true to form. He was just let down by the cadence. GG went off track and did the ultimate no-no, resorting to breast stroke and maybe a few strokes of dog paddle. The other competitors finished, did their interviews, and still had time to form a guard of honour. It was from this performance, I believe, that his cousin, Eric the Eel, gained inspiration to swim the 100-metre freestyle at the 2000 Olympics.

If we are going to continue with things that challenge the Guv, let's move onto dancing. He is possibly the only man of African descent born without the rhythm bone. You might laugh at this, but it is quite true. I have seen him embarrass his family with some of the moves he puts out. It is a genuine two-step with a single back lift of the foot. Quite like a grapevine in aerobics, yet less complicated. Consequently, he rarely frequents the dance floor.

On the field, GG will be remembered as the world's most capped player, captain of Australia in more Tests that any of the Wallabies captains before him. Trophies, tries, field goals . . . but I think what will forever be in the front of people's minds when you ask about George will be that tackle – the night where Jeff Wilson actually jumped into touch and made this little bloke so much money he didn't know what to do with it. So he decided to invest in coffee. Good idea. He has been living off that moment for the whole time I have been playing rugby with him. He should first thank Damian Smith, David Wilson and David Campese for the opportunity to put all those years of cover defence into practice. And what an outcome! He knocked the ball from Jeff Wilson's arms, and saved a certain try and the game. I was sitting in the stands as a squad member that night and remember the jubilation afterwards in the change room.

That night, I had nowhere to crash as my room had been given away. So what do you when you are standing in the reception of the team hotel still in your Aussie suit? You demand a key to GG's room. I was very polite, and slept on the floor in the bathroom, under the sink adjacent to the toilet. A slight problem was that the future Mrs Gregan was there, too, and an interesting glance was shared when it was time to spend the pennies. She held on. Fortunately, we are very close these days and we can look back on those things and have a laugh. The Gregan family and the Burke family have become firm friends, more so away from the rugby, sharing family times together with the kids.

My lasting memory of GG on the field was after the final whistle in the game versus New Zealand in Sydney in 2004. George put a tight spiral on the ball to end the game, turned to me and proceeded to give me a man hug. Now I don't shy away from a man hug, but what did make me frown was the moment he declared his love for me!

Of all the tales on the field and off, there is one thing that is true with George Gregan. He will be remembered as one of the finest athletes to grace the rugby field and will always be regarded as a great player and a great leader. But more importantly to those who are close to him, he is a great friend.

GEORGE GREGAN ON
SAM NEILL

In 1998, Sam Neill and I had a chance meeting at Sydney Airport, while we were waiting to collect our luggage. Now I must confess that my memory of this occasion differs significantly from Sam's, but the ultimate ending is the same. As I recall it, he had just returned from Los Angeles and I was with the Wallabies team that had just arrived home from South Africa, after losing the match in Johannesburg which decided that season's Tri Nations. We were scheduled to play the All Blacks at the Sydney Football Stadium on the following Saturday.

It was a bit surreal seeing the great New Zealand-born actor there, because I had just been watching him on the in-flight cinema. Almost as a reflex, I decided to politely invade his personal space (a practice commonly referred to within the team as 'banditing'). 'I just watched you in *Event Horizon* on my flight and I thought you were great in that . . . and in *Sleeping Beauty*, too,' I said enthusiastically.

Inevitably, he was a little tired after a long flight over the Pacific Ocean, so I could understand his less than enthusiastic response. 'Not two of my better pieces of work,' he muttered. The 'leave me alone' vibe was polite but clear, and I was about to apologise and retreat when the penny dropped with Sam that we were the Australian Wallabies who'd be playing against his All Blacks this coming weekend. (I think it was the fact that our uniforms and luggage were emblazoned with the Wallabies logo that gave it away!) Immediately, he began to 'bandit' me about rugby, explaining that he had returned to Sydney not just because of work but also to watch the Test.

'You must be looking forward to the game,' I said.

'Yes I am,' he replied. 'But I haven't got a ticket yet.'

I said we could organise some tickets for him. Then followed a brief exchange as to how he could collect them, and I discovered that his home in Sydney was not far from ours. So it was that on game day he walked around to our house with Fire, his beautiful Staffordshire bull terrier, to pick up the tickets from Erica and to suggest for us to get together following the Test.

The game came and went with a good close victory to the Wallabies, and afterwards Sam painted a vivid picture of finding himself sitting among all the Australian players' wives, girlfriends, parents and friends, and thus feeling obliged to cheer for us and to offer only occasional muffled applause for the All Blacks. This 'each way' support would be his role in future games, too, which – as I pointed out to him – was not necessarily a bad thing. At least he could always claim he was going for the winning team!

Over the years, Sam has attended many matches in Australia, New Zealand, South Africa, France, almost everywhere, and managed to be part of many special moments. The Wallabies may not have won every time, but he has certainly enjoyed cheering us on and getting to know many of the players. He and his good mate, Bryan Brown, were part of a celebrity 'expert' panel assembled by one of the television networks for the World Cup final in Sydney in 2003, and they were apparently very funny and good-natured about the game. Straight after coming off air, they wanted to see the team to express their pride in our performance. We had a private function happening at our team hotel with family and close friends – just the people you need to see after such an exhausting event – and plenty of drinks were being consumed; despite the disappointment of coming so close to victory, the mood was pretty good. The players had been away from their families and friends for an extended period of time, and this was a great way to catch up and relax.

Bryan and Sam were quickly mingling with the players and their loved ones, sharing a few drinks and laughs. It was after maybe an hour that Sam asked me if Bryan could say a few words to the team.

'Of course, he can,' I replied.

Bryan promptly jumped up on one of the tables and gave out a big whistle to get everyone's attention. 'I don't know about you guys,' he shouted as he looked around the room. 'But it made me bloody proud to be an Australian tonight, to see the effort you boys put into the game. Sure, you lost, but you gave everything you had and just came up short. That, to me, is pure Aussie! So let's toast these mighty Wallabies bastards!'

Everyone cheered and the celebrations continued. It was a truly memorable experience.

There are more stories I could share, but this book can only run to so many pages. It was an incredible thing, that meeting at a baggage carousel in Sydney! Sam and I have seen plenty of changes in our lives in the years since, but we have always made time to see each other. I'm looking forward to many more years of great food, wine and company – important ingredients in any strong friendship.

SAM NEILL ON GEORGE GREGAN

This is how I remember meeting George.

I was at Sydney Airport waiting for my bags, sleepless and probably a little hung-over; after all these years, I still find the idea of 'free' wine on a plane irresistible. I was dimly aware that standing around me was a bunch of tough-looking blokes wearing ties and funny blazers. I think I sort of shrugged inwardly and hoped they wouldn't squash my luggage for fun or something, and looked away.

Then, with something of a start, I realised one of them was talking to me. And talking fast. Puzzled, I took a look at him. The first thing I noticed was that, unlike the others, he was more or less normal-sized. The second was he looked a little balder and a bit more tanned than the rest. I got a closer look at his tie, no help there – and struggled to understand what he was saying. Sort of like this: 'G'dayhowareya something Sam I'm something something and I've something Red October something. Sydney? Something mate something waddayareckon?'

Now there are certain things to be said about this. Firstly, the business of obviously fully grown men wearing bad ties and

319

blazers en masse at 6.30 am – this, it turns out, is more or less peculiar to rugby. The people that run rugby, it seems, insist on this quaint custom. This is possibly a disciplinary measure; the theory being that an enormous bloke wearing a blazer and tie is more likely to behave himself in public, and won't, say, eat the armrest beside him while waiting for his meal. If this is the case, it obviously works; I never saw a Wallaby eat an aeroplane seat. And come to think of it, the odd time a rugby player gets into a scrape in perhaps a nightclub, it's invariably because they've somehow slipped out of the Magic Discipline Blazer and gone a bit doolally as a result.

The second thing is that George (for it was he) *is* in fact normal size. If you see him lined up with his team for the national anthem, he looks like a midget. He's not. It's just that the blokes beside him are generally the size of tidal waves – John Eales, for instance, fills an entire elevator on his own. Now, given that he's spent about twenty years crashing about with men that look and act like very fast D9 bulldozers, it does beg the question: how has George survived? I think I know the answer to that: he only *looks* normal. I once playfully punched George on the arm. A big mistake. It was like punching a concrete pile. My hand was in a frozen bag of peas for a day, and I was obliged to drink wine with my left hand only for the following week.

Anyway, back to the luggage carousel. No sign of the bags, and this bloke was still talking. 'Something something South Africa, something come around for a coffee something something do you want seats for the game?'

'Um,' I said intelligently, valiantly trying to get to grips with the grogginess. I was thinking, *What game? . . . What sport? . . . Who are these people? . . . Where am I? . . . They're all bigger than me, apart from the talking bald bloke (who looks friendly enough) . . . Better say yes, and maybe do a runner as soon as possible.*

'Yes,' I said. 'That'd be . . . great.' A bit feeble on the 'great' but reasonably convincing.

'So you follow rugby, Sam?' he said.

Ah . . . rugby, I thought. That explained everything.

And here, I'm ashamed to say, I lied. I'm not sure why. Maybe I thought he'd ask the big blokes to eat my suitcases. Or maybe I felt since that's what he did for a living, I should pretend to be a supporter. It might have been a tad rude to say, 'Good God no, rugby sucks.'

So instead I said, 'A bit.'

The truth is I hadn't followed rugby since about 1972. Despite it being our national obsession (I'm from New Zealand), I thought I had turned my back on the game forever. It seemed to me then irredeemably dull and tainted by apartheid: a boring, distasteful waste of time.

So here's the thing. I not only fibbed (for survival reasons), but I was wrong. I couldn't have been more wrong. After this, after getting to know George, I took a look at rugby again. I couldn't have been more surprised – the game had changed out of all recognition while I'd been away. It was fast and electrifyingly exciting. The last time I'd looked, 3–nil was considered a good day out. Now a typical Super 12 game might post a 43–38 result. Good Lord, they were actually giving the backs the ball now, and the backs in turn were not kicking for touch, but in fact *running* with it. Tries were scored, and lots of them!

But, back to the luggage carousel, and my new mate is still talking. I think he's asking questions about my movies. I'm mildly astonished that a rugby player knows who I am at all. But no, he's *telling* me stuff about my movies. 'Something something *Dead Calm*, mate, when you something something.'

Turns out, George is a big film buff (jazz buff, too). He can quote my lines from films I've forgotten I've been in. And in the right accent. He's a great mimic, George. I was deeply irritated getting back from South Africa last year having immersed myself in that peculiarly harsh English for a couple of months, only to find George could effortlessly outclass me with his Afrikaner voice. He also does various New Zealand accents hilariously.

Anyway, back to the airport. Still no bags, and he's still talking. And I have to say I'm beginning to like him. You don't often meet people who are so persistently friendly. I'm beginning to feel a little better. And a bit more kindly disposed towards rugby.

The bags come, he says goodbye, shakes my hand (a bone-crusher), gives me his number; and I say thanks, I will call and I will come to a game.

So a vote of thanks to the tardy baggage handlers of Sydney, without whose delay I wouldn't have met George – now a close mate – and I wouldn't have met his excellent wife Erica and I wouldn't have met his great (subsequent) kids. And I wouldn't have reconnected with rugby.

I did go to a game, and I was hooked. Now I'm a big rugby fan. And through George I've scored tickets to all sorts of things and seen some top rugby. The best games, of course, tend to be Bledisloe Cup matches. Here the two greatest sides in the world give it their all. The result is often academic to me. I am an All Blacks supporter (they're not only great, but I'm fairly sure some nutter would crucify my innocent dog if I supported anyone else). But I am also a Wallabies fan (an important distinction), because I love the way they play – with flair and enterprise and in great spirit. The only thing I don't like about them is how they all end their names in 'y' – Ealesy, Smithy, etc. Oh no, hang on; there's always Gits.

I've gone to other things through George, too. The after-match function is always interesting, even if they're sometimes about as much fun as a funeral. I usually go with Erica, who can always be relied on to liven things up after a shandy or two.

I ran into John Howard at one. Australia had won – he wouldn't have turned up otherwise – and he had the triumphant look of a man who had personally given the All Blacks a hiding. I found myself momentarily alone in his company, and given that this was post-Tampa, I thought I might as well say something. As simply as I knew how.

'John,' I said, 'you've got to let those little kiddies out of those concentration camps.'

His reply is forever etched in my mind. 'Sam, they won't leave without their parents.'

God spare us!

Bryan Brown and I got asked by George to the after-match when the Wallabies got beaten at the World Cup in Sydney. They were gutted; we were astonished that no one was there apart from the Wallabies and their families. No officials, no pollies (no John Howard, of course), no one to say, 'Good on you, boys.'

I talked sternly to Bryan; 'Bryan, you've got to make a speech. Tell them they did good. Get up there, Bryan!'

Bryan protested, 'Fuck off! You make a speech! You're better at speeches than me. Bastard!' Bryan was drunk, and I wasn't having a bar of it.

'Get up there, Bryan! You're the Aussie! Now!' Bryan got up on a table, precariously, and started. The audience went quiet.

'I just wanna say . . . I just wanna say . . . you Wallabies are a great fucken team, you play great fucken rugby . . . and we FUCKEN LOVE YA!'

It was as good a speech as I've ever heard. It brought the house down.

Over the years I always tried to get a heads-up from George about what to look for, what they were thinking and so on.

Useless, of course. 'Aw, look, the boys are feeling good. Something something we're gonna, mumble, something etc.' Funny thing is, I don't think I understand George any better now than I did at the carousel.

My mate's retired from Test rugby now. After an utterly incredible career. It's a bugger really – for me anyway. No more freebies to Tests, no more eyeballing pollies in scarves at after-match events. More than that, I'll miss the buzz of having a friend on the field flying through the thick of it. And I, along with millions of others, will miss George Gregan at play – his immense physical courage, his ability to read a game and to dictate the play, and all that exuberant stuff, too, including his outstanding skills at that most Australian of art forms: the sledge. And the word that always comes up for me is his dignity.

Still, the upside is there'll possibly be more time for a glass or three of wine together. I might as well say it – George is a big Two Paddocks fan. And why not? He is, after all, a smart guy. And it is one of the world's very finest wines at the end of the day.

The downside is he probably has more time for golf. Oh dear. I don't think even George could turn me round on that one.

GEORGE GREGAN ON THE ALL BLACKS

Over the years, I've developed something of a reputation for having a death stare. It's certainly true that I rarely yell at people. I did occasionally speak to a team-mate in a succinct manner, but that only happened when I felt that individual wasn't going at 100 per cent. If a player was being lazy or was operating outside the team's game plan, I didn't think there was any need to state the obvious – a serious look in that guy's direction was all that was required. Others called that look a death stare, but to me it just said, *C'mon, you're better than that!* If they all talk about it, I guess it must have made an impact.

If I had to nominate a specific time when I used the look to maximum effect, it wouldn't be with a team-mate but with an All Blacks coach, when I combined the look with a few words. It must have worked pretty well because Tana Umaga still talks about the incident as one of his favourite memories of me.

After the Bledisloe Test at Eden Park in '05, which we lost 34–24, the Wallabies had a happy hour at the team hotel and then the lads went in different directions. I'd been told the Kiwis would be drinking at a particular nightclub and I said to Chris

Whitaker, 'Let's go down and have a few beers with the All Blacks.' The fact that I'd got on so well with the Kiwis at the tsunami game a few months earlier was part of my motivation for suggesting this.

It was a bit late when we arrived, but Tana and a few of his men were still there. Also in attendance was Steve Hansen, the All Blacks forwards coach. He's a good, usually confident man, solidly built, about 180 centimetres tall, who goes by the nickname Shags. He also has a habit of calling people 'son'. 'Well done, son,' he might say, or, 'Good to see you, son.' He was at it this night, even calling Tana and Rodney So'oialo 'son'. Soon, he was doing the same to us, and I said to Whits, 'Mate, you're not going to cop this "son" stuff from Shags, are you?' Then Shags started calling Whits 'Anthems'.

'You've sung more anthems than you've started Tests, haven't you, son,' he chuckled. The combination of a couple of beers and a Test-match victory had clearly got to him. He thought he was really funny.

'Shags,' Whits said, looking a little agitated, 'you don't need to laugh at your own jokes. It's not that funny, and stop calling me Anthems.'

I backed Whits up with a stare as serious as any I'd ever put on in my life. 'Mate, it's not funny,' I said. 'Your humour's terrible; that's what the boys tell me.'

It was a jab that struck a nerve. Shags looked over at the nearby All Blacks and then looked back at us and said, 'Who told you that, son?'

'And another thing,' I said, my eyes now locked on his, 'I won't cop you calling me "son". You don't look like my dad, you're not my dad, I'm not your son. My name is George, and his name is Whits, and you're Shags.'

Steve was stunned. Before he could say anything, I continued,

'And if I were you, I'd stop calling your players "son", too. They feel they can't mention this to you, but they don't like it. Rodney just came over and had a word to me and so did Tana. They don't like being called "son" and they've asked me to say something to you.'

I didn't have a clue whether Tana was bothered by it, but I doubted it.

Shags looked devastated, then he grabbed his beer and rushed over to Tana. 'It's all right me calling you "son", isn't it?' he asked, without a trace of the cockiness from a moment earlier.

'No problem,' said Tana.

Back came Shags. 'I just spoke to the boys – they love being called "son". The joke's on you.'

'Mate,' I said, 'I saw the look on your face when you thought you'd upset Tana and Rodney. We had you hook, line and sinker.'

Steve Hansen's reaction said something about the aura of warriors such as Tana and Rodney. No one wants to upset them – whether they be a well-regarded coach in his forties or a Wallaby halfback!

For the rest of the night, we had some more good laughs, reflecting the respect between the Wallabies and All Blacks that has been forged over more than a hundred years of rugby. We can sledge each other, try to smash each other on the field, but afterwards we can shake hands, share a drink and a laugh if time permits (the time constraints imposed by modern rugby don't often allow this), and then look forward to the next battle. It was only when I'd finally got to spend some serious time with Tana and Andrew Mehrtens at the tsunami game in 2005 that I fully realised how much we Aussie and Kiwi rugby footballers have in common, on and off the park. There's a common spirit. It's really important the two teams never lose that.

ALL BLACKS
ANDREW MEHRTENS
AND TANA UMAGA
ON GEORGE GREGAN

Mehrts: In 2002, I had a mighty dust-up with referee Andre Watson at Sydney's Telstra Stadium during the first half of the Bledisloe Cup Test. On the way off the field at half-time, when we were down 8–3, I was arguing with Watson and Greegs gave me a wee bit of a wind-up. Unfortunately, I had a sense-of-humour failure and turned and glared at him, then went back to debating the point with the referee. To this day, Greegs talks about this as a time when I 'stingrayed' him, and we have a bit of a laugh about it. But I sensed – not during the game but straight after it – that it might have been one of the very few times he was worried that he'd over-stepped the mark, said the wrong thing at the wrong time.

For me, there is no overstepping the mark because if anyone's going to do that, it's me. But it made me wonder . . . maybe he wasn't quite the tough bastard halfback he wanted us to think he was.

*

Tana: George was a competitive terrier when he was out there – all you could hear was yap, yap, yap. But while he was intense on the field, off it he was laidback, relaxed, wanted to chill out. That was good for me because that's how I like to be. I don't like to be around a lot of fuss and a lot of people.

Still, you can sense that his competitive nature is working overtime. A good example of this was when he got into Steve Hansen in Auckland in 2005, when Steve started calling him and Chris Whitaker 'son'. Steve calls everyone 'son'. I remember George kept at him, saying, 'I'm not your son, mate, I'm not your son. Look at me, how can I be your son?' The rest of us were laughing. Steve and George are very similar, and it was all in good humour. Even Steve admitted that later.

Mehrts: In some ways, I reckon Greegs's on-field and off-field characters match up. You can have a crack at him or take the piss out of him and he'll just have a wee laugh and stay composed. On and off the field, he always seems like he has things under control. It's a bit clichéd to think that footballers are rugby players first, and the way they play the game moulds their personalities. I think more often it's the footballer's personality that shapes his rugby. With Greegs, I'd say his personality came out in his rugby – the composure, the way he was always calm yet fiercely competitive.

Socially, I've found him to be outgoing and very good with people, bubbly, a lot of personality . . . but not over the top. Can a person be in control and gregarious at the same time? Greegs seems to manage it.

We've found at Toulon that he's always clean and tidy and well prepared. Some blokes are happy to come to training in their gear and then head home for a shower straight afterwards. Not Greegs. His training bag has everything neatly compartmentalised: change of neatly pressed casual gear, a variety of lotions, toiletries in the zip pocket and so on. We all knew he's one of the toughest blokes to ever play the game, but when he arrived after the World Cup, he came armed with boxes and boxes of tape that he'd pilfered from the Wallabies physio, just in case he needed it, all immaculately stored in his kit. He wasn't prepared to trust the French tape. It prompted us to call him a hypochondriac, just to see if we'd get a bite. Nothing. He just lets it go, sensible and unflappable as usual.

He was always like that on the field, whether he was a Brumby or a Wallaby. He probably had to take more of a leadership role with the Brumbies. We always found the Wallabies to be a smart, savvy team and they probably didn't need as much prodding. Then again, the crowds for the Super 12 or Super 14 games were rarely as loud as for Test matches, so maybe we were just more likely to hear his voice barking out orders at a Super 14 match! He was the hub for both teams – they'd put on phase after phase and then, bang, Greegs would be in there and the ball was gone, cleared, and his backs were sweeping on to it. It was a pain in the arse, to be honest.

Tana: He marches to his own beat, which is something I respect. Everyone in New Zealand knows what he's done for Australia and how much of a nuisance he has been to the All Blacks. Here at Toulon, I've come to appreciate how he doesn't dwell on mistakes, how he learns from them. He is so experienced, and also very demanding of himself, providing knowledge and setting an example, which is such a help for me as a new coach. There's not much I can tell him that he doesn't already know, but there are a few things he can tell me that I don't know.

*

Mehrts: The tsunami game represented what rugby should be all about. It was the coming together of guys who had played against each other many times but had never had the chance to spend much quality time together. When I tell people how great that week was, they always assume we were out boozing all the time. But we weren't. Sure, we shared the odd beer and a couple of glasses of red, but it was more about the simple things, such as having a laugh and a game of cards on the team bus. All the Aussie guys were great – Phil Waugh, Chris Latham, Greegs; big Kef rocked up as well. We had so much fun and a lot of it was about the values and traditions of rugby. There was a bit of an amateur days feel about it, which was quite exciting.

We were only two days into the week and I was asking, 'When can we do a reunion?' The ironic thing is, I didn't want to go beforehand. I'd won back my place in the All Blacks in 2004 after missing a year and wanted to play every Super 12 game to push my case to stay in the side. But our officials said, 'We've got to send someone from each team,' and eventually, I thought, *Well, London could be cool.* I'd only ever been to London on All Blacks tours, when it gets a wee bit claustrophobic and you don't really get a chance to enjoy it. Then they started talking about who was going over – Greegs's name was mentioned and that made it more appealing. That week was brilliant and far exceeded my expectations – to the point where I'm eagerly looking forward to playing more of those style of matches while I'm still playing competitive rugby.

Tana: I'll never forget the build-up to the game, when we were able to spend the whole week together. That's when we really hit it off. And it wasn't just George; there was Victor Matfield and John Smit, Chris Latham, Moses Rauluni, Rod Macqueen, all the others.

Former All Black captain Andy Leslie has friends from when he played in Wales in the 1970s. If these guys come to New Zealand, or if Andy goes to Wales, they catch up. We don't really get the chance to build these kinds of friendships anymore with international rivals, which I think is sad. Usually, straight after the game, we have recovery or there are media and sponsors' obligations. We analyse our opponents on TV, so we know what they can do *on* a rugby field, but off the field we're restricted to crossing paths at a formal function, or briefly after the game if time permits. It takes a special effort for two teams to come together, such as what happened after the 2003 World Cup semifinal, or when George and Chris Whitaker came down to see Steve Hansen in 2005.

We all play the game because we love it and we care about it. It's part of what makes us who we are. The tsunami game was a chance for each of us to see the personal side of men who are usually our opponents, and to realise how we share a common bond through rugby. It was so new and refreshing, little wonder that after a couple of days Mehrts was talking about a reunion.

Mehrts: Thirty years from now, if someone asks me about Greegs, about what I think of him, how I remember him, hopefully I'll be able to say, 'He's still one of my good mates. I saw him a couple of weeks ago when he was over and we had a barbecue and played a round of golf in the pouring rain.' After that, I'll be thinking of how he still holds the Test caps record and how it was a privilege to have played in the same era, against him . . . and with him.

GEORGE GREGAN ON MATT GITEAU

I thought the first time I met Matt Giteau was in September 2002, at the Wallabies camp before our end-of-season tour, after he was picked in the Australian squad before he played a Super 12 game. But he tells me that this isn't the case, and does so in a way that offers a taste of the banter I've received and continue to receive from this cheeky little guy.

One of our first ever conversations concerned the fact that we're both from Eddies (St Edmund's College). One day in 1995 I'd returned as an 'old boy' to attend a school assembly. Gits was in Year 8 (a fact he emphasised!) and was in the audience as I handed out a few awards and gave a short speech on doing your best in your chosen field, be it sport, arts, academic endeavour, whatever. My speech apparently inspired Gits onto bigger and better things in rugby (so he said with his tongue firmly in his cheek).

What it seemed to have done in 2002 was help develop his ability to banter about the birthdates of certain team-mates he was about start playing with, the captain included!

That 2002 tour began in Argentina, and it was there that Gits acquired one of his many nicknames, the one that's probably my

335

favourite. He'd coloured his hair (which he continues to do and which I reckon he should be careful about – he only needs to look at his old man, Ron, who's a little light on top!) in a stripy blond pattern. Our team manager, Phil Thomson, was less than impressed with this new haircut and was keen for it to grow back to its natural colour. However, after we returned from an expedition to Iguaçú Falls (which, this time, unlike 1997, the entire team enjoyed), Gits arrived at breakfast the next morning with his eyebrows striped like a jaguar. Thommo just about had kittens and immediately let the young man know that he'd overstepped the mark and ordered him to get rid of the striped eyebrows by lunchtime.

Gits swiftly dyed them back to their natural hue, but they left a lasting impression on those of us lucky enough to get a peek. My memory is that he strongly resembled the baby jaguar out of *Dora the Explorer*. Our tour guide at the Falls the previous day had struggled when he tried to say 'jaguar'. Instead, he called them 'shagwahs'. From the moment Gits turned up for breakfast with those crazy eyebrows, he was Shagwah, too.

By the end of 2007, Gits had played more than fifty Tests. But it's still a little hard for me to imagine him as one of the Wallabies' senior players, especially as it seems like only yesterday (it was actually 2004!) that he fell a victim to one of my favourite South African pranks.

The Brumbies were in Cape Town during the Super 12, preparing to play the Stormers. We went for lunch and a coffee at Camps Bay, and Gits and I were sitting opposite the beaches. In the shallow water out towards the rocks were some dark shapes that looked like seals moving around. I let Gits know that until you've seen the Cape seals up close, you haven't done Cape Town. It was, I explained, a truly amazing experience that stays with you for life. At first, he was reluctant, but I kept prodding, and eventually he made the 400-metre journey past some sunbathers to discover that the incredible Cape seals were in fact . . . seaweed! When he returned, he didn't say a word, though he did hold up a finger that resembled the 'Cape bird'.

I've had a lot of fun with Gits, and spent a lot of time with him on tour and also in Canberra when he played for the Brumbies. (He moved to the Western Force in 2007.) He was one of the reasons that I played on after the 2003 World Cup: I wanted to see him develop as a footballer and a person. He has grown from a confident kid into a young man who is now a strong leader in every team he plays for. He's also learned how to order food off a menu, order and drink a short macchiato, speak a little French, prepare meals away from home . . . um . . . Oh well, it's a start!

He has great qualities as a footballer and as a person and that, to me, is the embodiment of the ideal rugby player. He was the guy between 2003 and 2007 who most helped me focus on what should really matter for a rugby player: striving for self-improvement and having some fun. We would continuously push each other, at training and in games, to achieve this improvement, and then we'd have a lot of laughs off the field.

To top it all off, my kids adore him. And what do they call him? Shagwah!

MATT GITEAU ON GEORGE GREGAN

The first time George Gregan and I met actually went this way. I'd just kicked the winning field goal in a big game for the under-13s at St Edmund's College, and that was the reason I was introduced to him when he came back, as a Test rugby star, to talk to the students at his old school. George was told what I'd done, shook my hand and said, 'Well done.' And that was it. I was certainly very polite. At that age, there was no way I was going to be smart in front of a person of George's stature.

To be honest, it would be pretty stunning if he did remember me from 1995. I'm sure I didn't make much of an impact on him. Proof of this came when he kept calling me Matty Henjak right through the first year I played with him. Such was his aura as the Australian captain and being such an influential figure at the Brumbies, it wasn't until near the end of the season that I finally summoned up the courage to tell him my last name was Giteau.

That was a weird start, but our relationship grew to the point that today it means a lot to me. George has taught me so much. When it came to rugby, I was inspired by his professionalism, by the way he was always the first one to arrive at training and the last one to leave. Every week, he paid due diligence to the team we were preparing to play. He did everything that he needed to and worked so hard, which is probably why he played for so long. Away from football, he'd invite me around for dinner and I met his family and saw another side of him. That's when I learned how down-to-earth he is; how Erica and Max and Charlie and Jazzy mean so much to him; how he stays positive, always looking forward. How he wants to help people.

The best way I can describe his sense of humour is 'dry'. Like most halfbacks, he's a bit of a pest, a bloke who likes to get a reaction out of people. He was forever calling me 'sweetheart', which was something that always got under my skin, and because he knew it was working, he kept at it. On the field and off, he'd find someone's weakness and just go at it.

He's too sensible to have too much to drink, but he has been known to shout everyone a Jägerbomb, or something similar, to give the impression he's in for a big night. Then, when the boys start downing their shots, he's out the door and on his way home.

He's a pretty self-assured bloke, no doubt about it, but there's one place where his confidence takes a knock. I remember once when we were away on a tour, our Brumbies and Wallabies team-mate Jeremy Paul took him on in a dance-off, with me as one of the judges. I gave it to Gregan, told him he'd won, but he didn't. He certainly second-guesses himself on the rare occasions he hits the dance floor.

Like all the senior players at the Brumbies, George was great when I made the decision to go to the Western Force at the start of 2007. I spoke to them all individually, and I think they all understood and were behind me. I was excited by the opportunity to contribute to an emerging club, and the Perth lifestyle appealed to me.

The two of us kept talking throughout the '07 Super 14 season, and in the last couple of weeks, after we played them in Canberra in round 12, I was able to remind him about what a dirty player he was. I passed the ball not long after the game started, and about three seconds later he ran up and shoved me over. We got the penalty, I kicked the goal, and that's three points I'll always have over him.

I know that he likes to tell the story of how, in my second year with the Brumbies, he conned me with the Camps Bay 'seals' at Cape Town, and I guess he did, though it's not true that I walked all the way up to them. I actually realised pretty quickly that it was only seaweed. From that cafe table, though, as we sat and talked and enjoyed a coffee, it did look like the weed was alive and jumping. Later, I discovered it was an old joke and I was just the latest Australian rugby footballer on tour to be taken in. I've used it myself on some of the new guys in the last couple of years, and it always works, so I can see why George thinks it's so funny.

If you want to spend time with George, it's best that you don't mind drinking coffee. Which brings me to one of the great myths about George Gregan. Despite everything you've heard about his skills as a barista, the fact is: his coffee-making is terrible. Same with his cooking. There were times when a group of us were invited around to his place and the vibe from everyone, behind his back, was the same: 'I don't want to go.' If Erica was cooking we couldn't get there quick enough, but not if George was in charge. 'But he's the captain,' we'd end up saying. 'He's been good enough to put on a meal for us, and his company's great.' So we'd all turn up to have a meal we wouldn't enjoy and drink coffee we didn't like.

I'm sure George'll be shattered to learn we don't rate his efforts in the kitchen, because he thinks he's a bit of a whiz in that area, but the truth needs to be told.

Or maybe he does know. Seems to me, whenever he goes into his coffee shops, he's always the one cleaning things up, asking customers if they want another biscuit. He's not the one making coffee. Erica's doing that – she's good at everything.

At the start of 2007, the World Cup year, George and I were both seen as halfbacks, but even though we were competing for the same position, he was continually working with me and trying to help me and the team. He was obviously the best halfback, but there was no animosity or bitterness in his mind because the coaches were trying something different; he was still willing to help me and teach me things. I'll never forget that.

Since he retired from the Wallabies we've talked quite a bit, but rarely about rugby. It's more about me asking how his family is, him checking out how I'm going, simple things like that. He is such a genuine guy. I will always have a lot of great memories of our time together with the Brumbies and the Wallabies.

GEORGE GREGAN ON DELWYN GRIFFITH

When I was introduced to Delwyn Griffith in 1995 by Rod Kafer, she was completing her sports medicine/sports science degree at Canberra University and was trying to get up as many practice hours on athletes as she could. This meant she was prepared to offer a very good student rate, which appealed to all of us – though Kafe's recommendation went further than that. I can still remember him saying, 'You know, she's pretty small but she'll really hurt you. She's an ex-AIS gymnast so she knows what a sports massage is and how to apply it.'

I went along to my first massage and quickly learned that Kafe couldn't have been more correct in his assessment. Delwyn was brutal . . . but extremely effective. I came out of her room that day a little the worse for wear, but the benefits I derived from the treatment were amazing. I had my last rub with Del in October 2007, on the day of the World Cup quarter-final against England in Marseille, and she was just as good then as at that first appointment. She's a great physician who is extremely professional in all aspects of her job.

Delwyn was fully booked up masssaging half the ACT Kooka-burras in 1995, and this continued when the Super 12 started and a steady stream of Brumbies were queuing up outside her door. We all felt the pain and welcomed the benefits of her treatment. By 2000, it was an obvious move for the Brumbies to employ her full-time and eventually she achieved her professional dream when she was part of the medical team who treated the 2007 Wallabies squad throughout our seven-week World Cup campaign.

Over the years I've spent countless hours on Del's table: she treated me for a range of injuries and was part of my post-game recovery. We used a variety of treatments, including acupuncture and pre- and post-game massage, and she was outstanding – not only in her massage skills, but also through her understanding of what areas to treat. Though she was brilliant from day one, I always felt she was looking to improve even more and was happy to try new things. And I can honestly say this about her and countless other wonderful therapists, physios and doctors who treated me during my career, at both provincial and international level: without them, I wouldn't have played for so long. These are the people who got up early or stayed up late to provide the extra treatment that would get me back on the field as soon as possible, to train or to play. Their efforts often go unnoticed by a lot of people, but at an elite level in sport they are essential if a team is going to be successful. For me, Del is the brightest of these stars, and not only because she worked with me the longest.

Looking back over all the time we spent together, at home and on tour, the thing that stands out most for me about Delwyn's character is her caring and understanding nature. She is a mother, and we saw a lot of her son, Elijah, in the team environment of the Brumbies. Around 2000 and 2001, a large number of players became fathers for the first time and Del was a great source of information and experience.

One day while she was giving me a massage – at the time Erica and I were expecting Max – she passed on a great tip about colic, an excess build-up of wind that can cause awful discomfort for newborns. She had endured some awkward times with Elijah because of the condition, but was able to resolve it through what she called 'baby massage'. Well, I was all ears during this treatment (I have to confess that I was prone to doze off sometimes) and asked a lot of questions: 'What do you look for? How do you know they're uncomfortable? What's the massage technique you use?'

Del answered every question clearly and, most importantly, showed me the technique required: a small anti-clockwise massage motion with your hand on the abdominal region, while your arm goes in a circle in a clockwise direction. If that sounds confusing, don't worry. I was confused too – until Del brought a baby doll along to our next session to demonstrate. What did I tell you – she's a true professional!

DELWYN GRIFFITH ON GEORGE GREGAN

When I first met George in 1995, I wasn't following rugby; my sporting background and sporting interests were gymnastics, athletics and triathlons. Many of my massage clients were distance runners, whom I enjoyed working with, and I followed their careers with interest. They were slight, lean athletes, not too physically demanding on my hands and arms. As I quickly learned from working with George, Rod Kafer and other players from the Kookaburras and then the Brumbies, footballers are a lot tougher to massage than distance runners and they have a very high pain threshold. I had to change my approach, and developed techniques using my forearms, elbows and body weight to apply the extra pressure required. At the same time, I became familiar with the soft-tissue injuries and tight muscles common to rugby players and used the techniques to treat these areas more effectively to help prevent any injuries occurring.

In 1996, following the start of the Super 12 competition, my client base of footballers expanded, and in 1997 I joined the Brumbies medical team part-time. It was the start of a formal association with the game that took me into the Wallabies set-up and to the 2007 World Cup. In all that time, I never met an athlete – in or outside of rugby – like George in terms of the way he respected and maintained his body.

My first impression of George was that he was softly spoken and very polite. I quickly learned that he was known as the Massage Shark, as he could get up to three massages during the week and another one on game day. He had a ritual he did before each treatment which involved him standing beside the table, stretching and poking at body parts to see what felt stiff or sore as he talked to me about what he wanted me to work on. He was very specific in his requests: 'left calf', 'right hip', 'right shoulder' and so on. He almost always asked for more than I had time for in one treatment session and often had a hydrotherapy session just before his massage so that he was looser and relaxed before he got on the table.

George's self-discipline is extraordinary. He always stuck religiously to his game-day routine – it didn't matter whether we were travelling or playing at home, if kick-off was at 7.30 pm, he'd arrive for a massage at precisely 1.30 pm, to help him prepare physically and mentally for the game.

It's true that he could be demanding, but in an inspirational way. The final home game for the Brumbies in 2007 was the last Super 14 game in Canberra for George, Steve Larkham and Jeremy Paul, and after the game the three boys spent at least an hour walking the field, shaking hands, signing autographs and saying goodbye to the fans. By the time they made it back to the change rooms, the rest of the players had completed their recovery session next door at the AIS and left the stadium. It was now 10.45 pm, an hour and a half since the game had ended, and we medical staff were waiting for George, Steve and Jeremy to come and do recovery. This is normally compulsory but we learned that because of the late hour, they'd been given the option to skip it. At 11 o'clock I rang the team doctor, who was in the change rooms, and asked what was happening. As we suspected, Steve and Jeremy were happy to give recovery a miss, but George was on his way. He arrived at 11.30 pm. We managed to get the recovery done a little quicker than usual, but even then – always the perfectionist! – we had to wait until he'd applied his moisturisers and cleaned his teeth before we could finally get home. It was after midnight, but we didn't really mind. It wasn't uncommon for George to go out of his way to let us know that our work was appreciated. I'll never forget the day in Auckland when he arranged a massage for me, or the times he took the medical team out to dinner to say thank you.

George's 'only the best' philosophy extended beyond his massages. One day, he turned up with a coffee machine, which was installed in the treatment room at the Brumbies headquarters, and from that day on he educated us on the techniques needed to make a good coffee. We were also educated on how to keep the machine clean! He talked us through how to aerate the milk without making a screeching noise, and getting a creamy result. George loves his macchiatos, and would often come in early to make one for each member of the medical staff.

Depending on how long there was to match day, George sometimes used the massage treatment as an opportunity to mentally relax. On these occasions, he often brought in a CD to listen to – almost certainly modern jazz. At other times, I could tell George was nervous or anxious leading up to a game because he'd become even more body aware and highlight every little niggle he had. At these times, he'd book in every day for treatment, alternating between massage and physiotherapy.

People often told me I had the dream job of massaging the Wallabies captain. But as George well knew, these massages usually involved me inflicting pain on him – digging my elbow into his gluteals, hamstrings and back. I was also told how lucky I was to be working in professional sport, and in many ways that was true. However, travelling was always tiring, and airports were a chore as flying with the team involved arriving a lot earlier and lugging extra team kit as well as your own gear.

We were often issued plane tickets in alphabetical order, and whenever that happened, Giteau, Gregan and Griffith had a giggle as we 'little' humans, sitting comfortably in our row, looked across the aisle to see three big forwards jammed in together with their shoulders touching and their knees pressed against the seats in front.

Working and travelling with the Brumbies and then the Wallabies often gave me the chance to closely observe the team dynamic. Early on, George copped his share of niggle from the likes of Joe Roff, Owen Finegan and Brett Robinson, and harmless tricks were often played on each other or plotted in the treatment room. But he managed to avoid all that during the second half of his career.

I remember once, after a long day of travelling to a game overseas, we had to collect our bags and all the team kit and then push trolley after trolley to the team bus. Everyone wanted to get to the hotel to shower and eat, but the senior players had been caught by the media. The players waiting on the bus whinged in good fun at the guys when they finally arrived – Stephen Larkham, for example, was promptly reminded that rugby is a team game and 'it's not all about you'. But when George got on the bus last, no one said a thing. It was like being in a classroom full of kids making a racket and then the teacher walks in and there's silence.

The respect George earned among his peers was extraordinary. He is an inspirational person and athlete; he keeps you thinking positively and motivated to achieve your goals. It has been such a pleasure working with him.

GEORGE GREGAN ON
PAT RAFTER

Everyone in Australia knows Pat Rafter – twice US Open champion (1997 and 1998), twice Wimbledon finalist (2000 and 2001), Davis Cup team member from 1994 to 2001, Australian of the Year in 2002. He is a superb Australian ambassador because he epitomises everything that is good about our country. He is also a great sport, a better mate, and a loving and caring father and husband. But there is a Pat Rafter that not many Australians know or get to see. This is where I come in.

I've known Pat since 1995, when we met at the Coolum Classic, a great golfing event featuring professionals and amateurs. The format was a lot of fun as it allowed a wide range of people – including sporting personalities, entertainers and others with real jobs – to play two rounds with a professional golfer. If they made the cut, they also played in an amateur final round with their pro. If you were a golf tragic (and everyone who attended was), then this was heaven on a stick!

Pat and I hit it off straight away, as we both love our golf, we have a keen interest in Aussie sport, and we were both managed at the time by IMG and were finishing off what had been a pretty good year. Pat won his first singles title in 1994, while I made my Wallabies debut. That shared love of golf has led us to enjoy many rounds together at a number of locations over the years. When Pat was living in Sydney, we were both members at Terrey Hills, and when we scheduled a game this proved handy for me because I would normally get a lift from him. On these occasions, I received an insight into what made this guy such a great tennis player – he was all about routine.

'Georgie, I'll pick you up at 8.30 am so we can get there just after 9,' he'd say, even though our tee time was 10 o'clock. 'Then we can hit a bucket of balls, have a few chips and putts, and then head out.'

I'd always respond, 'Of course, mate, but why so early? You've been hitting balls all week with Pete Lonard's personal coach. Surely you can just hit a few putts and maybe half a bucket of balls?'

'Hey mate, do you want the lift or not?' he'd reply.

Of course I did. It was just the start of a day out where there was always a little bit of gamesmanship going on.

Terrey Hills is a great course with very tricky greens. This particular day, after five holes Patty was four under par. I was three or four over, and it felt like I was playing with a pro. After nine, he was still two or three under – and a little shitty with himself for bogeying the eighth and the ninth. I was now six or seven over and totally amazed (and impressed) by his reaction to that first nine. The rest of the round came and went and he finished at one over for the day compared to my eleven or twelve over. He'd thumped me! So, of course, I got the drinks and food at the nineteenth, and then had to listen to poor old Patty bemoaning the fact that he'd 'choked' on the back nine.

'Mate, if that's what you consider a choke, then I want to choke like that every time we're out here,' I said.

Pat shrugged my comment off and replied, 'But it could have been so much better.'

Of course, this is Pat's competitiveness and search for constant improvement coming to the surface. But where, I'm sure you're asking, is that extra insight into his character I promised? It came at a time when he was already up by about ten strokes, when I was 60 to 80 metres away from the green – not a full approach shot but an in-between clubs shot.

Pat knew I'd developed a shank from these positions over the previous couple of months, so he quietly said to me, 'Hey mate, have you been practising these shots? You've been terrible from this distance lately.'

I didn't respond, but that little voice in my head was saying, 'Don't give the prick the satisfaction of watching you shank it.'

When you have the shanks, all you can think about is not hitting one. Which, for me, invariably means I'll either shank it or pull it hard left. With his throwaway line, Pat had me stuffed. He knew before he said it that I'd be thinking about it, but now I'd be thinking about it even more. He also knew that the way I was playing I would have preferred to chip and run the ball onto the green with a seven-iron rather than attempt to hit a 'feel' shot with my sand wedge. But now I couldn't ignore his challenge.

This time, it went hard left.

Afterwards, I swore to myself that I'd get over this 'sickness' I was suffering from 60 to 80 metres out from the green. I listened to good old Prefect Pat and practised this shot (with the help of a pro) until the only thoughts running through my head were the position I would commence my downswing and that my weight had to be a bit more on my left side. Eventually, I became quite comfortable from this position and pretty consistent too, and my mate's on-course banter had to shift to a different subject.

Although he still found plenty of flaws in my game at the right moments!

Pat loves the Brisbane Broncos rugby league team and was especially devoted to the Broncos' halfback and captain Allan 'Alfie' Langer. It was Alfie this and Alfie that the whole of the first night I met him – I really thought he was in love with the guy!

Fast forward to the 2006 league grand final, Brisbane versus Melbourne, which the Gregan family watched at the Rafters' home. I swear Pat was more nervous than the players. He rang me at 11 am to get my dinner order and to confirm the exact time we'd be arriving. 'You know, mate, it kicks off at seven so you'd better not be late.'

'Patty,' I said, 'it's 11 o'clock on a Sunday morning and the game kicks off in eight hours. Take it easy, mate.'

The Broncos went on to keep their Tiger Woods-like record when it comes to playing in the big one – six wins from six appearances between 1992 and 2006.

No doubt the players and coaches were ecstatic after their triumph, but I reckon there was one person in Sydney that evening who was even more excited than they were!

Pat is a great family man. When he and his wife, Lara, were living in Sydney with their two children, Joshua and India, Joshua went to the same pre-school as Max and Charlie, so we saw a lot of each other at drop-off and pick-up times. The kids had a lot of fun together, sharing swimming lessons in Pat and Lara's pool over summer and playing together in a park near our homes. Sometimes, we would catch up for an early dinner and the kids would run around after eating their meals. When it came time to leave, we were faced with the 'sleepover dilemma', which our kids always started.

'Can I sleep at Joshy's house?' Max would plead. Then Charlie would ask the same question . . . and it went on and on.

Patty would resolve the situation by allowing Max and Charlie a ride up to his house in his car, as long as they allowed their parents to take them home. All the kids could have another play at another time. This always went over a treat, although our kids, being good negotiators, never forgot that 'another time'.

'When are we going to Joshy's dad's house?' Max and Charlie would repeat over and over again until they got a firm date.

Pat has made a significant impression on our kids, as he has with most Australians. The Gregans were at the airport preparing to go on a family holiday, when there at the Bonds retail outlet was a big photo of Pat in his underwear. (He swears they don't use socks in the photo shoots!)

Charlie saw Patty in the shop window and yelled out at the top of her lungs, 'Look! Look! There's Joshy's dad!'

'And he's wearing his undies!' piped up Max.

Both of them fell around laughing hysterically.

The airport was packed and it was embarrassing and priceless at the same time. The Australian of the Year, two-time US Open champ, was just someone's dad posing in his undies . . .

PAT RAFTER ON GEORGE GREGAN

It's sometimes hard to remember when you first met someone whom you've often seen on television and also been in awe of. So although I don't exactly remember the first time I met George Gregan, I can tell you that in 1995 we had a beer and a great laugh together at the Schweppes Golf Classic at Coolum on the Sunshine Coast. Since that time back in '95 we have stayed in contact and forged a great relationship. In recent years, our kids have become close as well.

Now, in 2008, here we are in France, about to watch George play one of his last games for Toulon. It's cold and raining, but this game will decide if Toulon goes up to the top division so there's a lot riding on the result. The hospitality of the Gregans is second to none, but the kids have been together long enough for the claws to come out and I think it's time for the Rafters to head back to our little house in the country. Nevertheless, the good vibe of the past few days has been typical of the times we've spent together.

Although I never saw the real nitty-gritty of what goes on behind closed doors within the Wallabies, I was once invited for a quiet drink with the team after a loss to the All Blacks in Auckland. I said I'd go for a quick one, but hadn't realised that George would set me up. Soon I was 'driving the bus' – just one of their many drinking games. I tried to slip away, but with twenty-two pissed giants surrounding me I knew I was in trouble. It was explained to me that if I bailed before the end, I'd be tipped upside down and force-fed beer. Not a good position to be in. And all the while, little George was playing dumb in the background, apologising for 'not knowing that would happen'. That's one thing about George – he's a sly bugger but he acts as if he's completely innocent.

George got a little taste of what happens in tennis circles at another golf event at Coolum. I think George believed that tennis was played by nice boys and everyone on the circuit was friendly to each other, but he and Matty Burke soon discovered different. After I'd copped abuse for losing many Davis Cup matches and been called the General (because of my 'intensity' when it comes to organisation), we all started to unload on the rugby boys. It was 2003 and Australia had just lost the World Cup final to England. George was captain and thus responsible for the loss, so we twenty or so tennis players let him know just what we thought of the defeat. 'George lost the World Cup . . . Doo-dah! . . . Doo-dah!' we sang. Poor Burkey got hammered for not even making the team.

It may seem harsh, but it was all done in true Aussie fashion – with lots of laughter.

As for this piece, I know it's okay to bag the little fella – in fact, George has encouraged me to do so – but the truth is I really can't find anything negative to say about him. He's a top man.

GEORGE GREGAN ON
KATIE POWER

I met Katie at the first George Gregan Foundation fundraiser. There were lots of kids there from the Children's Hospital at Westmead, along with plenty of my Wallabies team-mates and other sporting celebrities enjoying the day and helping to raise funds for a much-needed playground at the hospital.

Katie was hard to miss. I'm partial to a bald head anyway, but this little girl had the most amazing smile I've ever seen. Erica and I just fell in love with her at first sight. She was having treatment for cancer and all her family were with her that day. She comes from a large Irish family who are warm and supportive, the perfect example of how a family should be. Here was a family going through such adversity and yet they only exuded positivity.

Katie is my hero. She faced cancer head on and just got on with life. Courage and determination are traits we all strive for, yet Katie was doing it naturally. She truly is inspirational. She reminds us all how important and necessary charitable work is, and why we should reach out to others and try to make a difference.

Following that day, Katie became the Foundation's youngest ambassador and it continues to be important to us to know how she's doing. I am delighted to say, bloody well. She just had her final scans, which came back clear, and everyone is hugely relieved. She now has beautiful long curls but that cheeky smile is just the same.

Katie touched my heart. I know she will continue to light up any room she walks into.

KATIE POWER ON GEORGE GREGAN

When I first met George Gregan, I was six and almost as tall as him. Now I'm nine and I must be at least a foot taller than him!

I first met George at his 'Bunny Doon' Golf Day. My family had been invited to this through the hospital, where I had spent the last six months undergoing intensive chemotherapy because I had a large Wilm's tumour on my kidney.

My first impression of George was . . . he's tiny! And really bald! At least I wasn't the only bald person in the room. I thought George would be so busy that he wouldn't notice us but I was definitely wrong. He came over to us with a big smile and we had a long chat. Mum said that she had to take a photo of us together so she could have a picture of the two baldies. George must have liked the idea because the next day our picture was in the *Sydney Morning Herald* and soon on his website.

The second time I met George I had hair. He didn't recognise me at first, but Mum reminded him that I was Katie from his web page. He was stunned! He greeted me with a warm hug and quickly brought me over to say hello to his wife, Erica. They couldn't believe how well I looked.

I can't pick my best time spent with George – every single time that I've met him, it's been great! My strongest memory of being with him is probably at the opening of the playground at Westmead Children's Hospital. He had chosen me to officially open the playground with him. George and I cut the ribbon together. It was a bit tricky because the scissors were quite blunt and we had a few snips at it until we finally got it. When the speeches were going on, George asked me to get up on stage with him. So I did. When George had finished his speech he gave me a lovely, warm, comfortable shoulder massage. He treated me like one of his own kids.

After the speeches were done, there was a concert and treasure hunt for the kids. There was food and drinks and a wonderful brand new playground. That day was fun. I had a great time!

George has taught me many things by his words, and especially by his actions. He taught me to never give up and to keep on trying. The thing that George has always done is to try to be happy. He says that you can always get through things that you don't want to do if you do them quickly.

George is a very funny guy. He always likes to see the good in things. When people are down, he makes them happy again. George is always laughing and telling jokes and is always so cheerful.

I reckon I will always keep in touch with him. I have known him for a long time, going all the way back to 2005, and we will always have a good relationship towards each other.

Seeing George playing football on TV just made me feel so happy and proud that I knew him. Of course, he wasn't playing for me because he has met a lot more people than me, but it felt like he was doing it for me. The pleasure built up inside me when I saw him on the television screen.

The last time I was with George was at the Sofitel Wentworth for a George Gregan Foundation function. That night, George and Erica had asked me to get up on stage, but I was quite tired and a bit teary. I really didn't want to get up there. George and Erica said that they didn't mind one bit if I didn't go up. The choice was mine. I decided to go up, and George and Erica were standing right on the edge of the stage. Whenever I looked over I saw their faces, all bright and beaming so hard that they were practically glowing!

Afterwards, I received my very own bouquet of flowers. They were from George and Erica as a thank you. I felt extremely special . . . ONCE AGAIN!

PS: When I was asked to write something for George's book, my Uncle Robbie told me he would like his name mentioned at least three times in this book.

Uncle Robbie, Uncle Robbie and Uncle Robbie.

Oops! That's four!

GEORGE GREGAN ON
PHIL KEARNS

Kearnsy has had other nicknames over the years. One of them is Turtles, which came from another Wallaby, Tim Gavin, or to be more precise from one of Tim's nephews, who just loved Phil. But no matter how hard the poor little guy tried, he couldn't quite get the surname right. He kept calling him Turtles instead of Kearns. Eventually this got back to the boys and, of course, we just loved it. This was back in 1998, when Phil had just got back into the Wallabies side after a long layoff with an Achilles tendon injury. His gait at times resembled a turtle on dry land and his frame . . . well, need I say more? We took to this nickname like a pack of wolves and I'm proud to say it remains one of his favourites.

The other nickname involves his personality. Turtles is a very organised chap; legend has it that Greenwich Mean Time is set off his watch. If you are running just on time, let alone a couple of minutes late, you can be sure the time sheriff will be tapping at his wrist. He also likes to plot your best path to a destination and calculate your time of arrival, and if any of these things are disturbed he turns into one big grumpy individual. No reason for your delay is acceptable, and he won't be swayed on the merits of an alternative route. You know the expression 'as stubborn as a mule'. Well, Turtles is sometimes known as Mule.

The Mule loves giving me a hard time on things such as punctuality, hygiene and apparel, but one of his favourite targets during our careers was Andrew Blades. (Before I go any further, I have to explain that when we were with the Wallabies, Bladesy was like a brother to me. On the field he was a quiet achiever, the most underrated tight-head prop of his time. We never had any problems with scrums when Bladesy was in our front row, because he was technically fantastic, always willing and able to match it with bigger opponents.) Bladesy and I roomed together during our time at Camp Wallaby at Caloundra. When we had some time off, we'd all try to get out for a meal and a few drinks, and, of course, the Mule always organised the venue, time of departure, time of arrival, even the menu. It's true that I often made him a little anxious about our ETD, but Bladesy deadset infuriated him. One night, our big prop tried using the old 'I was looking for my socks' routine, but that was like waving a red flag in front of a bull . . . or should I say, Mule! Kearnsy wouldn't let it go, and throughout the 32-minute journey to our destination he was muttering, 'Why is it so hard to put your socks out before you shower?' Then: 'You're not even wearing socks! Fathead!!'

Kearnsy and his wife, Julie, had planned to come on a canyoning trip in the Blue Mountains with Erica and me in December 1998, after the Wallabies' European tour. However, Phil was unable to do it due to his knee and Achilles injuries, so Jules was flying solo. I guess if you're married to a mule then some of his ways might rub off on you, and that's certainly the case with Jules. She is very determined, strong-willed and bloody competitive. The trip involved hiking down into the canyon, donning a wetsuit, abseiling down some waterfalls, and wading through water that couldn't have been more than 10°C. Then we had to hike back up the mountain at the end of the day.

The fun and games commenced as soon as the guide gave us our wetsuits. Erica's and Jules's suits were reasonably new and odourless, but mine was old and it stank worse than a set of soiled rugby jerseys. The girls loved it, especially Jules, who began calling me Skunk, followed up with her nasally laugh. I could see it was going to be a long day, but at least I had time on my side if I wanted to plan some retribution . . .

When we started abseiling, I made sure I went just before Julie so I could be responsible for guiding her down the rockface. This was supposed to be the driest possible path, away from the waterfall, but I chose the wettest possible path and made sure that water was banging into her helmet and drenching her wetsuit. She had to trust me, as you can't look up while you are abseiling, and that coupled with my encouragement – 'You're doing great, Jules, don't worry, I know it feels like you are in the middle of the waterfall, but you're not' – meant she had no option but to keep going. I repeated this for about three or four descents. She kept calling me Skunk (and kept laughing), so I wasn't backing off.

I think it was the fact that I was dealing with a member of the Kearns family that made me do it. In between abseils, we waded through the water with our helmets attached to our packs, which was exhausting work. After our final descent I asked everyone, 'How are you holding up? Is it just me, or are our packs starting feeling heavier?' Jules was quick to agree, putting it down to the water and fatigue. From that point on, during the walk back to the point where we were to begin our hike out, I started adding rocks to her helmet to make her pack even heavier. Every time I was about to weaken, she made another crack about the stinking wetsuit, so I went searching for another rock. I guess it was a small win for the Skunk, and we had a good laugh about it when we reached the hike-out point and she discovered what I'd been doing, but still she kept persisting with the name and the laugh so I had no alternative but to try for one more victory during our final two-hour hike.

By this stage of the afternoon, it would have been 30-plus degrees. The wife of the Mule would have it no other way than to lead her group courageously up the mountain. Yes, she was tired from the canyoning and carrying those extra rocks, but no way was she going to reveal that to the Skunk. Instead, she told me again that I stunk! I had hiked before, so I knew about a 'false peak' – where the ground ahead looks like the top but isn't. Jules hadn't and didn't. When I saw a false peak ahead, I encouraged Jules to 'stride right out' to reach the summit first, as a leader should. I knew she was knackered like the rest of us, but she wasn't going to show me she wasn't up to it. The false peak might as well have been renamed false hope, because that's all it gave her. When we finally met her at the top, she was almost broken . . . but still 'striding right out'.

It was a great day, one we still talk about because everyone thinks it was hilarious (nasal-laugh funny!) that I had to wear the world's smelliest wetsuit. For me, though, I can't help grinning to myself whenever I picture Jules getting pounded by those water-falls, carrying that extra load and chasing those false peaks.

PHIL KEARNS ON
GEORGE GREGAN

George Gregan is most famous for his tackle.

Back when he made his Test debut against Italy in 1994 he was most famous for his skin and hair. It had been a long time since the Wallabies had had an 'afro' in the team. I was an old timer in 1994 in that I'd been in the team since 1989. I'd heard about the next up-and-coming genius every year (as had previous generations) and mostly every year they'd disappoint. This kid had something else – a determination to learn, which meant he listened and had the drive to be good, whereas others thought they knew it all. He wasn't the most gifted or naturally brilliant but he had determination and tenacity and he clearly had ambition to be the best.

It was hard to shine when you came from Canberra. You had two big brothers in Queensland and New South Wales, and you didn't have regular games against the big boys to show your wares. Bob Dwyer was really the first coach to take the ACT boys seriously. Girvan, Cornish, McGuiness, Didier were all guys that Bob had picked directly from the ACT. When he picked the 'little dark kiddie', George's life changed.

Little Dark Kiddie was a name that stuck with the boys in the '99 team (we weren't very PC back then). When George was an up-and-comer and people asked, 'Which one's Gregan?' the reply was always, 'The little dark kiddie'. John McKay, our 1998-99 manager, perpetuated the name.

The more George stayed with the team, the more he learned, the more professional he became, and the more particular he got about his own preparation. I don't know if he was a clean and tidy kid but he single-handedly brought metrosexuality to the Wallabies. The days when players thought shampoo and conditioner were their neighbour's pet poodles were over. George got rid of the afro and, as time went by, began to take longer and longer to get ready whenever we went out. It couldn't be the hair that was taking the time – he didn't have any! In sheer frustration one day I asked, 'What the bloody hell are you doing?'

'Exfoliating,' he replied.

And he wasn't even ashamed about it!

Meanwhile, his mates experienced the kind of frustration any married man feels while he's waiting on his wife to decide what to wear before going out.

A group that included George and my wife, Julie, went canyoning in the Blue Mountains. The water is cold in those deep canyons so everyone was required to wear a wetsuit. The smart ones took their own; the less fortunate used the ones supplied by the guides. George, by this time of his career, had become a clean freak, even down to the fabric softener he used. He chose what he thought was the newest-looking wetsuit only to find that once warmed up it took on the foulest odour ever known to man, thanks to the hundreds of people that had worn it before him. The stench was horrific and nobody wanted to partner up with him. He also learned that as it gets cold in the water some people took the 'wee in your wetsuit option' to keep warm. That made George feel really uncomfortable – and didn't his companions take the piss! He pretended it didn't get to him. He pretended it was a joke. But it was eating away at him and the mind was ticking: How am I going to get them back?

As the group trudged up the mountain heading home, packs on their backs and helmet straps holding their helmets at the back of their necks, he suddenly saw an opportunity to strike. Here was a perfect chance to get the main culprit, Julie Kearns. He picked up a large rock and, during a break, gently placed it in the helmet hanging from the back of her neck. As the long uphill journey proceeded out of the canyon he kept asking her, 'How's your pack? Tough walk up, eh? Feels like there's a rock in your helmet, doesn't it?' She struggled for hours coming out of the canyon, and he told her at the top. He'd won!

He copped it – but kept in control, plotted his victory, executed it and won.

This story is typical of George's rugby career: the smaller kid, striving to be good, meets adversity along the way, plans to beat it, does and wins. How many times did we see a team led by Gregan down and out only to fight back with determination and discipline to be victorious?

Whilst the stats tell the story of his career, his longevity and resilience, most of the public won't know the real George. He didn't play the press game. He didn't suck up to the journalists and he didn't bow down to the administrators. As a result, they plotted together to dislodge him, to pressure him. The number of vicious attacks against George by some members of the press was phenomenal. It was well known that some key Australian Rugby administrators didn't like George as they didn't have the same easy relationship with him that they'd had with the previous skipper, John Eales. Some members of the press even commented how some writers did the ARU's dirty work in return for 'scoops'. Whilst George tried to treat it like water off a duck's back, it must have been hurtful, as it was for his family, friends and team-mates.

George withdrew from the public eye, limiting the dealings he had with the press to the absolute minimum, which meant the Australian public never really got to know him.

For me, the real George came to the fore after my daughter Andie had an accident in 2005. Whilst she was in hospital in intensive care, George and Erica looked after my other three children – Wilson, Finn and Matilda. That was kind enough in itself, but at the time Wallaby prop Richard Harry and his family were also staying with them as their house, three doors away, was being renovated. And next door to George and Erica were Erica's sister and their three kids, with no fence between the properties. It was Mosman's version of the Kennedy compound.

So there were George and Erica, their three kids, the Harrys and their four kids, and my three all living together in one house, plus the three next door who joined the fray.

With some help from 'Wallaby wives' Nicole Wilson, Bridget Little, Nicky Blades and Alana Kennedy, George and Erica ran it all like a well-oiled machine: feeding, dressing, making lunches for, dropping off at and picking up from school, bathing and putting to sleep thirteen kids. They even managed to entertain at the same time. I remember coming home one night from the hospital and they were hosting a dinner for Sam Neill. That's George – surprisingly calm, well organised, clean, disciplined, caring and composed, but most importantly, everything he does for those he cares about is done with love.

GEORGE GREGAN ON ROB SITCH AND JANE KENNEDY

My first encounter with Rob Sitch and Jane Kennedy was in July 2000, at one of Sam and Noriko Neill's dinner parties. It was about a week after the Wallabies had played the All Blacks in what was being hailed as the greatest Test match ever – we came back from a 21-point deficit after eight minutes to level the scores before half-time, only to lose the Test to a Jonah Lomu try in the final minute. It *was* an incredible match, and when Erica and I arrived at the party we were quickly aware that all the guests were up to speed on the game.

The dinner party was a typical Sam Neill affair in that his guests came from all walks of life but shared a common interest in good food, good wine and, most of all, good company. It is impossible to recall this night without sounding like a name-dropper, as there were a lot of genuinely famous people there: Tom Cruise, Temuera Morrison, Ewan McGregor, Rachel Ward, Bryan Brown, and Rob and Jane, whom Erica and I found ourselves talking to soon after we arrived. It's funny how you can instantly connect with people – that was certainly the case in this instance. We were quickly talking and laughing with them about their television shows, such as *Full Frontal* and *The Panel*, and the movie they directed and produced, *The Castle* (in my opinion, a real Aussie icon). We also felt somewhat reassured when they confessed they, like us, were a little starstruck by Sam's guest list. It was a bit crazy really, because people are people – it doesn't matter if you're famous or not; your personality will always shine through.

The night turned out to be an absolute cracker, because of the company and the atmosphere Sam and Noriko created. The highlights included a group singalong with ukuleles, Bryan Brown singing his farewell from on top of the dinner table, and Tom Cruise giving me a *Jerry Maguire*-type question-and-answer session about rugby union. Tom was right into rugby, as, inevitably, was Temuera Morrison. And it was during this party that our friendship with Rob and Jane was forged, for which we owe the Neills a big thank you!

In the years since, we've shared an uncanny number of similar experiences. This is especially true of our families – or it was until 2006, when they had twins. There'd only been a handful of weeks between the births of our kids – coincidences that became something of a running joke between us. But while Erica and I felt incredible joy and offered all the support we could when their fourth and fifth children arrived, we weren't prepared to join them in their reproduction escapade – we were busy enough with our little tribe! As it's turned out, they've come through their early experiences as a family of *seven* with flying colours.

Jane is a person from whom it is easy to draw inspiration. She is a board member of the George Gregan Foundation and has missed only one meeting since she took on that role (using her family as an excuse – very poor!). She also contributes to other charities in Melbourne, where they are based, but has still found time to do a little hands-on creative work for us. Meanwhile, Rob and his Working Dog team have produced, among other things, the innovative and funny television show *Thank God You're Here*, which has been highly successful not only in Australia but around the world. Jane and Rob are both extremely busy in their professional lives, but still love spending time at home with their family and friends; in this, they are much like Erica and me.

Whenever I played a Test in Melbourne we caught up for dinner – usually at their home, but once at a favourite restaurant of theirs. As soon as we entered, the owner came out to greet me. 'Hello, Mr Gregan, so nice to see you and your wife. Good luck this Saturday!' I responded in the appropriate manner and quickly learned that this guy was a big Wallabies fan. Rob and Jane stared at us in total disbelief. It took them a couple of drinks to recover and explain the magnitude of what had just happened. The owner was renowned for never engaging in small talk, even with regulars such as Rob and Jane. They had been eating there for over a decade and had never received more than a forced hello. Whenever they'd tried to start a conversation they'd inevitably come up with fresh air.

And every time since when they've returned for a meal, the owner has reverted back to type. Such is the power of rugby!

ROB SITCH ON GEORGE GREGAN

I've never seen George angry and I've never seen George mouth off at anyone. So it always surprised me when people talked about his ability to give a bit of lip on the field. Sure I'd seen his gums flapping beside the scrum, but from the distance of the stands or on the television at home it seemed like he was offering strategic advice or reminders of the drills they'd practised during the week. In fact, I'll go further and say I've never seen George be discourteous or offhand, period. I've seen him asked for autographs at the most inopportune times and the man seems incapable of being annoyed. If I were to delve into my subconscious, I probably thought that George's comments when he was standing beside the scrum, were imploring both sides to 'play in the spirit of the game, boys'. But still the references to his 'gift' for getting under the skin of his opponents kept coming.

But I wasn't thinking about that when we were having lunch together a few years back. George was his usual easygoing self and the conversation drifted from one topic to another until we settled on what amounts to a parlour game: giving golf handicaps to various aspects of your life. My friend Glenn Robbins invented this idea and if you play golf it's a beauty. Put simply, every golfer can describe their abilities instantly by their handicap – the number of shots you get given for a round. For men, the numbers range from 'scratch', zero, the mark of an expert and the highest accolade a golfer can aspire to, up to around thirty which is the limit for male golfers. If you're off twenty-six every golfer knows you're not much good, fourteen and they know you're handy, single figures and you can play, low single figures and you can really play, and finally scratch, which means you probably could have turned professional if you'd wanted to.

In fact scratch has a certain mythic quality for amateur golfers. In some ways it represents the Holy Grail. And for good reason. My old golf pro once told me that it took him three years of nearly full-time effort to get from a handicap of three down to scratch. That's a year a shot! If you get to scratch it's like you've been knighted by the Queen.

Anyway, George really took to the game and settled in for a long session. You can handicap yourself on trivial matters just as easily as important ones. The first handicap Glenn ever announced was his ability to find a park in the city. (He was off single figures by the way. I remember being quite impressed and even asked him for tips.) I was in the mid-teens for packing a boot. Not bad, especially when I explained that I thought I could go to single figures over the summer holiday season. Over the years, there've been plenty of handicaps in single figures, but none at scratch. To nominate scratch for yourself is such a big call it probably means that your skill level is world class. My best is low single figures for my ability to remember the names of Russian supermodels. Not a useful skill but one practised at a level that has really impressed my friends. No one challenged the handicap that's for sure.

George picked it up immediately and started to come up with

some fresh areas: What's your handicap as a parent? How good are you at ordering off a specials board?, Discipline with getting your car serviced?, Packing for an overseas trip? We went through the normal arc from the important to the ridiculous. Occasionally I thought he was being modest. He gave himself a handicap of eleven for tidiness around the home, which made Erica roll her eyes. She had him off single figures it seemed. In fact, neither of us gave ourselves many flattering handicaps. It's a natural thing between guys to self-deprecate slightly.

Then a thought occurred to me: what about George's on-field lip. What a perfect way to get to the truth! I'd word it deftly of course and give George plenty of wiggle room to fudge the answer a little. I wasn't trying to embarrass the guy, after all. I'd sneak my way into the question.

'Here's one, George,' I said. 'You know on the field, at the stoppages . . .?'

George's gaze was fixed as if to say, 'Keep going.'

'Well, out on the field during matches . . . like with all the chat and stuff . . .'

George hadn't moved a muscle.

I finally came out with it. 'What do you reckon your handicap is for sledging?'

After the briefest of pauses, and with the same fixed gaze, George responded, 'Scratch.'

APPENDIX

Name: George Gregan

Born: 19 April 1973, in Lusaka, Zambia

Position: Halfback

Clubs: Easts (Canberra, 1991–1993), Canberra Kookaburras (1994), Randwick (Sydney, 1995), RC Toulon (France, 2007–08), Suntory Sungoliath (Japan, 2008–)

Provincial: ACT (1993–1995), ACT Brumbies (Super 12 1996–2005; Super 14 2006–2007)

Australia Under-19s: 1992

Australia Under-21s: 1993

International Sevens: Australia (1994–1995)

Test Rugby: Australia (1994–2007)

TEST CAREER

Test Record
George Gregan's match-by-match record, from his debut in the first game of the two-Test series against Italy in Australia in 1994:

Test	Date	Opponent	Venue	Result	Tries	DG	Details
1	18-6-1994	Italy	Brisbane	23–20	–	–	
2	25-6-1994	Italy	Melbourne	20–7	–	–	
3	6-8-1994	Samoa	Sydney	73–3	1	–	
4	17-8-1994	New Zealand	Sydney	20–16	–	–	
5	30-4-1995	Argentina	Brisbane	53–7	–	–	
6	6-5-1995	Argentina	Sydney	30–13	–	–	
7	25-5-1995	South Africa	Cape Town	18–27	–	–	WC
8	31-5-1995	Canada	Port Elizabeth	27–11	–	–	WC, sub
9	3-6-1995	Romania	Stellenbosch	42–3	–	–	WC
10	11-6-1995	England	Cape Town	22–25	–	–	WC qf
11	9-6-1996	Wales	Brisbane	56–25	–	–	
12	29-6-1996	Canada	Brisbane	74–9	–	–	sub
13	13-7-1996	South Africa	Sydney	21–16	–	–	3N
14	27-7-1996	New Zealand	Brisbane	25–32	1	–	3N
15	3-8-1996	South Africa	Bloemfontein	19–25	–	–	3N
16	23-10-1996	Italy	Padua	40–18	–	–	
17	23-11-1996	Ireland	Dublin	22–12	–	–	
18	1-12-1996	Wales	Cardiff	28–19	–	–	
19	21-6-1997	France	Sydney	29–15	–	–	
20	28-6-1997	France	Brisbane	26–19	–	–	
21	5-7-1997	New Zealand	Christchurch	13–30	–	–	
22	12-7-1997	England	Sydney	25–6	1	–	
23	26-7-1997	New Zealand	Melbourne	18–33	1	–	3N
24	2-8-1997	South Africa	Brisbane	32–20	–	–	3N
25	16-8-1997	New Zealand	Dunedin	24–36	–	–	3N
26	23-8-1997	South Africa	Pretoria	22–61	–	–	3N
27	1-11-1997	Argentina	Buenos Aires	23–15	–	–	
28	8-11-1997	Argentina	Buenos Aires	16–18	–	–	
29	15-11-1997	England	London	15–15	1	–	
30	22-11-1997	Scotland	Edinburgh	37–8	1	–	
31	6-6-1998	England	Brisbane	76–0	1	–	
32	13-6-1998	Scotland	Sydney	45–3	–	–	
33	20-6-1998	Scotland	Brisbane	33–11	–	–	
34	11-7-1998	New Zealand	Melbourne	24–16	–	–	3N

Test	Date	Opponent	Venue	Result	Tries	DG	Details
35	18-7-1998	South Africa	Perth	13–14	1	–	3N
36	1-8-1998	New Zealand	Christchurch	27–23	–	–	3N
37	22-8-1998	South Africa	Johannesburg	15–29	–	–	3N
38	29-8-1998	New Zealand	Sydney	19–14	–	–	
39	18-9-1998	Fiji	Sydney	66–20	–	–	
40	26-9-1998	Samoa	Brisbane	25–13	–	–	
41	21-11-1998	France	Paris	32–21	–	–	
42	28-11-1998	England	London	12–11	–	–	
43	12-6-1999	Ireland	Brisbane	46–10	–	–	
44	19-6-1999	Ireland	Perth	32–26	–	–	
45	26-6-1999	England	Sydney	22–15	–	–	
46	17-7-1999	South Africa	Brisbane	32–6	–	–	3N
47	24-7-1999	New Zealand	Auckland	15–34	1	–	3N
48	14-8-1999	South Africa	Cape Town	9–10	–	–	3N
49	28-8-1999	New Zealand	Sydney	28–7	–	–	3N
50	3-10-1999	Romania	Belfast	57–9	–	–	WC
51	10-10-1999	Ireland	Dublin	23–3	–	–	WC
52	23-10-1999	Wales	Cardiff	24–9	2	–	WC qf
53	30-10-1999	South Africa	London	27–21	–	–	WC sf
54	6-11-1999	France	Cardiff	35–12	–	–	WC f
55	17-6-2000	Argentina	Brisbane	53–6	–	–	
56	24-6-2000	Argentina	Canberra	32–25	–	–	
57	8-7-2000	South Africa	Melbourne	44–23	–	–	
58	15-7-2000	New Zealand	Sydney	35–39	–	–	3N
59	29-7-2000	South Africa	Sydney	26–6	–	–	3N
60	5-8-2000	New Zealand	Wellington	24–23	–	–	3N
61	26-8-2000	South Africa	Durban	19–18	–	–	3N
62	30-6-2001	Lions	Brisbane	13–29	–	–	
63	7-7-2001	Lions	Melbourne	35–14	–	–	
64	14-7-2001	Lions	Sydney	29–23	–	–	
65	28-7-2001	South Africa	Pretoria	15–20	–	–	3N
66	11-8-2001	New Zealand	Dunedin	23–15	–	–	3N
67	18-8-2001	South Africa	Perth	14–14	–	–	3N
68	1-9-2001	New Zealand	Sydney	29–26	–	–	3N

APPENDIX

Test	Date	Opponent	Venue	Result	Tries	DG	Details
69	1-11-2001	Spain	Madrid	92–10	–	–	capt
70	10-11-2001	England	London	15–21	–	–	capt
71	17-11-2001	France	Marseille	13–14	–	–	capt
72	25-11-2001	Wales	Cardiff	21–13	–	–	capt
73	22-6-2002	France	Melbourne	29–17	–	–	capt
74	29-6-2002	France	Sydney	31–25	–	1	capt
75	13-7-2002	New Zealand	Christchurch	6–12	–	–	3N, capt
76	27-7-2002	South Africa	Brisbane	38–27	–	–	3N, capt
77	3-8-2002	New Zealand	Sydney	16–14	–	–	3N, capt
78	17-8-2002	South Africa	Johannesburg	31–33	–	1	3N, capt
79	2-11-2002	Argentina	Buenos Aires	17–6	–	–	capt
80	9-11-2002	Ireland	Dublin	9–18	–	–	capt
81	16-11-2002	England	London	31–32	–	–	capt
82	23-11-2002	Italy	Genoa	34–3	–	–	capt
83	7-6-2003	Ireland	Perth	45–16	2	–	capt
84	14-6-2003	Wales	Sydney	30–10	–	–	capt
85	21-6-2003	England	Melbourne	14–25	–	–	capt
86	12-7-2003	South Africa	Cape Town	22–26	–	–	3N, capt
87	26-7-2003	New Zealand	Sydney	21–50	–	–	3N, capt
88	2-8-2003	South Africa	Brisbane	29–9	–	–	3N, capt
89	16-8-2003	New Zealand	Auckland	17–21	–	–	3N, capt
90	10-10-2003	Argentina	Sydney	24–8	–	–	WC, capt
91	18-10-2003	Romania	Brisbane	90–8	–	–	WC, capt
92	1-11-2003	Ireland	Melbourne	17–16	–	1	WC, capt
93	8-11-2003	Scotland	Brisbane	33–16	1	–	WC qf, capt
94	15-11-2003	New Zealand	Sydney	22–10	–	–	WC sf, capt
95	22-11-2003	England	Sydney	17–20	–	–	WC f, capt
96	13-6-2004	Scotland	Melbourne	35–15	–	–	capt
97	19-6-2004	Scotland	Sydney	34–13	–	–	capt
98	26-6-2004	England	Brisbane	51–15	–	–	capt
99	3-7-2004	Pacific Islands	Adelaide	29–14	–	–	capt
100	31-7-2004	South Africa	Perth	30–26	–	–	3N, capt
101	7-8-2004	New Zealand	Sydney	23–18	–	–	3N, capt
102	21-8-2004	South Africa	Durban	19–23	–	–	3N, capt

Test	Date	Opponent	Venue	Result	Tries	DG	Details
103	6-11-2004	Scotland	Edinburgh	31–14	–	–	capt
104	13-11-2004	France	Paris	14–27	1	–	capt
105	20-11-2004	Scotland	Glasgow	31–17	1	–	capt
106	27-11-2004	England	London	21–19	–	–	capt
107	25-6-2005	Italy	Melbourne	69–21	1	–	capt
108	2-7-2005	France	Brisbane	37–31	–	–	capt
109	9-7-2005	South Africa	Sydney	30–12	–	–	capt
110	23-7-2005	South Africa	Johannesburg	20–33	–	–	capt
111	30-7-2005	South Africa	Pretoria	16–22	–	–	3N, capt
112	13-8-2005	New Zealand	Sydney	13–30	–	–	3N, capt
113	20-8-2005	South Africa	Perth	19–22	–	–	3N, capt
114	3-9-2005	New Zealand	Auckland	24–34	–	–	3N, capt
115	5-11-2005	France	Marseille	16–26	–	–	capt
116	12-11-2005	England	London	16–26	–	–	capt
117	19-11-2005	Ireland	Dublin	30–14	–	–	capt
118	26-11-2005	Wales	Cardiff	22–24	–	–	capt
119	11-6-2006	England	Sydney	34–3	–	–	capt
120	17-6-2006	England	Melbourne	43–18	–	–	sub
121	24-6-2006	Ireland	Perth	37–15	1	–	capt
122	8-7-2006	New Zealand	Christchurch	12–32	–	–	3N, capt
123	15-7-2006	South Africa	Brisbane	49–0	–	–	3N, capt
124	29-7-2006	New Zealand	Brisbane	9–13	–	–	3N, capt
125	5-8-2006	South Africa	Sydney	20–18	–	–	3N, capt
126	19-8-2006	New Zealand	Auckland	27–34	–	–	3N, capt
127	9-9-2006	South Africa	Johannesburg	16–24	–	–	3N, capt
128	26-5-2007	Wales	Sydney	29–23	–	–	sub
129	2-6-2007	Wales	Brisbane	31–0	–	–	sub
130	9-6-2007	Fiji	Perth	49–0	–	–	
131	16-6-2007	South Africa	Cape Town	19–22	–	–	3N
132	30-6-2007	New Zealand	Melbourne	20–15	–	–	3N
133	7-7-2007	South Africa	Sydney	25–17	–	–	3N
134	21-7-2007	New Zealand	Auckland	12–26	–	–	3N
135	8-9-2007	Japan	Lyon	91–3	–	–	WC
136	15-9-2007	Wales	Cardiff	32–20	–	–	WC

Test	Date	Opponent	Venue	Result	Tries	DG	Details
137	23-9-2007	Fiji	Montpellier	55–12	–	–	WC, capt
138	29-9-2007	Canada	Bordeaux	37–6	–	–	WC, sub
139	6-10-2007	England	Marseille	10–12	–	–	WC qf

Notes

1. 'sub' indicates Gregan came on as replacement; 'WC' indicates World Cup match; 'WC qf' indicates World Cup quarter-final; 'WC sf' indicates World Cup semifinal; 'WC f' indicates World Cup final; '3N' indicates Tri Nations Test; 'capt' indicates Gregan was captain.

2. All tries were worth five points, drop goals (DG) were worth three points. In total, Gregan scored 18 tries and three drop goals, for 99 career points.

3. Gregan played Tests at the following venues in Australia: Ballymore, Brisbane (Tests 1, 5, 11, 12, 20, 33, 40, 43, 55); Olympic Park, Melbourne (Test 2); Sydney Football Stadium (3, 4, 6, 13, 19, 22, 32, 38); Suncorp Stadium, Brisbane (14, 24, 31, 46, 88, 91, 93, 98, 108, 123, 124, 129); Melbourne Cricket Ground (23, 34, 132); Subiaco Oval, Perth (35, 44, 67, 83, 100, 113, 121, 130); Parramatta Stadium, Sydney (39); Sydney's Stadium Australia, known as Telstra Stadium from 2002 to 2007 (45, 49, 58, 59, 64, 68, 74, 77, 84, 87, 90, 94, 95, 97, 101, 109, 112, 119, 125, 128, 133); Canberra Stadium (56); Melbourne's Telstra Dome, known as Colonial Stadium from 2000 to 2002 (57, 63, 73, 85, 92, 96, 107, 120); the Gabba, Brisbane (62, 76); Adelaide Oval (99).

4. In the games Gregan came on as a substitute, the Australian starting halfbacks were Peter Slattery (v Canada, 1995), Sam Payne (v Canada, 1996), Sam Cordingley (v England, 2006; v Fiji 2007), Matt Giteau (v Wales, 2007).

In the period from Gregan's first Test to his last, Australia played 17 Tests in which Gregan did not appear:

Test	Date	Opponent	Venue	Result	Reason	Halfback
1	22-7-95	New Zealand	Auckland	16–28	dropped	Steve Merrick
2	29-7-95	New Zealand	Sydney	23–34	dropped	Steve Merrick
3	22-6-96	Wales	Sydney	42–3	dropped	Sam Payne
4	6-7-96	New Zealand	Wellington	6–43	dropped	Sam Payne
5	9-11-96	Scotland	Edinburgh	29–19	dropped	Sam Payne

Test	Date	Opponent	Venue	Result	Reason	Halfback
6	22-9-98	Tonga	Canberra	74–0	rested	Chris Whitaker
7	14-10-99	United States	Limerick	55–19	rested	Chris Whitaker
8	4-11-00	France	Paris	18–13	injured	Sam Cordingley
9	11-11-00	Scotland	Edinburgh	30–9	injured	Sam Cordingley
10	18-11-00	England	London	19–22	injured	Sam Cordingley
11	25-10-03	Namibia	Adelaide	142–0	rested	Chris Whitaker
12	17-7-04	New Zealand	Wellington	7–16	injured	Chris Whitaker
13	11-6-05	Samoa	Sydney	74–7	injured	Chris Whitaker
14	4-11-06	Wales	Cardiff	29–29	injured	Matt Giteau
15	11-11-06	Italy	Rome	25–18	injured	Matt Giteau
16	19-11-06	Ireland	Dublin	6–21	injured	Matt Giteau
17	25-11-06	Scotland	Edinburgh	44–15	injured	Matt Giteau

Notes

1. 'Reason' indicates the cause of Gregan's omission; 'Halfback' is the Australian starting halfback in that Test.

2. Gregan missed the Wallabies' European tours in 2000 and 2006 to rehabilitate injuries suffered during the previous just-completed Australian season.

Gregan's record against the teams he faced during his Test career:

Team	Played	Won	Drawn	Lost	Tries	DG	Points
Argentina	8	7	–	1	–	–	–
British & Irish Lions	3	2	–	1	–	–	–
Canada	3	3	–	–	–	–	–
England	16	8	1	7	3	–	15
Fiji	3	3	–	–	–	–	–
France	10	7	–	3	1	1	8
Ireland	9	8	–	1	3	1	18
Italy	5	5	–	–	1	–	5
Japan	1	1	–	–	–	–	–
New Zealand	27	12	–	15	3	–	15
Pacific Islands	1	1	–	–	–	–	–
Romania	3	3	–	–	–	–	–

Team	Played	Won	Drawn	Lost	Tries	DG	Points
Samoa	2	2	–	–	1	–	5
Scotland	8	8	–	–	3	–	15
South Africa	30	14	1	15	1	1	8
Spain	1	1	–	–	–	–	–
Wales	9	8	–	1	2	–	10
Total	*139*	*93*	*2*	*44*	*18*	*3*	*99*

Gregan appeared in 48 Tri Nations Tests between 1996 and 2007, and was part of winning Wallabies teams in nine Tri Nations Tests against New Zealand (out of 23) and in 11 Tri Nations Tests against South Africa (out of 25, including one draw). Australia won the Tri Nations in 2000 and 2001.

Test Landmarks

Gregan appeared in 20 World Cup matches, and is the only Australian player to participate in four World Cups. The only man to appear in more World Cup games is English prop Jason Leonard, who played in 22 matches between 1991 and 2003. John Eales, Michael Lynagh and David Campese appeared in 15 World Cup games; Jason Little, Tim Horan and Joe Roff in 14.

Gregan's 78th Test appearance established a new mark for most Tests played by a halfback.

Gregan was the second Australian to play 100 Tests, after David Campese (101 Tests). In playing his 115th Test, Gregan broke Jason Leonard's record for most Test appearances for one team. Leonard also played five Tests for the British and Irish Lions, meaning that Gregan had to wait until his 120th Test to achieve the overall Test appearance record. He broke this record by coming off the bench against England at the Telstra Dome in 2006. As of May 2008, eight players have appeared in 100 Tests, as follows:

APPENDIX

Player	Tests
George Gregan (Australia)	139
Jason Leonard (England, Lions)	119
Fabien Pelous (France)	118
Philippe Sella (France)	111
Gareth Thomas (Wales, Lions)	103
Stephen Larkham (Australia)	102
David Campese (Australia)	101
Alessandro Troncon (Italy)	101

Note

Leonard played five of his 119 Tests for the Lions. Thomas played three Tests of his 103 Tests for the Lions. As at May 2008, most Tests for New Zealand is 92, by Sean Fitzpatrick; then 81, by Justin Marshall. Most Tests for South Africa is 94, by Percy Montgomery; then 89 by Joost van der Westhuizen.

Test Captaincy

Gregan's 138th Test, against Fiji at the 2007 World Cup, was his 59th Test as captain, equalling the mark for most Tests as captain set by England's Will Carling. Before Gregan, the highest number of Tests as Australian captain was 55, by John Eales. As at May 2008, the only other man to captain his country in 50 or more Tests is the All Blacks' Sean Fitzpatrick (51 Tests as captain). The next highest by an Australian captain is 36 Tests, by Nick Farr-Jones, then Andrew Slack (19 Tests as captain), Greg Davis (16) and John Thornett (16). Gregan led the Wallabies in 21 Tri Nations Tests, for seven wins (five against South Africa, two against New Zealand) and 14 losses. Gregan captained the Southern Hemisphere team that defeated the Northern Hemisphere 54–19 in the IRB Rugby Aid match staged at Twickenham on 5 March 2005.

Gregan's Test captaincy record against each team he faced as Wallabies skipper:

Team	Tests	Wins	Losses
Argentina	2	2	–
England	8	3	5
Fiji	1	1	–
France	6	3	3
Ireland	5	4	1
Italy	2	2	–
New Zealand	11	3	8
Pacific Islands	1	1	–
Romania	1	1	–
Scotland	5	5	–
South Africa	13	6	7
Spain	1	1	–
Wales	3	2	1
Total	*59*	*34*	*25*

George Gregan's Team-mates in Test Rugby

93 Tests with Gregan Stephen Larkham; *76* Joe Roff; *74* George Smith; *71* Chris Latham; *69* Matthew Burke; *65* Jeremy Paul; *62* Phil Waugh; *60* John Eales, Daniel Herbert; *58* David Wilson; *57* Matt Cockbain, Nathan Sharpe; *56* Toutai Kefu; *54* Stirling Mortlock; *52* Lote Tuqiri; *51* Owen Finegan; *49* Dan Vickerman; *46* Al Baxter; *44* David Giffin, Matt Giteau, Ben Tune; *42* Michael Foley, Jason Little; *41* Tim Horan, Bill Young; *40* David Lyons; *39* Brendan Cannon, Mat Rogers; *37* Elton Flatley; *35* Richard Harry, Wendell Sailor; *33* Matt Dunning; *31* Andrew Blades; *32* Justin Harrison; *30* Mark Chisholm, Nathan Grey; *27* Ben Darwin, Rocky Elsom, Phil Kearns; *26* Chris Whitaker; *25* Dan Crowley; *24* Patricio Noriega; *22* Willie Ofahengaue; *21* Drew Mitchell, Clyde Rathbone; *20* Adam Freier; *19* Mark Gerrard;

18 Morgan Turinui; *17* Glenn Panoho, John Roe; *16* David Campese, Mark Connors, Pat Howard; *15* Tom Bowman, Ewen McKenzie, Stephen Moore; *14* Brett Robinson, Guy Shepherdson; *13* Tim Gavin, Stephen Hoiles, Greg Holmes, Rod Moore, Wycliff Palu; *12* Adam Ashley-Cooper, Troy Coker, Damian Smith, Nick Stiles; *11* Sam Cordingley, Hugh McMeniman, Daniel Manu; *10* Tiaan Strauss, Jim Williams; *9* Michael Brial, Julian Huxley, David Knox, Garrick Morgan, Scott Staniforth; *8* Andrew Heath, Rodney Kafer; *7* Fletcher Dyson, James Holbeck, Matthew Pini; *6* Rodney Blake, Graeme Bond, Tony Daly, Mitch Hardy, Steve Kefu, Michael Lynagh, Rod McCall, Tai McIsaac; *5* Scott Fava, Radike Samo, John Welborn; *4* Berrick Barnes, Marco Caputo, David Croft, Sean Hardman, Sam Payne, Cameron Shepherd, Warwick Waugh; *3* Scott Bowen, Mark Hartill, Lloyd Johansson, Benn Robinson, Peter Slattery; *2* David Fitter, Daniel Heenan, Matt Henjak, Troy Jaques, Darren Junee, Sam Norton-Knight, Tatafu Polota-Nau, Nathan Spooner, Richard Tombs, Tim Wallace; *1* Mark Bartholomeusz, Mark Bell, Cameron Blades, Al Campbell, Ryan Constable, Manny Edmonds, Fili Finau, Nic Henderson, James Horwill, Digby Ioane, Alex Kanaar, Lachlan MacKay, Alistair Murdoch, Brett Sheehan, Josh Valentine.

Note
For the purpose of this list, a 'team-mate' is defined as a player who appeared in a Test in which Gregan also took part.

SUPER 12/SUPER 14

Super 12/Super 14 Record
Gregan played 136 games for the ACT Brumbies. He appeared in 17 other matches for ACT, scoring five tries in these non-Super 12/Super 14 games. His 100th game for ACT came in 2003, a

37–22 win over the Stormers at Canberra on 14 March, and his 100th Super 12 game was a 29–37 loss to the Waratahs in Sydney on 24 April 2004.

Gregan's year-by-year record for the Brumbies in Super 12 (1996–2005) and Super 14 (2006–2007):

Year	Played	Tries	DG	Points	Brumbies' finish
1996	11	1	–	5	Fifth
1997	13	7	–	35	Lost final 23–7 to Blues
1998	5	–	–	–	10th
1999	11	5	–	25	Fifth
2000	13	1	–	5	Lost final 20–19 to Crusaders
2001	13	–	2	6	Beat Sharks 36–6 in final
2002	13	1	–	5	Lost final 31–13 to Crusaders
2003	12	4	–	20	Lost semifinal 42–21 to Blues
2004	13	–	–	–	Beat Crusaders 47–38 in final
2005	7	–	1	3	Fifth
2006	12	2	1	13	Sixth
2007	13	–	–	–	Fifth
Total	136	21	4	117	

Gregan missed six Super 12 games in 1998 and three in 2005 because of injury. He missed one game in 2005 to travel to London for the IRB Rugby Aid match, and one game in 2006 because of suspension. Two of his 136 appearances came from the bench: one in 2004 and one in 2005. He appeared in 80 consecutive Super 12 games between round nine in 1998 and round one in 2005.

The table for most Super 12/Super 14 appearances (as at the end of the 2008 Super 14 competition):

Player	Games
George Gregan (Brumbies)	136
Caleb Ralph (Crusaders/Blues/Chiefs)	135
Reuben Thorne (Crusaders)	129
Anton Oliver (Highlanders)	127
Tana Umaga (Hurricanes)	122
Stephen Larkham (Brumbies)	116
Jeremy Paul (Brumbies)	112

Note

Following the 2008 Super 14, other Brumbies to appear in 100 or more Super 12/Super 14 games are George Smith (107 games), Stirling Mortlock (105) and Bill Young (100).

Super 12/Super 14 Captaincy

Gregan led the Brumbies on 10 occasions prior to 2001 (when Brett Robinson was the first-choice captain), in 38 games from 2001 to 2003, and once in 2005 (when regular captain Stirling Mortlock and regular vice-captain Owen Finegan were unavailable). To the end of the 2008 Super 14 competition, this total of 49 is the most appearances by a Brumbies captain. Next best is Mortlock (44 games as captain, from 2004 to 2008) and Robinson (43, from 1996 to 2000).

SELECTED BIBLIOGRAPHY

BOOKS

Gordon Bray (editor), *The Australian Rugby Companion*, Viking, Melbourne, 2002.

Matthew Burke with Ian Heads, *Matthew Burke: A Rugby Life*, Macmillan, Sydney, 2005.

Mike Cleary, *Wounded Pride: The Official Book of the Lions Tour to Australia 2001*, Mainstream Publishing, Edinburgh, 2001.

Bob Dwyer, *Full Time*, Pan Macmillan, Sydney, 2004.

Peter FitzSimons, *The Rugby War*, HarperSports, Sydney, 1996.

Peter FitzSimons, *John Eales: The Biography*, ABC Books, Sydney 2001.

Peter Jenkins, *Wallaby Gold: 100 Years of Australian Test Rugby*, Random House, Sydney, 1999.

Martin Johnson, *The Autobiography*, Headline, London, 2004.

Stephen Larkham, *Stephen Larkham's World Cup Diary*, Viking, Melbourne, 2004.

Rod Macqueen with Kevin Hitchcock, *One Step Ahead*, Random House, Sydney, 2001.

Michael McKernan, *The Brumbies: The Super 12 Years*, Allen & Unwin, Sydney, 2006.

Paul Morgan & John Griffiths (editors), *IRB World Rugby Yearbook 2007*, Vision Sports Publishing, London, 2006.

John O'Neill, *It's Only A Game: The Autobiography of John O'Neill*, Random House, Sydney, 2007.

Ian Robertson (editor), *The Complete Book of the Rugby World Cup 1999*, Hodder & Stoughton, London, 1999.

Ian Robertson (editor), *Sweet Chariot: The Complete Book of the Rugby World Cup 2003*, Mainstream Publishing, Edinburgh, 2003.

Greg Thomas (editor), *Schweppes Rugby '97: Rugby's Southern Hemisphere Yearbook*, Mandarin, Melbourne, 1997.

NEWSPAPERS

Daily Telegraph-Mirror (Sydney), *Herald Sun* (Melbourne), *Mail on Sunday* (London), *Otago Daily Times* (Dunedin), *Sunday Herald Sun* (Melbourne), *Sunday News* (Auckland), *The Age* (Melbourne), *The Australian* (Sydney), *The Canberra Times*, *The Courier-Mail* (Brisbane), *The Daily Telegraph* (London), *The Daily Telegraph* (Sydney), *The Guardian* (London), *The Independent* (London), *The Observer* (London), *The Press* (Christchurch), *The Sunday Age* (Melbourne), *The Sunday Mail* (Brisbane), *The Sunday Telegraph* (Sydney), *The Sunday Telegraph* (London), *The Sunday Times* (London), *The Sun-Herald* (Sydney), *The Sydney Morning Herald*, *The Times* (London).

MAGAZINES

Australian Rugby News & Review, *Inside Rugby*, *Rugby News*, *Rugby World*, *The Bulletin* and a number of Brumbies and Wallabies match programs.

WEBSITES

bbc.co.uk, brumbies.com.au, lassen.co.nz/pickandgo, planet-rugby.com, rctoulon.com, rugby.com.au, rugbyheaven.com.au, scrum.com, stuff.co.nz, plus many of the websites produced by newspapers listed above.